SPORTSMANSHIP

Patrick McCaskey

A Sports and Faith Series Book

Photographs appearing in *Sportsmanship* were sourced from the Library of Congress, Getty Images, New York Public Library, UPI/Alamy, Chicago Police Department, and Canons Regular Saint John Cantius. Please see the Photographs and Illustrations Credit Table on page 335 for more information.

The opinions and ideas expressed are those of the author who is entirely responsible for its content. The author has composed *Sportsmanship* at his own expense, using his own resources and technology. This publication is not associated in any way with the Chicago Bears Football Team.

Sportsmanship is Book 5 of the Sports and Faith Series.

CONTENTS

The Beatitudes of Football..V
PART ONE: NOTEWORTHY EVENTS........................1
Chicago Bears' Calendar..1
PART TWO: THE GAME.....................................56
First Quarter..56
Second Quarter...65
Halftime..76
Third Quarter..87
Fourth Quarter..97
Overtime 102
Giving Thanks..112
PART THREE: Praiseworthy 124
My Favorite Writers..140
Lines from My Favorite Comedians...........................186
PART FOUR: Biblical Poems....................................190
Matthew 190
Mark..203
Luke..211
John 247
PART FIVE: Speeches..258
Chicago Bears' History.......................................260
Faith Based Education..274
Reading and Writing..287
Sports and Faith...302
PART SIX: Resolutions..315
Resolution for Pete Newell and Joe Petricca 315
Resolution for Loyola Academy 317
Resolution for Kevin Matthews 319
Resolution for Ben Ruf.......................................320

Resolution for Mark Balasa.....................322
Resolution for Rich Conyers 324
Resolution for Nancy Saviola 326
Resolution for the Metropolitan Water
Reclamation District...............................328
Resolution for Cheshire Academy............329
Resolution for John Perkins....................331
Resolution for Bill Kanzer.......................333
Photo Credits...335
Index..336

Sportsmanship

"Regardless of what happens on the field, let's behave like champions in sports and spirit. Let's not analyze. Let's not denigrate. Let's not second guess. Let's not diagnose injuries before we've read the x-rays. Let sportsmanship prevail."

—Patrick McCaskey

The Beatitudes of Football

Matthew 5:3-12

Blessed are the champions in sports and spirit, for they watch the games with sportsmanship.

Blessed are they who attend funerals, for they provide condolences.

Blessed are those who do not fight, for they will not be penalized.

Blessed are they who hunger and thirst for fitness, for they have a healthy lifestyle.

Blessed are the helpful, for they will improve the game.

Blessed are they who play clean, for they are doing God's will.

Blessed are the foot-washers, for they will be called servants of God.

Blessed are they who go to Church, for they hear the wonderful news of salvation.

Blessed are you when they mock and scorn you because of your faith. These are opportunities to live the gospel.

Beatitudes Illustrated

Blessed are the champions in sports and spirit, for they watch the games with sportsmanship.
When I was a Notre Dame High School senior, the 1967 regional championship basketball game was at Maine South. It was very hot in the gym. So naturally I stripped to the waist. The following Monday, Father Markos called me in to his office. He said to me, "That won't happen again will it Mister McCaskey?" I replied, "No, it won't Father."

When we take part in sports, it can often improve our health and wellbeing. And when we watch sports, whether it's at our kids' or grandkids' games—or as a member of a larger community in a stadium or other venue, we should watch with sportsmanship.

Blessed are they who attend funerals, for they provide condolences.
"Bury the Dead" is one of the Corporal Works of Mercy. When Bob Costas spoke at Stan Musial's funeral, he quoted Yogi Berra: "Always go to your friends' funerals, otherwise they won't come to yours."

Blessed are those who do not fight, for they will not be penalized.
From the movie "A League of Their Own," who can forget the words of exasperated manager Jimmy Dugan (played by Tom Hanks): "there's no crying, there is no crying in baseball." In football, there is no fighting, there is no fighting in football. Fighting crosses the line, disrupts the game, encourages disrespectful behavior, and hurts the image of the club.

Blessed are they who hunger and thirst for fitness, for they have a healthy lifestyle.
Athletes must eat well and train hard. Sports become more competitive at each level. The effort required to achieve success is extraordinary, especially at the

professional level. Every day at the Chicago Bears' headquarters, Halas Hall, we witness the importance of conditioning.

Blessed are the helpful, for they will improve the game.

Some players are great contributors; they help make the whole team better. If you watch Walter Payton highlight clips, you might miss one of his best qualities—the way he got up after being tackled. Often, the clips end too soon. Many running backs looked like they could barely get up after a tackle. But Payton was absolutely exuberant. That rubbed off on the other players. He didn't go down easily and he got up in a flash.

Blessed are they who play clean, for they are doing God's will.

Playing "above board" is important. The rules of the game help keep players healthy. And healthy, clean play makes the NFL work. Attention is often given rookies coming onboard to expand their resumes on the positive side—to build character

Blessed are the foot-washers, for they will be called servants of God.

Players like Charles Tillman, Olin Kreutz, Brian Urlacher, Matt Forte, and others recognized by their teammates for multiple Brian Piccolo awards are good for the locker room. They are good off the field as well. I've seen many athletes and others on our staff reach out at hospitals to encourage sick kids, appear at schools to promote reading and homework, and visit youth centers to encourage students to stay in school.

Blessed are they who go to Church, for they hear the wonderful news of salvation.

Not all Bears are altar boys or sing in the choir, but many are guided by faith. Our players organize their own Bible studies. For those who want to participate, we have Mass and chapel services before our games. It's not our place to force religion on anyone, but we help our players continue their prayer lives when playing for the Bears.

Blessed are you when they mock and scorn you because of your faith. These are opportunities to live the gospel.

Athletes are reminded that life can be humbling at times. Exceptional hitters rarely get on base more than a third of their times up. Great golfers sometimes miss "the cut." An NBA superstar can be "off" on some nights. And yes, even Tom Brady can throw a wounded duck every now and then.

PART ONE: NOTEWORTHY EVENTS

THE CHICAGO BEARS CELEBRATED THE FIRST 100 YEARS OF THE NFL. HERE IS A SPECIAL CALENDAR OF NOTEWORTHY EVENTS IN BEARS' HISTORY.

Chicago Bears' Calendar

[With thanks to Dan Barile, Larry Mayer, Matt Simeone, and Dan Yuska.]

January

On January 1, 1919, George Halas was the Most Valuable Player in the Rose Bowl; he had a touchdown reception and a 77-yard interception return. Halas's Great Lakes Bluejackets beat the Mare Island Marines, 17–0.

On January 2, 1936, Bronko Nagurski signed a contract to play his 7th season with the Bears.

On January 3, 1966, Wendell Davis was born. He was a 1st round draft choice of the Bears in 1988. He played wide receiver for the Bears from 1988 through 1993.

On January 4, 1942, before the Bears played the professional all-stars from the balance of the league at the Polo Grounds in New York, George Halas spoke to the team. This team was, in his words, the culmination of his dream, the best that there had been. This was a never recaptured moment; he was overcome with emotion, an unforgettable experience. The Bears won 35–24.

On January 5, 1923, Virginia McCaskey was born. She has seen the Bears win eight Championships: 1932, 1933, 1940, 1941, 1943, 1946, 1963, and 1985.

On January 6, 1985, the George Halas Trophy was first presented to the NFC Champions.

On January 7, 1962, Ron Rivera was born. He was a 2nd round draft choice of the Bears in 1984. He played linebacker for the Bears from 1984 through 1992. He was a Bears' assistant coach in 1997 and 1998 and from 2004 through 2006. He played on the Bears' 1985 Championship team.

On January 8, 2015, Ryan Pace became the Bears' general manager.

On January 9, 2018, Matt Nagy was introduced as the Bears' head coach at a press conference.

On January 10, 1972, Frank Halas died at the age of 89. He worked for the Bears from 1922 through 1972. He was the Bears' traveling secretary. He is number three on the Bears' longevity list behind Max Swiatek and George Halas.[1]

On January 11, 1895, Paddy Driscoll was born. He played halfback, kicker, and punter for the Bears in 1920 and from 1926 through 1929. He was first-team All-Pro for the Bears twice. He made the NFL 1920s All-Decade Team. He was a Bears' assistant coach from 1941 through 1955 and from 1958 through 1962. He was a Bears' assistant coach for the 1941, 1943, and 1946 Bears' Championship teams. He was the Bears' head coach in 1956 and 1957. He is a Pro Football Hall of Famer.

On January 12, 1986, the Bears played the Los Angeles Rams at Soldier Field in the NFC Championship Game. The Bears won 24–0.

On January 13, 1971, Curtis Conway was born. He was a 1st round draft choice of the Bears in 1993. He

---

1 Max Swiatek was hired by George Halas and served in many capacities from 1934 until 2001.

played wide receiver for the Bears from 1993 through 1999.

On January 14, 2007, the Bears played the Seattle Seahawks at Soldier Field in a playoff game. The Bears won 27–24 in overtime.

On January 15, 2004, Lovie Smith became the Bears' head coach. Smith took the Bears to Super Bowl XLI on February 4, 2007, where they faced off against Tony Dungy's Indianapolis Colts at Dolphin Stadium in Miami Gardens. It was the first Super Bowl contest that featured two African-American coaches. The Colts won 29–17.

On January 16, 2011, the Bears played the Seattle Seahawks at Soldier Field in a playoff game. The Bears won 35–24.

On January 17, 1933, J. C. Caroline was born. He was a 7th round draft choice of the Bears in 1956. He played running back, defensive back, and special teams for the Bears from 1956 through 1965. He played on the Bears' 1963 Championship team. He played in one Pro Bowl.

On January 18, 1936, Bo Farrington was born. He was a 16th round draft choice of the Bears in 1960. He played offensive end for the Bears from 1960 through 1963. He played on the Bears' 1963 Championship team.

On January 19, 1993, Dave Wannstedt became the Bears' head coach.

On January 20, 1982, Mike Ditka became the Bears' head coach.

On January 20, 2002, John Aveni died. He was a 27th round draft choice of the Bears in 1959. He played kicker and end for the Bears in 1959 and 1960.

On January 20, 2009, Austin Denney died. He played tight end for the Bears from 1967 through 1969.

On January 21, 2007, the Bears played the New Orleans Saints at Soldier Field in the NFC Championship Game. The Bears won 39–14.

On January 22, 1944, Mirro Roder was born. He was the Bears' kicker in 1973 and 1974. He was an immigrant from Czechoslovakia. Dick Butkus taught him how to speak English.

On January 23, 1914, Joe Maniaci was born. He played fullback for the Bears from 1938 through 1941. He played on the Bears' 1940 and 1941 Championship teams.

On January 24, 1999, Dick Jauron became the Bears' head coach.

On January 25, 2007, Ken Kavanaugh died. He was a 3ʳᵈ round draft choice of the Bears in 1940. He played end for the Bears in 1940 and 1941 and from 1946 through 1950. He played on the Bears' 1940, 1941, and 1946 Championship teams. He was first-team All-Pro two times. He made the NFL 1940s All-Decade Team. He was a Bears' assistant coach in 1951.

On January 26, 1986, the Bears played the New England Patriots for the NFL Championship in New Orleans. The Bears won 46–10.

On January 27, 2002, Eggs Manske died. He played end for the Bears in 1937, half the season in 1938, and 1939 through 1940. He played on the Bears' 1940 Championship team.

On January 28, 1922, the Chicago Staleys became the Chicago Bears at a League Meeting.

On January 29, 1977, Jack Manders died. He played halfback, fullback, and kicker for the Bears from 1933 through 1940. He played on the 1933 and 1940 Bears' Championship teams.

On January 30, 1926, the Bears played the Portland All-Stars in Portland. Red Grange scored two touchdowns. The Bears won 60–3.

On January 31, 1934, Ted Karras was born. He played guard for the Bears from 1960 through 1964. He was the starting left guard on the Bears' 1963 Championship team.

February

On February 1, 1900, Joey Sternaman was born. He played quarterback for the Bears in 1922, the last 3 games in 1923, 1924, and 1925 and from 1927 through 1930.[2]

On February 2, 1895, George Halas was born. He played end and was co-coach for the Staleys and the Bears from 1920 through 1929. He played for and was co-coach of the Staleys' 1921 Championship team. He made the NFL 1920s All-Decade team. He was coach of the Bears from 1933 through 1942, 1946 through 1955, and 1958 through 1967. He was coach of the Bears' 1933, 1940, 1941, 1946, and 1963 Championship teams. He was owner from 1921 through 1983. He was owner of the Bears' 1921, 1932, 1933, 1940, 1941, 1943, 1946, and 1963 Championship teams. He is a Pro Football Hall of Famer. His Bears' number, 7, is retired.

On February 2, 1943, Virginia Halas and Edward McCaskey were married near Baltimore in Bel Air.

On February 3, 2018, Brian Urlacher was elected to the Pro Football Hall of Fame on the first ballot.

---

[2] Sternaman coached and played for the Duluth Kelleys for their 1923 season of 7 games and then came over to the Bears to finish out the Chicago season.

On February 4, 2007, in Super Bowl XLI between the Bears and the Colts, Devin Hester became the first player in Super Bowl history to return the game's opening kickoff for a touchdown: 92 yards.

On February 5, 2011, Richard Dent was voted for enshrinement into the Pro Football Hall of Fame.

On February 6, 1913, Bob Snyder was born. He played halfback, quarterback, and kicker for the Bears from 1939 through 1941 and 1943. He played on the Bears' 1940, 1941, and 1943 Championship teams.

On February 7, 1970, Chris Gardocki was born. He was a 3rd round draft choice of the Bears in 1991. He was the Bears' punter from 1991 through 1994.

On February 8, 1936, the Bears drafted Joe Stydahar in the 1st round of the first collegiate player draft. He played tackle for the Bears from 1936 through 1942 and from 1945-1946. He played on the Bears' 1940, 1941, and 1946 Championship teams. He was first-team All-Pro four times. He was a Bears' assistant coach in 1963 and 1964. He was a Bears' assistant coach for the 1963 Championship team. He is a Pro Football Hall of Famer. Dan Fortmann presented Stydahar for induction in 1967.

On February 9, 1895, Dutch Sternaman was born. He played halfback and was co-coach of the Staleys and the Bears from 1920 through 1929. He played and was co-coach for the Staleys' 1921 Championship team. He was first-team All-Pro twice. He was co-owner from 1921 through 1932.

On February 10, 1959, Dennis Gentry was born. He was a 4th round draft choice of the Bears in 1982. He played running back, wide receiver, and returner for the Bears from 1982 through 1992. He played on the Bears' 1985 Championship team.

SPORTSMANSHIP

On February 11, 1986, the Shufflin' Crew's "Super Bowl Shuffle" was certified gold by the Record Industry Association of America.

On February 12, 1961, Mark Bortz was born. He was an 8th round draft choice of the Bears in 1983. He played guard for the Bears from 1983 through 1994. He played on the Bears' 1985 Championship team. He has played in the most Bears' playoff games.

On February 13, 1978, Mike Brown was born. He was a 2nd round draft choice of the Bears in 2000. He played safety for the Bears from 2000 through 2008. He played in one Pro Bowl. He was All-Pro twice.

On February 14, 1966, Min Halas died. She started working for the Bears in 1922. In addition to her clerical duties, she compiled scrapbooks that she kept all of her life. Every day, she would go through the newspapers, hoping to find some reference to the Bears. When she did, she clipped it out and threw it into an old bread box. Then during the off-seasons, she would paste these clippings into what became an annual scrapbook.

On February 15, 1975, Bears' general manager Jim Finks named Carl Marasco as director of player personnel.

On February 16, 1958, George Halas returned as the Bears' head coach. This was the start of his fourth and last 10-year term.

On February 17, 2011, Dave Duerson died. He was a 3rd round draft choice of the Bears in 1983. He played safety for the Bears from 1983 through 1989. He played on the Bears' 1985 Championship team. He played in four Pro Bowls. He was All-Pro twice. He was the NFL Man of the Year in 1987.

On February 18, 1922, George Halas and Min Bushing got married. Almost immediately after their marriage, my grandmother started working in the Bears' office three days a week, sometimes as many as five. In addition to her clerical duties, she started compiling scrapbooks that she kept all of her life. Every day, she would go through the newspaper, hoping to find some reference to the Bears. When she did, she clipped it out and threw it into an old bread box. Then during the off-season, she would paste these clippings into what became an annual scrapbook.

On February 19, 1971, Glyn Milburn was born. He was a returner and a wide receiver for the Bears from 1998 through 2001. He played in one Pro Bowl for the Bears.

On February 20, 1967, Tom Waddle was born. He played wide receiver for the Bears from 1989 through 1994. He was a Piccolo Award winner.

On February 21, 1960, offensive captain and veteran guard Abe Gibron announced that he was retiring from the Bears. He was a Bears' player his last two seasons. He would return to the Bears as an offensive assistant coach for three seasons, a Bears' defensive assistant coach for four seasons, and the Bears' head coach for three seasons.

On February 22, 1991, Khalil Mack was born. He started playing outside linebacker for the Bears in 2018.

On February 23, 1981, Charles Tillman was born. He was a 2nd round draft choice of the Bears in 2003. He played cornerback for the Bears from 2003 through 2014. He was a three-time Piccolo Award winner. He played in two Pro Bowls. He was All-Pro once. He won the Walter Payton NFL Man of the Year Award once.

On February 24, 1987, Prince and the Revolution's "Kiss" won the Grammy for best R&B vocal performance by a duo or group, besting the "Super Bowl Shuffle."

On February 25, 1958, Jeff Fisher was born. He was a 7th round draft choice of the Bears in 1981. He played cornerback and returner for the Bears from 1981 through 1984.

On February 26, 1940, Mac Percival was born. He was the Bears' kicker from 1967 through 1973. He tied Roger LeClerc's record of five field goals in one game. He was All-Pro once.

On February 27, 1975, Marcus Robinson was born. He was a 4th round draft choice of the Bears in 1997. He played wide receiver for the Bears from 1997 through 2002. He set the Bears' record for receiving yards with 1400 in 1999.

On February 28, 1953, Roland Harper was born. He was a 17th round draft choice of the Bears in 1975. He played fullback for the Bears from 1975 through 1978 and from 1980 through 1982. He was a Piccolo Award winner.

On February 29, 2016, Rudy Bukich died. He played quarterback for the Bears in 1958 and 1959 and from 1962 through 1968. He played on the Bears' 1963 Championship team.

March

On March 1, 1926, the Bears opened offices at 111 West Washington in Chicago.

On March 2, 1916, Lee Artoe was born. He was an 11th round draft choice of the Bears in 1940. He played tackle for the Bears from 1940 through 1943. He played on the Bears' 1940, 1941, and 1943 Championship teams.

On March 3, 1997, the Bears moved to Halas Hall at Conway Park in Lake Forest.

On March 4, 1953, Doug Plank was born. He was a 12th round draft choice of the Bears in 1975. He played safety for the Bears from 1975 through 1982.

On March 5, 2010, the Bears signed free agent defensive end Julius Peppers who was voted to the Pro Bowl in each of his first three seasons with the team.

On March 6, 1991, Herman Lee died. He played offensive tackle for the Bears from 1958 through 1966. He played on the Bears' 1963 Championship team.

On March 7, 1927, Eddie Macon was born. He was a 2nd round draft choice of the Bears in 1952. He played halfback for the Bears from 1952 through 1953. He was the first black player for the Bears.

On March 8, 1962, Shaun Gayle was born. He was a 10th round draft choice of the Bears in 1984. He played safety for the Bears from 1984 through 1994. He played on the Bears' 1985 Championship team. He was a Brian Piccolo Award winner.

On March 9, 1898, Laurie Walquist was born. He played quarterback for the Bears in 1922 and from 1924-1931. He was an assistant coach for the Bears in 1933-1934. He was an assistant coach for the Bears' 1933 Championship team.

On March 10, 1919, Bulldog Turner was born. He was a 1st round draft choice of the Bears in 1940. He played center and linebacker for the Bears from 1940 through 1952. He played on the Bears' 1940, 1941, 1943, and 1946 Championship teams. He was first-team All-Pro seven times. He played in two Pro Bowls. He made the NFL 1940s All-Decade team. He was a Bears' assistant coach from 1953 through 1958. He is a Pro Football Hall of Famer. His Bears' number, 66, is retired.

On March 11, 1915, Hamp Pool was born. He was a 9th round draft choice of the Bears in 1940. He played end for the Bears from 1940 through 1943. He played on the Bears' 1940, 1941, and 1943 Championship teams.

On March 11, 1994, Charlie Bivins died. He played running back for the Bears from 1960 through 1966. He played on the Bears' 1963 Championship team.

On March 12, 1966, Keith Molesworth died. He played for the Bears from 1931 through 1937. He played on the Bears' 1932 and 1933 Championship teams.

On March 13, 1918, George McAfee was born. He played halfback for the Bears in 1940 and 1941 and from 1945 through 1950. He played on the Bears' 1940, 1941, and 1946 Championship teams. He was All-Pro once. He made the NFL 1940s All-Decade team. He is a Pro Football Hall of Famer. His Bears' number, 5, is retired.

On March 14, 1936, Carl Brumbaugh rejoined the Bears. He had played on the Bears' 1932 and 1933 Championship teams.

On March 15, 1951, Steve Schubert was born. He played wide receiver and returner for the Bears from 1975-1979.

On March 16, 1917, Dante Magnani was born. He played running back for the Bears in 1943, 1946, and 1949. He played on the Bears' 1943 and 1946 Championship teams.

On March 17, 1912, Joe Stydahar was born. He was a 1st round draft choice of the Bears in 1936. He played tackle for the Bears from 1936 through 1942 and from 1945-1946. He played on the Bears' 1940, 1941, and 1946 Championship teams. He was All-Pro six times. He made the NFL 1930s All-Decade team. He was a Bears' assistant coach in 1963 and 1964. He was an assistant coach for the Bears' 1963 Championship team. He is a Pro Football Hall of Famer.

On March 18, 1920, George Chamberlain met with George Halas, in Chicago. Chamberlain was the general superintendent of the A. E. Staley Company in Decatur. Chamberlain offered Grandpa the opportunity to learn the starch business and be the company's athletic director and football coach. He could play on the Staley football and baseball teams.

On March 19, 1970, George Halas was elected president of the National Football Conference as the NFL-AFL merge.

On March 20, 2018, the Bears signed veteran cornerback Kyle Fuller to a 4-year contract.

On March 21, 1959, Jay Hilgenberg was born. He played center for the Bears from 1981 through 1991. He played on the Bears' 1985 Championship team. He played in the Pro Bowl seven times. He was All-Pro five times.

On March 22, 1960, Jim Covert was born. He was a 1st round draft choice of the Bears in 1983. He played offensive left tackle for the Bears from 1983 through 1990. He made the All-Rookie team. He won the Brian Piccolo Award. He played on the Bears' 1985 Championship team. He was a Bears' captain. He played in two Pro Bowls. He was All-Pro twice. He made the NFL 1980s All-Decade Team. He is a Pro Football Hall of Famer.

On March 23, 1977, Joe Stydahar died. He was a 1st round draft choice of the Bears in 1936. He played tackle for the Bears from 1936 through 1942 and from 1945 through 1946. He played on the Bears' 1940, 1941, and 1946 Championship teams. He was All-Pro six times. He made the NFL 1930s All-Decade team. He was a Bears' assistant coach in 1963 and 1964. He was

an assistant coach for the Bears' 1963 Championship team. He is a Pro Football Hall of Famer.
On March 24, 1990, Danny Trevathan was born. He started playing linebacker for the Bears in 2016.
On March 25, 1956, the Bears signed their 8th round draft choice Dominic "Dick" Klawitter, who at the time was considered one of the biggest men in football at 6-foot-7 and weighing 282 pounds. Klawitter was a Chicago native, prepping at Bowen High School on the city's Southside before attending South Dakota State University.
On March 26, 1987, George Halas was inducted into the National Business Hall of Fame.
On March 27, 1960, Tim Wrightman was born. He was a 3rd round draft choice of the Bears in 1982. He played tight end for the Bears in 1985 and 1986. He was on the Bears' 1985 Championship team.
On March 28, 1930, Joe Fortunato was born. He was a 7th round draft choice of the Bears in 1952. He played linebacker for the Bears from 1955 through 1966. He played in five Pro Bowls. He was All-Pro four times. He made the NFL 1950s All-Decade Team. He played on the Bears' 1963 Championship team. He was a Bears' assistant coach in 1967 and 1968.
On March 29, 1968, James Williams was born. He played offensive tackle for the Bears from 1991 through 2002. He played in one Pro Bowl.
On March 30, 1935, Willie Galimore was born. He was a 5th round draft choice of the Bears in 1956. He played halfback for the Bears from 1957 through 1963. He played on the Bears' 1963 Championship team. His Bears' number, 28, has been retired.
On March 31, 1956, George Halas and Curly Lambeau held a rally to keep the Packers in Green Bay.

April

On April 1, 2015, the Bears signed outside linebacker Sam Acho to a 1-year contract.

On April 2, 1917, Hugh Gallarneau was born. He was a 3ʳᵈ round draft choice of the Bears in 1941. He played halfback and returner for the Bears from 1941 through 1942 and from 1946 through 1947. He played on the Bears' 1941 and 1946 Championship teams.

On April 3, 1959, Les Frazier was born. He signed with the Bears as a free agent in 1981. He played cornerback and returner for the Bears from 1981 through 1985. He was a starting cornerback on the Bears' 1985 Championship team.

On April 4, 1967, Guy Chamberlin died. He played end for the 1920 Decatur Staleys and the 1921 Chicago Staleys. He played on the Staleys' 1921 Championship team. He was All-Pro for the Staleys once. He made the NFL 1920s All-Decade Team. He is a Pro Football Hall of Famer.

On April 5, 2011, Anthony Adams received the Ed Block Courage Award. He played defensive tackle for the Bears from 2007 through 2011. Since 2013, he is a host for the television show "Inside the Bears."

On April 5, 2016, Robbie Gould received the Ed Block Courage Award. Robbie was the Bears' kicker from 2005 through 2015. He played in one Pro Bowl. He was All-Pro once.

On April 6, 1914, Dick Plasman was born. He was a 3ʳᵈ round draft choice of the Bears in 1937. He played end for the Bears from 1937 through 1941 and 1944. He played on the Bears' Championship teams in 1940 and 1941. He is the last player in the NFL to play without a helmet. He did that in the 1940 NFL Championship game.

SPORTSMANSHIP

On April 7, 1948, Ross Brupbacher was born. He was a 4th round draft choice of the Bears in 1970. He played linebacker for the Bears from 1970 through 1972 and 1976.

On April 8, 1910, George Musso was born. He played guard and tackle for the Bears from 1933 through 1944. He played on the Bears' 1933, 1940, 1941, and 1943 Championship teams. He was All-Pro twice. He was a Bears' Captain for nine seasons. He made the NFL 75th Anniversary All-Time team. He is a Pro Football Hall of Famer.

On April 9, 2019, Bears' tight end Zach Miller was presented with the Ed Block Courage Award.

On April 10, 2012, Bears' Hall of Fame linebacker Brian Urlacher was presented with the Ed Block Courage Award.

On April 11, 1916, Dan Fortmann was born. He was a 9th round draft choice of the Bears in 1936. He played guard for the Bears from 1936 through 1943. He played on the Bears' 1940, 1941, and 1943 Championship teams. He was All-Pro six times. He made the NFL 1930s All-Decade team. He is a Pro Football Hall of Famer.

On April 12, 1972, Ronnie Bull, who at the time was number five on the all-time Bears' rushing leaders list, announced his retirement after 10 years in the NFL. He was the 1962 NFL Rookie of the Year. He played on the Bears' 1963 Championship team.

On April 13, 1964, George Halas became the first person outside of the Green Bay organization to be honored by the team for his contributions to the game.

On April 14, 2014, the Bears agreed to terms with cornerback Kyle Fuller on a 4-year contract.

On April 15, 2000, the Bears drafted Brian Urlacher in the 1st round and Mike Brown in the 2nd round.

On April 16, 2000, the Bears drafted Paul Edinger in the 6th round. He was the Bears' kicker from 2000 through 2004.

On April 17, 1999, the Bears drafted Cade McNown in the 1st round and Rex Tucker, D'Wayne Bates, and Marty Booker in the 3rd round.

On April 18, 1938, Richie Petitbon was born. He was a 2nd round draft choice of the Bears in 1959. He played safety for the Bears from 1959 through 1968. He played on the Bears' 1963 Championship team. He played in four Pro Bowls. He was All-Pro three times.

On April 18, 1975, Pat Mannelly was born. He was a 6th round draft choice of the Bears in 1998. He was the Bears' long snapper from 1998 through 2013. He was the Bears' special teams captain seven times. He was an Ed Block Courage Award winner.

On April 19, 1915, Connie Mack Berry was born. He played end for the Bears from 1942 through 1946. He played on the Bears' 1943 and 1946 Championship teams.

On April 20, 2015, Doug Buffone died. He was a 4th round draft choice of the Bears in 1966. He played linebacker for the Bears from 1966 through 1979.

On April 21, 1938, Angelo Coia was born. He was a 20th round draft choice of the Bears in 1960. He played offensive end for the Bears from 1960 through 1963. He played on the Bears' 1963 Championship team.

On April 22, 1995, the Bears drafted Rashaan Salaam in the 1st round. He played running back for the Bears from 1995 through 1997. He set the Bears' rookie rushing record with 1,074 yards.

On April 23, 2018, Matt Forte and Devin Hester signed 1-day contracts so that they could retire as Bears.

On April 24, 1978, Hunk Anderson died. He played guard for the Bears from 1922 through 1925. He made the NFL 1920s All-Decade team. He was a Bears' assistant coach from 1940 through 1942 and from 1946 through 1950. He was an assistant coach for the Bears' 1940 and 1946 Championship teams. He was co-head coach of the Bears from 1942 through 1945. He was co-head coach for the Bears' 1943 Championship team.

On April 25, 1927, Jim Parmer was born. He was a Bears' scout from 1973 through 1991. He was a Bears' scout for the 1985 Championship team.

On April 26, 1961, the NFL signed a 2-year $9,300,000 TV contract.

On April 27, 1919, Ed McCaskey was born. He worked for the Bears from 1967 through 2003. He was vice president, treasurer, chairman, and chairman emeritus.

On April 28, 1968, Mark Carrier was born. He was a 1st round draft choice of the Bears in 1990. He played safety for the Bears from 1990 through 1996. He was the NFL Defensive Rookie of the Year. He played in three Pro Bowls. He was a Brian Piccolo Award winner.

On April 29, 1983, Tommie Harris and Jay Cutler were born. Tommie Harris played defensive tackle for the Bears from 2004 through 2010. Jay Cutler played quarterback for the Bears from 2009 through 2016.

On April 30, 2016, the Bears selected running back Jordan Howard in the 5th round of the draft with the 150th pick overall. Howard broke the franchise's rookie rushing record with 1,313 yards and was voted to the Pro Bowl.

Patrick McCaskey

1963 Chicago Bears' Championship Roster

9	Bill Wade	Quarterback
10	Rudy Bukich	Quarterback
17	Richie Petitbon	Safety
22	Billy Martin	Returner
23	Dave Whitsell	Cornerback
24	Rosey Taylor	Safety
25	J.C. Caroline	Cornerback
26	Bennie McRae	Cornerback
28	Willie Galimore	Running Back
29	Ronnie Bull	Running Back
31	Joe Fortunato	Outside Linebacker
33	Larry Morris	Outside Linebacker
34	Joe Marconi	Running Back
35	Rick Casares	Fullback
43	Larry Glueck	Safety
46	Angela Coia	Wide Receiver
47	Johnny Morris	Wide Receiver
49	Charlie Bivins	Running Back
50	Mike Pyle	Center
60	Roger Davis	Guard
61	Bill George	Middle Linebacker
63	Bob Wetoska	Tackle
65	Tom Bettis	Outside Linebacker
67	Ted Karras	Guard
70	Herman Lee	Tackle
71	Earl Leggett	Tackle
72	Jim Cadile	Guard
73	Steve Barnett	Tackle
74	Bob Kilcullen	End
75	Fred Williams	Tackle
76	John Johnson	Tackle
78	Stan Jones	Tackle
80	Bob Jenks	Kicker
81	Doug Atkins	End
83	Roger LeClerc	Kicker
84	Bo Farrington	Wide Receiver
87	Ed O'Bradovich	End
88	Bobby Joe Green	Punter
89	Mike Ditka	Tight End

May

On May 1, 1984, the Bears drafted Wilber Marshall in the 1st round and Ron Rivera in the 2nd round. The Bears traded for Steve Fuller. All three players were on the Bears' 1985 Championship team. Steve Fuller was in the Super Bowl Shuffle.

On May 2, 1908, Joe Zeller was born. He played guard and end for the Bears from 1933 through 1938. He played on the Bears' 1933 Championship team.

On May 3, 1956, Cliff Thrift was born. He played linebacker for the Bears in 1985. He played on the Bears' 1985 Championship team.

On May 4, 1932, Harlon Hill was born. He was a 15th round draft choice of the Bears in 1954. He played wide receiver for the Bears from 1954 through 1961. He was the NFL Rookie of the Year. He played in three Pro Bowls. He was All-Pro twice. He was the NFL Most Valuable Player once.

On May 5, 2011, George McCaskey became the Bears' chairman.

On May 6, 2015, the Bears signed 2nd round draft pick Eddie Goldman, a nose tackle from Florida State University, to a 4-year contract.

On May 7, 1936, Bobby Joe Green was born. He was the Bears' punter from 1962 through 1973. He played on the Bears' 1963 Championship team. He played in the 1970 Pro Bowl.

On May 8, 1930, Doug Atkins was born. He played defensive end for the Bears from 1955 through 1966. He played on the Bears' 1963 Championship team. He played in eight Pro Bowls. He was All-Pro for the Bears nine times. He made the NFL 1960s All-Decade team. He is a Pro Football Hall of Famer. Ed McCaskey presented Doug for induction in 1982.

On May 9, 1937, Bob Jeter was born. He played cornerback for the Bears from 1971 through 1973.

On May 10, 1980, George Halas received an honorary law degree from Lake Forest College.

On May 11, 2017, the Bears signed draft pick Tarik Cohen.

On May 12, 1995, the Bears broke ground for Halas Hall at Conway Park in Lake Forest.

On May 13, 1936, Bob Kilcullen was born. He was an 8th round draft choice of the Bears in 1957. He played defensive end for the Bears from 1957 through 1966. He played on the Bears' 1963 Championship team. He presented Stan Jones for induction into the Pro Football Hall of Fame in 1991.

On May 14, 1998, Bill Bishop died. He was an 8th round draft choice of the Bears in 1952. He played defensive tackle for the Bears from 1952 through 1960. He played in one Pro Bowl for the Bears.

On May 15, 1918, John Siegal was born. He was a 17th round draft choice of the Bears in 1939. He played wide receiver for the Bears from 1939 through 1943. He played on the Bears' 1940, 1941, and 1943 Championship teams.

On May 16, 1963, Bernie Masterson died. He played quarterback for the Bears from 1934 through 1940. He played on the Bears' 1940 Championship team.

On May 17, 1969, the Bears traded Richie Petitbon to the Los Angeles Rams for Lee Calland; a 1970 4th round draft choice, Ross Brupbacher; and a 1971 3rd round draft choice, Bob Newton.

On May 18, 2013, rookie Kyle Long signed a 4-year deal with the Bears.

On May 19, 1966, Keith Jennings was born. He played tight end for the Bears from 1991 through 1997.

On May 20, 2017, the Bears' Care Gala took place in the United Club at Soldier Field.[3] It was for the benefit of breast and ovarian cancer research and treatment programs in Chicago.

On May 21, 1940, Ed O'Bradovich was born. He was a 7th round draft choice of the Bears in 1962. He played defensive end for the Bears from 1962 through 1971. He played on the Bears' 1963 Championship team.

On May 22, 1980, Jason McKie was born. He played fullback for the Bears from 2003 through 2009.

On May 23, 1995, Dan Fortmann died. He was a 9th round draft choice of the Bears in 1936. He played guard for the Bears from 1936 through 1943. He played on the Bears' 1940, 1941, and 1943 Championship teams. He was All-Pro six times. He made the NFL 1930s All-Decade team. He is a Pro Football Hall of Famer.

On May 24, 1919, George Halas was on the roster of the New York Yankees when they beat the Chicago White Sox, 2–1, in Chicago. In July, Halas would be sent down to the Minors for the rest of the baseball season. He would be playing semipro football with the Hammond Pros that fall. Then he would land a job in the spring of 1920 managing, coaching, and playing for the Decatur Staleys![4]

On May 25, 1978, Brian Urlacher was born. He was a 1st round draft choice of the Bears in 2000. He played linebacker for the Bears from 2000 through 2012. He was the NFL Defensive Rookie of the Year. He was the

---

[3] The United Club is a hospitality area for Soldier Field. Located on the east side of the stadium, the three-level United Club offers impressive sightlines and access to the indoor club lounge.

[4] Gary Sarnoff, "George Halas," Society for American Baseball Research, viewed at https://sabr.org/bioproj/person/586380d8 on August 7, 2019.

NFL Defensive Player of the Year in 2005. He played in eight Pro Bowls. He was All-Pro five times. He made the NFL 2000s All-Decade team. He is a Pro Football Hall of Famer.

On May 26, 2000, Hamp Pool died. He was a 7th round draft choice of the Bears in 1940. He played end for the Bears from 1940 through 1943. He played on the Bears' 1940, 1941, and 1943 Championship teams.

On May 27, 1968, George Halas retired from coaching after 40 seasons with 324 wins, 151 defeats, and 31 ties.

On May 28, 1993, Bobby Joe Green died. He was the Bears' punter from 1962 through 1973. He played on the Bears' 1963 Championship team. He played in the 1970 Pro Bowl.

On May 29, 2009, the Bears signed defensive lineman Israel Idonije to a 2-year contract extension.

On May 30, 1943, Gale Sayers was born. He was a 1st round draft choice of the Bears in 1965. He played running back and returner for the Bears from 1965 through 1971. He played in four Pro Bowls. He was All-Pro five times. He was the NFL Comeback Player of the year in 1969. He made the NFL 1960s All-Decade team. He made the NFL 75th Anniversary All-Time team. He is a Pro Football Hall of Famer. George Halas presented Gale for induction in 1977. His Bears' number, 40, is retired.

On May 31, 2012, Bears' President and Chief Executive Officer Ted Phillips joined NFL commissioner Roger Goodell at a ceremony at Soldier Field honoring the facility as the first NFL stadium to be certified as "green" by the U.S. Green Building Council.

June

On June 1, 1949, Craig Clemons was born. He was a 1st round draft choice of the Bears in 1972. He played safety for the Bears from 1972 through 1977.

On June 2, 1972, Dwayne Joseph was born. He was on the Bears' practice squad in 1994. He played defensive back for the Bears in 1995. He was on injured reserve in 1996. He was a Bears' player relations man from 1998 through 2003. He was a Bears' scout from 2012 through 2015.

On June 3, 1957, the Bears signed their 3rd round draft pick UCLA quarterback Ronnie Knox. It was an unprecedented 3-year contract for an NFL rookie ($50,000 for 3 years)

On June 4, 1979, Alex Brown was born. He was a 4th round draft choice of the Bears in 2002. He played defensive end for the Bears from 2002 through 2009.

On June 5, 1956, the Bears announced the signing of J. C. Caroline. He played defensive back and special teams for the Bears from 1956 through 1965. He played on the Bears' 1963 Championship team.

On June 6, 1938, Billy Martin was born. He was a 4th round draft choice of the Bears in 1960. He played halfback for the Bears from 1962 through 1964. He played on the Bears' 1963 Championship team.

On June 7, 1964, Richie Petitbon and Dave Whitsell, both defensive backs on the Bears' 1963 Championship team, signed contracts to return to Chicago in 1964.

On June 8, 1957, George Halas announced Perry Jeter, the Bears' punt and kickoff return specialist re-signed with the team. Jeter, 5 feet 7 inches and 184 pounds, was the shortest back in the NFL at that time.

On June 9, 1977, Olin Kreutz was born. He was a 3rd round draft choice of the Bears in 1998. He played center for the Bears from 1998 through 2010. He played in six Pro Bowls. He was All-Pro twice. He made the NFL 2000s All-Decade team. He was a Piccolo Award winner five times.

On June 10, 1961, the Bears signed fullback Rick Casares and offensive tackle Stan Fanning. Casares played for the Bears from 1955 through 1964. He played on the Bears' 1963 Championship team. Fanning played for the Bears from 1960 through 1962.

On June 11, 1954, Gary Fencik was born. He played safety for the Bears from 1976 through 1987. He played on the Bears' 1985 Championship team. He played in two Pro Bowls. He was All-Pro three times. He is the Bears' all-time leading interceptor with 38.

On June 12, 2001, Jerry Angelo started working for the Bears. He was the Bears' general manager from 2001 through 2011.

On June 13, 1903, Red Grange was born. He played halfback for the Bears in 1925 and from 1929 through 1934. He played on the Bears' 1932 and 1933 Championship teams. He was All-Pro three times. He made the NFL 1920s All-Decade Team. He was a Bears' assistant coach from 1933 through 1940. He was a Bears' assistant coach for the Bears' 1933 and 1940 Championship teams. He was a Bears' television broadcaster. He is a Pro Football Hall of Famer. Jimmy Conzelman presented Grange for induction in 1963. His Bears' number, 77, is retired.

On June 14, 1936, Dave Whitsell was born. He played cornerback for the Bears from 1961 through 1966. He played on the Bears' 1963 Championship team.

On June 15, 1939, Solly Sherman, star University of Chicago halfback and quarterback, signed his first contract with the Bears. He played for the Bears in

1939 and 1940. He played on the Bears' 1940 Championship team.

On June 16, 1970, Brian Piccolo died. He played running back for the Bears from 1966 through 1969. Bear players vote for their teammates who best exemplify the courage, loyalty, teamwork, dedication, and sense of humor for the Brian Piccolo Award. His Bears' number, 41, has been retired.

On June 17, 1971, the Bears promoted director of player personnel Bobby Walston to assistant to President George "Mugs" Halas Junior.

On June 18, 1969, Jay Leeuwenburg was born. He played tackle and guard for the Bears from 1992 through 1995. His father, Rich, played tackle for the Bears in 1965.

On June 19, 1951, Bill Knox was born. He played defensive back for the Bears from 1974 through 1976.

On June 20, 1981, Dick Plasman died. He was a 3rd round draft choice of the Bears in 1937. He played running back for the Bears from 1937 through 1944. He played on the Bears' 1940 and 1941 Championship teams. He was the last NFL player to play without a helmet. He did that in the 1940 Championship game.

On June 21, 1947, Dave Hale was born. He was a 12th round draft choice of the Bears in 1969. He played on the defensive line for the Bears from 1969 through 1973.

On June 22, 1947, Bobby Douglass was born. He was a 2nd round draft choice of the Bears in 1969. He played quarterback for the Bears from 1969 through 1974 and was traded early in the 1975 season.

On June 23, 1938, Roger Davis was born. He was a 1st round draft choice of the Bears in 1960. He played guard for the Bears from 1960 through 1963. He was the starting right guard on the Bears' 1963 Championship team.

On June 24, 1922, the American Professional Football Association became the National Football League at a League meeting.

On June 25, 1981, the Bears announced the re-signings of center Dan Neal and cornerback Terry Schmidt for the 1981 season.

On June 26, 1895, Min Halas was born. She started working for the Bears in 1922. In addition to her clerical duties, she started compiling scrapbooks that she kept all of her life. Every day, she would go through the newspapers, hoping to find some reference to the Bears. When she did, she clipped it out and threw it into an old bread box. Then during the off-season, she would paste these clippings into what became an annual scrapbook.

On June 27, 1944, Doug Buffone was born. He was a 4th round draft choice of the Bears in 1966. He played linebacker for the Bears from 1966 through 1979.

On June 27, 1957, Ted Phillips was born. He is the Bears' President and Chief Executive Officer.

On June 28, 2016, Buddy Ryan died. He was the defensive coordinator for the Bears from 1978 through 1985. He was the defensive coordinator of the Bears' 1985 Championship team.

On June 29, 1968, Paddy Driscoll died. He played halfback, kicker, and punter for the Bears in 1920 and from 1926 through 1929. He was All-Pro for the Bears three times. He made the NFL 1920s All-Decade Team. He was a Bears' assistant coach from 1941 through 1955 and from 1958 through 1962. He was a Bears' assistant coach for the 1941, 1943, and 1946 Bears' Championships teams. He was the Bears' head coach in 1956 and 1957. He is a Pro Football Hall of Famer.

Jimmy Conzelman presented Driscoll for induction in 1965.

On June 30, 1957, the Bears starting quarterback Ed Brown re-signed with the team for the 1957 season. He played quarterback and punter for the Bears from 1954 through 1961. He played in one Pro Bowl.

July

On July 1, 1979, Adrian Peterson was born. He was a 6th round draft choice of the Bears in 2002. He played running back for the Bears from 2002 through 2009.

On July 2, 1925, Don Kindt was born. He was a 1st round draft choice of the Bears in 1947. He played offensive and defensive back for the Bears from 1947 through 1955. He played in one Pro Bowl.

On July 3, 1943, Steve DeLong was born. He was a 1st round draft choice of the Bears in 1965. He played on the defensive line for the Bears in 1972. He was the Bears' third choice in the 1st round of the 1965 draft behind Dick Butkus and Gale Sayers.

On July 4, 1931, Rick Casares was born. He was a 2nd round draft choice of the Bears in 1954. He played fullback for the Bears from 1955 through 1964. He played on the Bears' 1963 Championship team. He played in five Pro Bowls. He was All-Pro twice.

On July 4, 1937, Rosey Taylor was born. He played safety and returner for the Bears from 1961 through 1968 and into early 1969. He played on the Bears' 1963 Championship team.

On July 5, 1941, John Johnson was born. He was a 6th round draft choice of the Bears in 1963. He played defensive tackle for the Bears from 1963 through 1968. He played on the Bears' 1963 Championship team.

On July 6, 1972, Bears' defensive end Ed O'Bradovich announced his retirement after ten seasons with the

Bears. He was one of the NFL's most durable performers, and his interception in the 1963 Championship game against the Giants led to the winning touchdown.

On July 7, 1958, Matt Suhey was born. He was a 2nd round draft choice of the Bears in 1980. He played fullback for the Bears from 1980 through 1989. He played on the Bears' 1985 Championship team.

On July 8, 1954, Phil McKinnely was born. He played offensive tackle for the Bears in 1982.

On July 9, 1969, the Bears signed their top draft choice offensive tackle Rufus Mayes of Ohio State University.

On July 10, 1980, the Bears signed their 1st round draft pick Otis Wilson. He was a starting outside linebacker on the Bears' 1985 Championship team.

On July 11, 1957, the Bears announced the re-signings of veteran linebacker Joe Fortunato and guard Tom Roggeman.

On July 12, 1975, the Bears started training camp at Lake Forest College.

On July 13, 1986, Gary Famiglietti died. He was a 3rd round draft choice of the Bears in 1938. He played running back for the Bears from 1938 through 1945. He played on the Bears' 1940, 1941, and 1943 Championship teams.

On July 14, 1914, Bob Swisher was born. He played halfback for the Bears from 1938 through 1941 and 1945. He played on the Bears' 1940 and 1941 Championship teams.

On July 15, 1941, Bob Jencks was born. He played end and kicker for the Bears from 1963 through 1964. He played on the Bears' 1963 Championship team.

On July 16, 1940, Jim Cadile was born. He was a 4th round draft choice of the Bears in 1962. He played guard for the Bears from 1962 through 1972.

On July 17, 1979, Bears' running back Johnny Musso announced his retirement.

On July 18, 1981, the Bears signed 2nd round draft pick linebacker Mike Singletary and free agent cornerback Les Frazier. Both of them were starters on the Bears' 1985 Championship team.

On July 19, 1919, Norm Standlee was born. He was a 1st round draft choice of the Bears in 1941. He played running back for the Bears in 1941. He played on the Bears' 1941 Championship team.

On July 20, 1927, Dick Stanfel was born. He was the Bears' offensive line coach from 1981 through 1992. He was the offensive line coach for the Bears' 1985 Championship team. He is a Pro Football Hall of Famer.

On July 21, 1976, Bears' tackle Bob Asher announced his retirement. He had played offensive tackle for the Bears from 1972 through 1975.

On July 22, 1918, Rudy Mucha was born. He played guard for the Bears from mid-season 1945 through 1946. He played on the Bears' 1946 Championship team.

On July 23, 1957, Kris Haines was born. He played wide receiver for the Bears. He came over from the Redskins during the 1979 season and played for the Bears through 1981.

On July 24, 1962, Kevin Butler was born. He was a 4th round draft choice of the Bears in 1985. He was the Bears' kicker from 1985 through 1995. He played on the Bears' 1985 Championship team.

On July 25, 1954, Walter Payton was born. He was a 1st round draft choice of the Bears in 1975. He played running back for the Bears from 1975 through 1987. He played on the Bears' 1985 Championship team. He played in nine Pro Bowls. He was All-Pro eight times. He was the NFL Most Valuable Player twice. He was the NFL Man of the Year once. He made the NFL 1970s All-Decade team. He made the NFL 1980s All-Decade team. He made the NFL 75th Anniversary All-Time team. He is a Pro Football Hall of Famer. His Bears' number, 34, is retired.

On July 26, 1951, Ralph Jones died. He was the Bears' head coach from 1930 through 1932. He was the head coach of the Bears' 1932 Championship team.

On July 27, 1974, Ed McCaskey presented Bill George for induction into the Pro Football Hall of Fame.

On July 27, 1991, Bob Kilcullen presented Stan Jones for induction into the Pro Football Hall of Fame.

On July 28, 1979, former University of Illinois Coach Pete Elliott presented Dick Butkus for induction into the Pro Football Hall of Fame.

On July 29, 1986, Joe Kopcha died. He played guard for the Bears from 1929 through 1935. He played on the Bears' 1932 and 1933 Championship teams.

On July 29, 1995, Ed McCaskey presented Jim Finks for induction into the Pro Football Hall of Fame.

On July 30, 1977, George Halas presented Gale Sayers for induction into the Pro Football Hall of Fame.

On July 30, 1988, Ed O'Bradovich presented Mike Ditka for induction into the Pro Football Hall of Fame.

On July 31, 1971, football executive Upton Bell presented Bill Hewitt posthumously for induction into the Pro Football Hall of Fame.

On July 31, 1993, Jarrett Payton presented Walter Payton for induction into the Pro Football Hall of Fame.

August

On August 1, 1981, Al Davis presented George Blanda for induction into the Pro Football Hall of Fame.

On August 1, 1998, Kim Singletary presented Mike Singletary for induction into the Pro Football Hall of Fame.

On August 2, 1975, George Halas presented George Connor for induction into the Pro Football Hall of Fame.

On August 3, 2002, Ed O'Bradovich presented Dan Hampton for induction into the Pro Football Hall of Fame.

On August 4, 2018, Bears former linebacker coach, Bob Babich, presented Brian Urlacher for induction into the Pro Football Hall of Fame.

On August 5, 1967, Dan Fortmann presented Joe Stydahar for induction into the Pro Football Hall of Fame.

On August 6, 2011, Joe Gilliam presented Richard Dent for induction into the Pro Football Hall of Fame.

On August 7, 1982, Ed McCaskey presented Doug Atkins and George Halas presented George Musso for induction into the Pro Football Hall of Fame.

On August 8, 1944, the Bears started training camp at Saint Joseph's College in Rensselaer, Indiana.

On August 9, 1941, the Bears depart from Wrigley Field and make the 113-mile drive to Saint John's Military Academy in Delafield, Wisconsin, for 18 days of training camp.

On August 10, 1911, Bernie Masterson was born. He played quarterback for the Bears from 1934 through 1940. He played on the Bears' 1940 Championship team.

On August 11, 1937, Pete Manning was born. He was an 8th round draft choice of the Bears in 1960. He played end for the Bears in 1960 and 1961.

On August 12, 1966, the Bears played the Green Bay Packers in Milwaukee in a preseason game. The Bears won 13–10.

On August 13, 1977, the Bears played the Oakland Raiders at Oakland-Alameda County Coliseum in a preseason game. The Bears won 20–13.

On August 14, 1964, Neal Anderson was born. He was a 1st round draft choice of the Bears in 1986. He played running back for the Bears from 1986 through 1993. He played in four Pro Bowls. He was All-Pro once.

On August 15, 1935, Lionel Taylor was born. He played end for the Bears in 1959.

On August 16, 1961, Tom Thayer was born. He was a 4th round draft choice of the Bears in 1983. He played guard for the Bears from 1985 through 1992. He played on the Bears' 1985 Championship team. He provides commentary for the Bears' radio broadcasts.

On August 17, 1997, there was a ceremony in Aurora, Illinois, as the United States Postal Service honored George Halas by placing him on stamps.

On August 18, 2010, Steve DeLong died. He was a 1st round draft choice of the Bears in 1965. He played defensive end for the Bears in 1972.

On August 19, 1951, Allan Ellis was born. He was a 5th round draft choice of the Bears in 1973. He played cornerback for the Bears from 1973 through 1980. He played in one Pro Bowl for the Bears.

On August 20, 1909, Beattie Feathers was born. He played halfback for the Bears from 1934 through 1937. He was the first 1,000-yard rusher in the NFL. He made the NFL 1930s All-Decade team.

On August 21, 1959, Jim McMahon was born. He was a 1st round draft choice of the Bears in 1982. He played quarterback for the Bears from 1982 through 1988. He was NFC Rookie of the Year. He was a Piccolo Award winner. He was All-NFC in 1985. He played on the Bears' 1985 Championship team. He played in one Pro Bowl for the Bears.

On August 22, 1937, Bob Wetoska was born. He played offensive line for the Bears from 1960 through 1969. He played on the Bears' 1963 Championship team.

On August 22, 1961, Dennis McKinnon was born. He played receiver and returner for the Bears from 1983 through 1989. He played on the Bears' 1985 Championship team.

On August 23, 2015, the Bears unveiled the statue of team founder, owner, coach, and player George Halas during a private ceremony just outside the entrance of Halas Hall.

On August 24, 1973, Pete Stinchcomb died. He was All-Pro quarterback for the Staleys in 1921 and for the Bears in 1922. He played on the Staleys' 1921 Championship team.

On August 25, 1928, John Dottley was born. He was a 2nd round draft choice of the Bears in 1950. He played fullback for the Bears from 1951 through 1953. He played in one Pro Bowl.

On August 26, 1973, the Bears played the Buffalo Bills in a preseason game. The Bears won 13–10.

On August 26, 1984, the Bears played the Buffalo Bills in the Hoosier Dome in a preseason game. The Bears won 38–7.

On August 26, 2005, the Bears played the Buffalo Bills at Soldier Field in a preseason game. The Bears won 16–12.

On August 27, 1971, Jim Flanigan was born. He was a 3rd round draft choice of the Bears in 1994. He played defensive tackle for the Bears from 1994 through 2000.

On August 28, 2005, the Bears traded tight end John Owens and a 7th round draft choice in 2006 to the Miami Dolphins for linebacker Brendon Ayanbadejo. Brendon played in two Pro Bowls for the Bears as a special teamer.

On August 29, 1931, Herman Lee was born. He played offensive tackle for the Bears from 1958 through 1966. He was the starting offensive left tackle on the Bears' 1963 Championship team.

On August 29, 2007, Aldo Forte died. He was a 21st round draft choice of the Bears in 1939. He played guard and tackle for the Bears from 1939 through 1941 and in 1946. He played on the Bears 1940 and 1941 Championship teams.

On August 30, 1963, Keith Ortego was born. He played wide receiver for the Bears from 1985 through 1987. He played on the Bears' 1985 Championship team.

On August 31, 1934, the Bears played the College All Stars at Soldier Field in the first College All Star Game. The final score was 0–0.

SPORTSMANSHIP

1985 Chicago Bears' Championship Roster

4	Steve Fuller	Quarterback
6	Kevin Butler	Kicker
8	Maury Buford	Punter
9	Jim McMahon	Quarterback
18	Mike Tomczak	Quarterback
20	Thomas Sanders	Running Back
21	Leslie Frazier	Cornerback
22	Dave Duerson	Safety
23	Shaun Gayle	Defensive Back
24	Jeff Fisher	Defensive Back
26	Matt Suhey	Fullback
27	Mike Richardson	Cornerback
29	Dennis Gentry	Running Back
31	Ken Taylor	Def. Back/ Punt Returner
33	Calvin Thomas	Running Back
34	Walter Payton	Running Back
45	Gary Fencik	Free Safety
48	Reggie Phillips	Defensive Back
50	Mike Singletary	Middle Linebacker
51	Jim Morrissey	Linebacker
52	Cliff Thrift	Linebacker
53	Dan Rains	Linebacker
54	Brian Cabral	Linebacker
55	Otis Wilson	Left Linebacker
57	Tom Thayer	Guard
58	Wilber Marshall	Right Linebacker
59	Ron Rivera	Linebacker
60	Tom Andrews	Tackle
62	Mark Bortz	Guard
63	Jay Hilgenberg	Center
70	Henry Waechter	Line
71	Andy Frederick	Tackle
72	William Perry	Tackle
73	Mike Hartenstine	Tackle/End
74	Jim Covert	Tackle
75	Stefan Humphries	Tackle
76	Steve McMichael	Tackle
78	Keith Van Horne	Tackle
79	Kurt Becker	Guard
80	Tim Wrightman	Tight End
81	James Maness	Wide Receiver
83	Willie Gault	Wide Receiver
84	Brian Baschnagel	Wide Receiver

85 Dennis McKinnon Wide Receiver
86 Brad Anderson   Wide Receiver
87 Emery Moorehead Tight End
88 Pat Dunsmore   Tight End
89 Mitch Krenk   Tight End
89 Keith Ortego   Wide Receiver
95 Richard Dent   End
98 Tyrone Keys   End
99 Dan Hampton   Tackle/End

HUPMOBILE

September

On September 1, 2018, the Bears acquired Khalil Mack, the standout pass rusher and former NFL Defensive Player of the Year, in a trade from the Oakland Raiders.

On September 2, 1982, the George Halas Junior Sports Center was dedicated at Loyola University.

On September 3, 1923, Ed Sprinkle was born. He played for the Bears from 1944 through 1955. He played on the Bears' 1946 Championship team. He made the NFL 1940s All-Decade team. He is a Pro Football Hall of Famer.

On September 4, 1925, Mugs Halas was born. He started working for the Bears in 1950. He was the Bears' treasurer, general manager, and president.

On September 5, 1971, George Trafton died. He played center for the Staleys and the Bears from 1920 through 1932. He played on the Staleys' 1921 Championship team and the 1932 Bears' Championship team. He was All-Pro six times. He made the NFL 1920s All-Decade team. He is a Pro Football Hall of Famer.

On September 5, 2000, George Musso died. He played offensive guard, tackle, and nose tackle for the Bears from 1933 through 1944. He played on the Bears' 1933, 1940, 1941, and 1943 Championship teams. He made the NFL 75th Anniversary All-Time team. He is a Pro Football Hall of Famer.

On September 6, 1964, Harry Stuhldreher presented Ed Healey, William Umstadd presented Link Lyman, and Ernie Nevers presented George Trafton for induction into the Pro Football Hall of Fame.

On September 7, 1963, Jimmy Conzelman presented Red Grange, David Lawrence presented George Halas, and Don Miller presented Bronko

Nagurski for induction into the original class of the Pro Football Hall of Fame.

On September 8, 1985, the Bears beat the Tampa Bay Buccaneers, 38–28, on a blistering hot day in Chicago's Soldier Field. It was the first NFL regular season game for rookies William Perry, Kevin Butler, and others who would contribute to the Bears Championship Season.

On September 9, 2012, the Bears played the Indianapolis Colts at Soldier Field. It was the beginning of Pat Mannelly's 15th Bears' season. The Bears won 41–21. Pat broke the Bears' player record for years of service.

On September 9, 2018, Matt Nagy paid tribute to George Halas by calling a T Formation for his first play as Bears' head coach.

On September 10, 1953, Revie Sorey was born. He was a 5th round draft choice of the Bears in 1975. He played guard for the Bears from 1975 through 1983.

On September 11, 1988, the Bears played the Indianapolis Colts at the Hoosier Dome. The Bears won 17–13. It was the start of the Bears' fifth straight division title.

On September 12, 1965, Jimmy Conzelman presented Paddy Driscoll, Andy Kerr presented Dan Fortmann, and Lou Little presented Sid Luckman for induction into the Pro Football Hall of Fame.

On September 13, 2013, Rick Casares died. He was a 2nd round draft choice of the Bears in 1954. He played fullback for the Bears from 1955 through 1964. He played on the Bears' 1963 Championship team. He was All-Pro twice for the Bears. He played in five Pro Bowls for the Bears.

On September 14, 1987, Dennis McKinnon's 94-yard punt return touchdown helped the Bears beat the

Giants 34–19 on Monday Night Football in a matchup of previous two Super Bowl winners. At the time, it was the longest punt return in MNF history.

On September 15, 1996, Joe Maniaci died. He played fullback for the Bears from the early season 1938 through 1941. He played on the Bears' 1940 and 1941 Championship teams.

On September 16, 1962, the Bears played the San Francisco 49ers in San Francisco. The Bears won 30–14. It was the first time that the Bears had white Cs on their helmets in a regular season game.

On September 16, 1973, the Bears played the Dallas Cowboys at Soldier Field. It was the first time that the Bears had orange Cs on their helmets in a regular season game.

On September 17, 1920, the original meeting for what is now the National Football League took place. The site was Ralph Hay's Hupmobile Showroom in Canton, Ohio. That's why the Pro Football Hall of Fame is located there. Since there weren't enough chairs for Hay and Halas and the other founding fathers, they sat on the fenders and the running boards of the cars.

On September 17, 1966, Dick Gallagher presented George McAfee and Ed Healey presented Bulldog Turner for induction into the Pro Football Hall of Fame.

On September 18, 2013, Allan Ellis died. He was a 5th round draft choice of the Bears in 1973. He played cornerback for the Bears from 1973 through 1980. He played in one Pro Bowl for the Bears.

On September 19, 1957, Dan Hampton was born. He was a 1st round draft choice of the Bears in 1979. He played on the defensive line for the Bears from 1979 through 1990. He was a Piccolo Award winner. He played on the Bears' 1985 Championship team. He played in four Pro Bowls. He was All-Pro six times. He was the NFL Defensive Player of the Year in 1982. He was the NFC Defensive Lineman of the Year in 1984. He was the George Halas Courage Award Winner in 1990. He made the NFL 1980s All-Decade team. He is a Pro Football Hall of Famer.

On September 20, 1986, Chet Chesney died. He played center for the Bears in 1939 and 1940. He played on the Bears' 1940 Championship team.

On September 21, 1956, George Halas was presented with the Distinguished Public Service Award, the Navy's highest civilian decoration at halftime of the Armed Forces Game. Halas originated the Armed Forces Benefit Game idea while he was a captain in the Naval Reserve.

On September 22, 1898, Hunk Anderson was born. He played guard for the Bears from 1922 through 1925. He made the NFL 1920s All-Decade team. He was a Bears' assistant coach from 1940 through 1942 and from 1946 through 1950. He was an assistant coach for the Bears' 1940 and 1946 Championship teams. He was a Bears' co-head coach from 1942 through 1945. He was a co-head coach on the Bears' 1943 Championship team.

On September 23, 1997, George Halas's home when he started the Bears in Chicago, 4356 Washington Boulevard, received a marker of distinction.

On September 24, 1950, the Bears played the San Francisco 49ers in San Francisco. The Bears won 32–20.

On the flight back to Chicago, the team plane ran into a thunderstorm that bounced the plane all over the sky. George Halas was sitting next to Paddy Driscoll. Harper Davis heard Halas exclaim that the Bears would never fly again. (The next trip to the Coast to play the Rams for a playoff game, the Bears took the train and lost the game. Bears' flights resumed.)

On September 25, 1932, the Bears opened the 1932 season with a 0–0 tie against the Green Bay Packers. The Bears would have three consecutive ties to start the season and six total during the 1932 season that saw the Bears capture the NFL Championship.

On September 26, 1935, Johnny Morris was born. He was a 12th round draft choice of the Bears in 1958. He played receiver and returner for the Bears from 1958 through 1967. He played on the Bears' 1963 Championship team. He played in one Pro Bowl. He was All-Pro once.

On September 27, 2010, George Blanda died. He was a 12th round draft choice of the Bears in 1949. He played kicker and quarterback for the Bears from 1949 through 1958. He is a Pro Football Hall of Famer.

On September 28, 1985, Laurie Walquist died. He played quarterback for the Bears in 1922 and from 1924-1931. He was an assistant coach for the Bears from 1933-1934. He was an assistant coach for the Bears' 1933 Championship team.

On September 29, 1985, the Bears played the Washington Redskins at Soldier Field. The Bears scored 31 points in the second quarter (their most ever in any quarter) and won 45–10.

On September 30, 2018, Mitch Trubisky threw 6 touchdown passes as the Bears defeated the Tampa Bay Buccaneers 48–10 at Soldier Field. Mitch is the only Bear to throw five touchdown passes in one half.

October

On October 1, 1936, Roger LeClerc was born. He was a 15th round draft choice of the Bears in 1959. He played kicker and linebacker for the Bears from 1960 through 1966. He played on the Bears' 1963 Championship team.

On October 2, 2011, Matt Forte rushed for 205 yards in a 34–29 win over the Carolina Panthers. The 205 yards tied Forte for the second most in a game in franchise history with Hall of Famers Walter Payton and Gale Sayers.

On October 3, 1920, the Staleys played the Moline Tractors at Staley Field in Decatur.[5] Dutch Sternaman had three touchdown runs. Hugh Blacklock kicked two extra points. It was the first game in the history of the franchise. The Bears won 20–0.

On October 3, 1993, the Bears played the Atlanta Falcons at Soldier Field. The Bears won 6–0. It was the Bears 1,000[th] game.

On October 4, 1930, Bill Wade was born. He played quarterback for the Bears from 1961 through 1966. He played on the Bears' 1963 Championship team. He played in one Pro Bowl for the Bears. He was All-Pro twice. He was a Bears' assistant coach in 1967.

On October 5, 1941, Larry Glueck was born. He was a 3rd round draft choice of the Bears in 1963. He played defensive back for the Bears from 1963 through 1965. He played on the Bears' 1963 Championship team.

---

[5] In the beginning, play was often extended with teams outside the league. The Moline Universal Tractors was one such team. Eventually, games were limited to league members only play.

On October 6, 1921, Mister Augustus Staley gave the team $5,000 worth of advertising to move the team to Chicago with the stipulation that the team nickname Staleys be retained for that season. In 1921, the team was the Chicago Staleys.

On October 7, 1984, Walter Payton became the NFL all-time rushing leader, breaking the record that Cleveland's Jim Brown set in 1965. The Bears beat the Saints, 20–7, behind Payton's 154 yards.

On October 8, 1909, Bill Hewitt was born. He played end for the Bears from 1932 through 1936. He was All-Pro for the Bears three times. He played on the 1932 and 1933 Bears' Championship teams. He made the NFL 1930s All-Decade Team. He is a Pro Football Hall of Famer. His Bears' number, 56, is retired.

On October 9, 1958, Mike Singletary was born. He was a 2nd round draft choice of the Bears in 1981. He played linebacker for the Bears from 1981 through 1992. He played on the Bears' 1985 Championship team. He played in 10 Pro Bowls. He was All-Pro nine times. He was NFL Man of the Year in 1990. He was NFL Defensive Player of the Year twice. He was NFC Player of the Year three times. He made the NFL 1980s All-Decade team. He is a Pro Football Hall of Famer.

On October 10, 2010, Solly Sherman died. He played quarterback for the Bears in 1939 and 1940. He played on the Bears' 1940 Championship team.

On October 11, 1990, George Corbett died. He played running back for the Bears from 1932 through 1938. He played on the Bears' 1932 and 1933 Championship teams.

On October 12, 1947, the Bears played the Philadelphia Eagles at Wrigley Field. The Bears won 40–7. It was the first time that a Bears' game had been televised.

On October 13, 1952, Greg Latta was born. He played tight end for the Bears from 1975 through 1979.

On October 14, 2001, the Bears played the Arizona Cardinals at Soldier Field. The Bears won 20–13.

On October 15, 1939, the Bears played the Chicago Cardinals at Wrigley Field. Bill Osmanski had an 86-yard run from scrimmage. The Bears won 44–7.

On October 16, 1938, Charlie Bivins was born. He played running back for the Bears from 1960 through 1966. He played on the Bears' 1963 Championship team.

On October 17, 1957, Steve McMichael was born. He played defensive tackle for the Bears from 1981 through 1993. He played on the Bears' 1985 Championship team. He played in two Pro Bowls.

On October 18, 1939, Mike Ditka was born. He was a 1st round draft choice of the Bears in 1961. He played tight end for the Bears from 1961 through 1966. He played on the Bears' 1963 Championship team. He was the NFL Rookie of the Year. He played in five Pro Bowls for the Bears. He was All-Pro five times. He made the NFL 75th Anniversary All-Time team. He is a Pro Football Hall of Famer. He was the Bears' head coach from 1982 through 1992. He was the head coach of the Bears' 1985 Championship team. He was the NFL Coach of the Year twice. His Bears' number, 89, is retired.

On October 19, 1930, Charlie Sumner was born. He was a 22nd round draft choice of the Bears in 1954. He played safety for the Bears from 1955 through 1960.

On October 20, 2013, Devin Hester returned a punt 81 yards for a touchdown to tie the NFL record for most return touchdowns with 19, tying Hall of Famer Deion Sanders.

On October 21, 1944, Andy Livingston was born. He was a running back for the Bears from 1964 through 1968.

On October 22, 1961, the Bears played the San Francisco 49ers at Wrigley Field. Bill George switched from middle linebacker to middle guard to neutralize the 49ers' shotgun formation. The Bears won 31–0.

On October 23, 1962, Mike Tomczak was born. He played quarterback for the Bears from 1985 through 1990. He played on the Bears' 1985 Championship team.

On October 24, 1969, Carl Brumbaugh died. He played quarterback for the Bears from 1930 through 1938. He played on the Bears' 1932 and 1933 Championship teams.

On October 25, 1987, the Bears trailed the Buccaneers 20–0 in the first quarter. Then the Bears rallied for a 27–26 win in Tampa.

On October 26, 1928, Ed Brown was born. He was a 6th round draft choice of the Bears in 1952. He played quarterback for the Bears from 1954 through 1961. He played in two Pro Bowls for the Bears.

On October 27, 1929, Bill George was born. He was a 2nd round draft choice of the Bears in 1951. He played middle guard and linebacker for the Bears from 1952 through 1965. He played on the Bears' 1963 Championship team. He played in nine Pro Bowls. He was All-Pro eight times. He made the NFL 1950s All-Decade team. Ed McCaskey presented him for induction into the Pro Football Hall of Fame in 1974. His Bears' number, 61, is retired.

On October 28, 1956, the Bears played the San Francisco 49ers in San Francisco. The Bears won 38–21. It was the Bears' 300th victory.

On October 29, 1933, the Bears played the New York Giants at Wrigley Field. The Bears won 14–10.

On October 30, 1998, Bulldog Turner died. He was a 1st round draft choice of the Bears in 1940. He played center and linebacker for the Bears from 1940 through 1952. He played on the Bears' 1940, 1941, 1943, and 1946 Championship teams. He was first-team All-Pro seven times. He played in two Pro Bowls. He made the NFL 1940s All-Decade team. He was a Bears' assistant coach from 1953 through 1958. He is a Pro Football Hall of Famer. His Bears' number, 66, is retired.

On October 31, 1983, George Halas died. He played end and was co-coach for the Staleys and the Bears from 1920 through 1929. He played for and was co-coach of the Staleys' 1921 Championship team. He made the NFL 1920s All-Decade team. He was coach of the Bears from 1933 through 1942, 1946 through 1955, and 1958 through 1967. He was coach of the Bears' 1933, 1940, 1941, 1946, and 1963 Championship teams. He was owner from 1921 through 1983. He was owner of the Bears' 1921, 1932, 1933, 1940, 1941, 1943, 1946, and 1963 Championship teams. He is a Pro Football Hall of Famer. His Bears' number, 7, is retired.

November

On November 1, 1999, Walter Payton died. He was a 1st round draft choice of the Bears in 1975. He played running back for the Bears from 1975 through 1987. He played on the Bears' 1985 Championship team. He played in nine Pro Bowls. He was All-Pro eight times. He was the NFL Most Valuable Player once. He made the NFL 1970s All-Decade team. He made the NFL 1980s All-Decade team. He made the NFL 75th

Anniversary All-Time team. He is a Pro Football Hall of Famer. His Bears' number, 34, is retired.

On November 2, 1958, the Bears and the Rams established an NFL attendance record drawing 90,833 paid (100,470 actual) in the LA Coliseum. The Rams won 41–35.

On November 3, 1908, Bronko Nagurski was born. He played for the Bears from 1930 through 1937 and 1943. He was All-Pro four times. He played on the 1932, 1933, and 1943 Bears' Championship teams. He made the NFL 1930s All-Decade team and the NFL 75th Anniversary All-Time team. He is a Pro Football Hall of Famer. His number, 3, has been retired.

On November 4, 1923, the Bears played the Oorang Indians at Wrigley Field. When the Indians were on the Bears' 2-yardline, Jim Thorpe fumbled. George Halas recovered and ran with Thorpe in pursuit. When Thorpe zigged, Halas zagged. When Thorpe zagged, Halas zigged. Halas ran 98 yards for a touchdown. The Bears won 26–0.

On November 5, 1970, Ryan Wetnight was born. He played tight end for the Bears from 1993 through 1999.

On November 6, 1909, John Doehring was born. He played running back for the Bears from 1932 through 1934 and from 1936 through 1937. He played on the Bears' 1932 and 1933 Championship teams.

On November 7, 1999, the Bears played the Green Bay Packers at Lambeau Field. It was the first game after Walter Payton had died. The Bears blocked the Packers' game-winning field goal attempt. The Bears won 14–13.

On November 8, 1913, Ray Nolting was born. He played halfback for the Bears from 1936 through 1943. He played on the Bears' 1940, 1941, and 1943 Championship teams.

On November 9, 2015, Jay Cutler surpassed Hall of Famer Sid Luckman's franchise record for career touchdown passes with 138.

On November 10, 1963, the Bears shutout the Los Angeles Rams 6-0 at Wrigley Field behind two Roger LeClerc field goals.

On November 11, 1983, Mike McCaskey was named the Bears' president.

On November 12, 2006, the Bears played the New York Giants in New Jersey. Devin Hester returned a Giants' missed field goal 108 yards for a touchdown. The Bears won 38–20.

On November 13, 2005, the Bears played the San Francisco 49ers at Soldier Field. Nathan Vasher returned a 49ers' missed field goal 108 yards for a touchdown. The Bears won 17–9.

On November 14, 1943, the Bears played the New York Giants in New York. Sid Luckman became the first professional to pass for more than 400 yards in a game. He passed for 433 yards and 7 touchdowns. The Bears won 56–7.

On November 15, 2000, Mayor Richard M. Daley announced the City of Chicago's Lakefront Improvement Plan. The project replaced parking lots with 17 acres of new parkland, built an underground parking structure to serve the Museum Campus and Soldier Field, created easier access to the Museum Campus and added other amenities giving Chicagoans and tourists the ability to enjoy the lakefront year-around.

On November 16, 1975, Walter Payton posted the first of his Bears-record 100-yard rushing games, gaining 105 yards against the 49ers in San Francisco.

On November 17, 1963, the Bears played the Green Bay Packers at Wrigley Field. J. C. Caroline made a great tackle on a kickoff. The Bears won 26–7. In the film session the next week, the team gave J. C. Caroline a great round of applause. He died on November 17, 2017.

On November 17, 1985, the Bears played the Dallas Cowboys in Dallas. The Bears won 44–0. It was the Bears' 500th victory.

On November 18, 2010, the Bears played the Miami Dolphins at Sun Life Stadium. The Bears won 16–0.

On November 19, 1922, the Bears played the Rock Island Independents at Wrigley Field. George Halas played across the line from Ed Healey. Halas held Healey; Healey told Halas not to do that anymore. Halas did it anyway, slipped in the mud, and rolled over. He just missed receiving a punch from Healey. Healey's fist went into the mud up to his wrist. Halas didn't hold anymore that day. The Bears won 3–0.

On November 20, 1977, the Bears played the Minnesota Vikings at Soldier Field. Walter Payton had 40 carries for 275 yards and 1 touchdown. The Bears won 10–7.

On November 21, 1916, Sid Luckman was born. He played quarterback for the Bears from 1939 through 1950. He played on the Bears' 1940, 1941, 1943, and 1946 Championship teams. He was All-Pro six times. He was the NFL Most Valuable Player in 1943. He made the NFL 1940s All-Decade team. He is a Pro Football Hall of Famer. His Bears' number, 42, is retired.

On November 22, 1925, the Bears signed Red Grange and played the Green Bay Packers at Wrigley Field. The Bears won 21–0.

On November 23, 1978, George Wilson died. He played end for the Bears from 1937 through 1946. He was All-Pro once. He played on the Bears' 1940, 1941, 1943, and 1946 Championship teams. He was a Bears' assistant coach in 1947 and 1948.

On November 24, 1931, Stan Jones was born. He was a 5th round draft choice of the Bears in 1953. He played tackle, guard, and defensive tackle for the Bears from 1954 through 1965. He played on the Bears' 1963 Championship team. He played in seven Pro Bowls. He was All-Pro three times. He is a Pro Football Hall of Famer.

On November 25, 1984, the Bears defeated the Vikings 34–3 in Minneapolis to clinch their first Central Division crown.

On November 26, 1925, Red Grange played in his first game for the Bears. A crowd of 36,000 saw the Bears and the Cardinals tie 0–0 in Cubs Park (re-named Wrigley in 1926) with Grange held to 36 yards. The Bears started a coast-to-coast tour that ended after 19 games on January 31, 1926.

On November 27, 1922, George Halas forgave the debt of $100 from the Rock Island Independents' owner, Walter Flanagan. The Bears acquired Ed Healey. It was the first trade in the history of the League.

On November 28, 1964, the Bears drafted Dick Butkus and Gale Sayers in the 1st round.

On November 29, 1925, the Bears played the Columbus Tigers at Wrigley Field. Red Grange gained 140 yards. The Bears won 14–13.

On November 30, 1898, Link Lyman was born. He played tackle for the Bears from 1926 through 1928, from 1930 through 1931, and from 1933 through 1934. He played on the Bears' 1933 Championship team. He was All-Pro for the Bears twice. He is a Pro Football Hall of Famer.

December

On December 1, 1986, Bobby Layne died. He was a 1st round draft choice of the Bears in 1948. He played quarterback for the Bears in 1948.

On December 2, 1934, Beattie Feathers became the first professional to rush for 1,000 yards in a season (1,004).

On December 3, 1944, the Bears played the Chicago Cardinals-Pittsburgh Steelers at Forbes Field. The Bears won 49–7.

On December 4, 1921, the Staleys played the Buffalo All-Americans at Wrigley Field. Guy Chamberlin had a 70-yard interception return for a touchdown. Dutch Sternaman kicked an extra point and a field goal. The Staleys won 10–7. The Staleys won the Championship based on the standings.

On December 5, 1927, John Helwig was born. He was an 11th round draft choice of the Bears in 1950. He played for the Bears from 1953 through 1956.

On December 6, 1915, Ray McLean was born. He played halfback and kicker for the Bears from 1940 through 1947. He played on the Bears' 1940, 1941, 1943, and 1946 Championship teams.

On December 7, 1941, the day of the attack on Pearl Harbor, the Bears played the Chicago Cardinals at Comiskey Park. The Bears won 34–24.

On December 8, 1940, the Bears played the Washington Redskins in Washington, D.C., for the championship. Ten Bears scored touchdowns. The Bears won 73–0.

On December 9, 1942, Dick Butkus was born. He was a 1st round draft choice of the Bears in 1965. He played linebacker for the Bears from 1965 through 1973. He played in eight Pro Bowls. He was All-Pro eight times. He was the NFL Defensive Player of the Year twice. He made the NFL 1960s All-Decade team. He made the NFL 1970s All-Decade team. He made the NFL 75th Anniversary All-Time team. He is a Pro Football Hall of Famer. His Bears' number, 51, is retired.

On December 10, 1933, Larry Morris was born. He played linebacker for the Bears from 1959 through 1965. He played on the Bears' 1963 Championship team. He was the Most Valuable Player of the 1963 Championship game. He made the NFL 1960s All-Decade team.

On December 10, 1984, Luke Johnsos died. He attended Carl Schurz High School and Northwestern University. He played end for the Bears from 1929 through 1936. He played on the 1932 and 1933 Championship teams. He was co-head coach with Hunk Anderson during the war years from 1942 through 1945. He was an assistant coach from 1937 through 1941 and from 1946 through 1968. He was co-head coach for the Bears' 1943 Championship team.

On December 11, 1949, the Bears played the Chicago Cardinals at Wrigley Field. Johnny Lujack passed for 468 yards. The Bears won 52–21.

On December 12, 1965, the Bears played the San Francisco 49ers at Wrigley Field. Gale Sayers scored six touchdowns. The Bears won 61–20.

On December 13, 1960, Richard Dent was born. He was an 8th round draft choice of the Bears in 1983. He played defensive end for the Bears from 1983 through 1993 and 1995. He played on the Bears' 1985 Championship team. He was the Most Valuable Player of Super Bowl XX. He played in four Pro Bowls. He was All-Pro four times. He is a Pro Football Hall of Famer.

On December 14, 1941, the Bears played the Green Bay Packers at Wrigley Field in a playoff game for the conference championship. The Bears and the Packers agreed that the game should be played to a sudden death finish in the event of a tie. The Bears won 33–14.

On December 15, 1946, the Bears played the New York Giants at the Polo Grounds for the championship. Sid Luckman threw a 21-yard touchdown pass to Ken Kavanaugh. Luckman had a 19-yard bootleg touchdown run. The Bears won 24–14.

On December 16, 1979, Mugs Halas died. He started working for the Bears in 1950. He was the Bears' treasurer, general manager, and president.

On December 16, 1979, the Bears played the Saint Louis Cardinals at Soldier Field. The Bears won 42–6 and qualified for the playoffs.

On December 17, 1933, the Bears played the New York Giants at Wrigley Field for the championship. Jack Manders scored 10 points. The Bears won 23–21.

On December 18, 1932, the Bears played the Portsmouth Spartans at the Chicago Stadium for the championship. Bronko Nagurski threw a 2-yard touchdown pass to Red Grange. The Bears won 9–0.

On December 19, 1961, Mike Ditka was named NFL Rookie of the Year. He had caught 12 touchdown passes and he had 1,076 yards receiving.

On December 20, 2010, the Bears played the Minnesota Vikings at TCF Bank Stadium. Devin Hester had a 64-yard punt return for a touchdown. The Bears won 40–14 and clinched the NFC North crown.

On December 21, 1941, the Bears played the New York Giants at Wrigley Field for the championship. The Bears won 37–9.

On December 22, 1965, Gale Sayers was named rookie of the year and George Halas was named coach of the year.

On December 23, 1905, Joe Kopcha was born. He played guard for the Bears from 1929 through 1935. He played on the Bears' 1932 and 1933 Championship teams.

On December 24, 1962, Jim Morrissey was born. He was an 11th round draft choice of the Bears in 1985. He played linebacker for the Bears from 1985 through 1993. He played on the Bears' 1985 Championship team.

On December 25, 1996, Bill Osmanski died. He was a 1st round draft choice of the Bears in 1939. He played fullback for the Bears from 1939 through 1947. He played on the Bears' 1940, 1941, 1943, and 1946 Championship teams. He made the NFL 1940s All-Decade team.

On December 26, 1943, the Bears played the Washington Redskins at Wrigley Field for the championship. Sid Luckman threw five touchdown passes: two to Harry Clark, two to Dante Magnani, and one to Jim Benton. Bronko Nagurski scored his last Bears' touchdown, a 3-yard run. The Bears won 41–21.

On December 27, 1913, Bill Steinkemper was born. He played tackle for the Bears in 1943. He played on the Bears' 1943 Championship team.

On December 28, 1894, Ed Healey was born. He played tackle for the Bears from 1922 through 1927. He was All-Pro five times. He made the NFL 1920s All-Decade team. He is a Pro Football Hall of Famer.

On December 29, 1963, the Bears played the New York Giants at Wrigley Field for the championship. Bill Wade had two touchdown runs. The Bears had five interceptions. The Bears won 14–10.

On December 30, 2015, Doug Atkins died. He played defensive end for the Bears from 1955 through 1966. He played on the Bears' 1963 Championship team. He played in eight Pro Bowls. He was All-Pro for the Bears nine times. He made the NFL 1960s All-Decade team. He is a Pro Football Hall of Famer.

On December 31, 1988, the Bears played the Philadelphia Eagles at Soldier Field in a playoff game. It was very foggy. The Bears won 20–12.

PART TWO: THE GAME

THE GAME IS ALL ABOUT CHARACTER AND SPORTS-MANSHIP.

First Quarter

"Sometimes I was allowed to accompany my grandfather to the Pink Poodle press room at Wrigley Field where he met with reporters after the games. Once, after he had let out a string of profanities following a particularly painful loss, he remembered that I was sitting next to him. Then he said, "Now fellas, all of that was off the record."

—Patrick McCaskey

Father Nicholas Marro

Dolores Madlener wrote the popular "Church Clips" column for many years in the *Catholic New World* newspaper, which was later renamed *Chicago Catholic*. Madlener also penned a feature called "5 Minutes with Father" that introduced readers to priests in the Archdiocese of Chicago. In Madlener's "5 Minutes with Father" column from July 27-August 9, 2014, she gave readers a glimpse into the life of Father Nicholas "Nick" Marro.[6] Father Marro was a parish priest and unofficial chaplain for the Chicago Bears from 1984-2011. Father Marro "fit" right in with the Bears, he was 6-foot-1 and 265 pounds!

Father Marro's grandparents were Italian immigrants. His father, Nicholas, worked in the mills

---

Dolores Madlener, "Five Minutes with Father," *Chicago Catholic*, issue of July 27 —August 9, 2014, viewed at
http://legacy.chicagocatholic.com/cnwonline/2014/0727/5min.aspx
on September 17, 2019.

around Providence, Rhode Island. Nicholas was a church sexton. His mother, Katherin, helped out at the parish school and church.[7] Going back to his childhood, Father Marro was interested in sports— particularly baseball and football. Father John Francis Farley, an excellent baseball player in the Diocese of Providence, encouraged Father Marro when discerning his vocation. Marro enrolled at the seminary high school.

Like many good priests, the road to the priesthood was not easy for Father Marro. He failed a class at the Major Diocesan seminary in Baltimore and had to go home and tell his mother that he had flunked out! It didn't take long for him to "take another road" and get into a Scalabrini seminary.   The Scalabrinians (Missionaries of Saint Charles Borromeo) are a Roman Catholic order whose mission is to maintain Catholic faith and practice among immigrants (Italians originally) to the New World. Although Marro's interest in the Seminary was still strong, at one time he snuck off to the Baltimore Colts for a tryout.[8]

He was ordained in New York in 1963 and he came to Chicago. His parish work in the Chicago Archdiocese included assignments at Saint Charles Borromeo, Santa Lucia-Santa Maria Incoronata, and Saint Callistus. In 1984, he was asked to minister to the Chicago Bears. He was with the Chicago Bears for 1 year and next season they were NFL Champions. For home games, he said Mass with the Bears at 7 a.m. and then

---

[7] A church sexton is historically someone who looks after the physical plant.

[8] Father Marro said his priesthood was always first on his mind and not in doubt at the time of the tryout.

returned to his parish to say his regular Masses there. He headed back to Soldier Field for the game and then back again to his parish. He tied his work with the Bears and his parish together. In Madlener's article, Father Marro said he was especially fond of the McCaskey family and the players and coaches. For health reasons, Father Marro resigned from the Bears in 2011.

Father Marro was grateful for making it through the seminary and thanked the Blessed Virgin Mary for that. He was a priest who understood the miracles that God can perform and he told his students at Saint Lucy's: "Don't underestimate what God can do." Father Marro was a fan of Thomas Merton.

Marro made the most of his "friends in high places." Jerry Reinsdorf allowed him to use White Sox Park for Saint Lucy fundraisers. Bears players came by to sign autographs. He'd have Bears' footballs and jerseys to auction off.

Mike Ditka and Tom Thayer read for Mass. Being a chaplain was very important as well. He "did some weddings" of Bears players like Matt Suhey and Maury Buford. He baptized the children of many Bears. Many of the players asked Father Marro for a blessing as they were about to head into a game. When the Bears team struggled a few years after the 1985 season, he quipped that maybe it was time for the team to get a new chaplain, "maybe a Rabbi."

Father Marro died on July 18, 2019, at the age of 84. Memories from the 1985 Bears about his role with the team and what he meant to them personally were conveyed in articles. Several of the players remember him with great fondness and as one of their own.

Super Bowl XX

In preparation for Super Bowl XX, we camped on the Mississippi River near the Mark Twain Courtyard. Many of us visited Bourbon Street, where there was a great need for missionary work. On our walks we sang "What a Friend We Have in Jesus."

Coach Ditka wanted me to take care of the people who really matter: the coaches and the players. My responsibility was to take care of them in terms of meals, meetings, and practices.

When I came into the locker room before one practice, Walter Payton told one of the security guards to check me out. He did, and everyone involved had a good laugh.

When I met Jim McMahon's father, the day before the Super Bowl, I said to him, "You should have given Jim more spankings."

He replied, "I know."

Father Marro was in New Orleans to say Mass for us. We had Mass and Chapel Service on Saturday and Sunday. I had the privilege of being the lector at both Masses. The Epistle was 1 Corinthians 12:12-30.

In his homily, Father Marro described this passage as a Super Bowl sermon. It is about how everyone is important to the Body of Christ, the team. "The body is one and has many members, but all the members, many though they are, are one body; and so it is with Christ."

Throughout the season, and particularly in the week before the Super Bowl game, everyone in the Bears' organization: management, coaches, and players, contributed to the Championship.

The Bears won Super Bowl XX, 46–10.

The players who made the Pro Bowl had to leave New Orleans for Hawaii early the next morning. They were not able to attend the downtown Chicago ticker tape parade that reminded me of all the confetti that was thrown after the wedding of Grace Kelly & Prince Ranier.

Perhaps Saint Paul offers the appropriate comment from the previously mentioned Epistle. "We honor the members we consider less honorable by clothing them with greater care, thus bestowing on the less presentable a propriety which the more presentable already have."

Joe Stydahar

When the first college draft was staged in 1936, the Bears chose tackle "Jumbo" Joe Stydahar from West Virginia. West Virginia alum playing end for the Bears, Bill Karr, had tipped off George Halas on Stydahar's potential. Stydahar was fast and powerful at 6-foot-4 and 233 pounds. Wearing number 13 and often playing helmetless, Stydahar was a tackle for the Bears for 7 years (1936-1942). He was off to war and started back again in 1945 for 2 more seasons. Stydahar served as a Navy Lieutenant Gunnery Officer in 1943 and 1944.

George Halas called Stydahar a man of outstanding character. Hunk Anderson who coached him on the line called him one of the all-time greats of pro football.[9]

After his playing career, Stydahar went on to coach the Los Angeles Rams from 1950-1952 and the Chicago Cardinals from 1953-1954. He returned to the Bears as line coach in 1963 and 1964. He was credited with overhauling the Bears defensive line for their 1963 Championship season.[10]

Frank Deford

Sportswriter Frank Deford wrote about sports records and how often they are broken. Deford suggested that it is an article of faith that today's athletes are the best ever. Unlike the arts, where a musical composition, a statue, or a painting lives on for hundreds of years, sports performances are eclipsed often. "In sports, you've got till next Tuesday to stay number one."[11]

Champions often display great sportsmanship when they congratulate a new record holder who has replaced their mark. But a champion's mark in life can go beyond the record book. Deford himself has made such a mark.

Deford wrote many books including *Alex: The Life of a Child*, about his daughter, Alexandra. "Alex"

---

[9] Heartley W. "Hunk" Anderson with Emil Klosinki, *Notre Dame Chicago Bears and Hunk* (Oviedo, Florida: Florida Sun-Gator Publishing, 1976) 167.

[10] Cooper Rollo, "Bears Defensive Line Overhauled by Stydahar," *Chicago Tribune*, August 28, 1963.

[11] Frank Deford, *Over Time: My Life as a Sportswriter* (New York: Grove Press, 2012) 281.

battled and died from cystic fibrosis at age 8. Published in 1983, her inspiring story touched millions as both a book and movie. Deford and his wife, Carol, worked with others to grow the Cystic Fibrosis Foundation which has contributed to new therapies and significant discoveries. The Foundation's work is improving the lives of those who have the disease, increasing life spans, and working towards a cure. Deford remarked that he always enjoyed signing copies of *Alex: The Life of a Child* and hearing people's stories. Deford died on May 28, 2017, at age 78.

Mrs. Quinn Sold the House

In 1952, Mr. and Mrs. Quinn bought the house at 714 Rose Avenue in Des Plaines: the city of destiny, decency, dignity, and determination. Their son Jim and my brother Mike were classmates at
's School and Notre Dame High School (NDHS). Their daughter Maureen and my sister Ellen were classmates at Saint Mary's. Their daughter Sheila and I were also classmates there. Their daughter Honora and my brother Ned were classmates at Saint Mary's for 2 years. Then the parish was divided and Ned went to Saint Emily's School.

In the fall of 1960, I went with my parents to watch my brothers Mike and Tim play football for NDHS. The Dons played the Immaculate Conception Knights in Elmhurst next to some railroad tracks and a large quarry. Mike and Jim Quinn played on the varsity. Tim played on the sophomore team. I was in sixth grade. My parents introduced me to Mr. and Mrs. Quinn. Mr. Quinn asked if I knew his daughter Sheila. I looked at the ground and said yes. My father had a good laugh.

SPORTSMANSHIP

My first visit to the Quinns' home wasn't until the fall of 1962. Ken Okon and I were in Sister Arthesma's eighth grade class at Saint Mary's. A car killed him while he rode his bike across Northwest Highway near the Cumberland train station. I was a pallbearer at the funeral Mass at Saint Emily's Church. I walked Sheila home after school.

I was wearing a suit because of the funeral and I walked my bike with Sheila along Prairie Avenue. We talked about the funeral and many other things. When we got to her house, we kept talking and I kept holding my bike. After an hour or so, Sheila's sister Maureen came out of the house and invited us inside. I agreed to go inside if Sheila would explain to her family why I was wearing a suit. This she did.

On many occasions, I had the privilege of walking Sheila home from school. Sometimes Dale Haase and Gayle McCarthy would walk with us. I played center on the school basketball team. Sheila was a cheerleader. It was natural for us to watch Dave Bradds play center for the Ohio State University basketball team on television at the Quinns'. Chores at my house were a chore. When I helped at the Quinns', I felt like a hero.

Maureen was homecoming queen at Maine West High School. Debbie Quinn was Junior Miss Des Plaines. Sheila was also homecoming queen at Maine West. Diana Quinn was in the homecoming court there. Honora was in the court of the College All-Star queen the year the game was cancelled. It was not Honora's fault. Many young men nervously said good night in the Quinns' front hallway. Sheila also had three younger brothers, Terry, Kevin, and Kenny, but I didn't notice them very much.

My brother Mike and I would go over to the Quinns' every Christmas. We were known as the ghosts of Christmas past. For Christmas of 1971, we stayed until dawn. Diana did her impersonation of a female Paul Lynde. Jack Kelly, who was a classmate of my brother Mike and Jim Quinn, tried and tried to get the guitar chords for the Kingston Trio song, "Scotch and Soda." He was working for the FBI. He had come a long way from his days as a Saint Mary's School patrol boy.

Mr. Quinn died in the fall of 1982. He was one of my heroes. In late July 1988, Mrs. Quinn sold the house and bought a condominium in Schaumburg. I respect her right to have made this decision. The Quinns' phone number was 824-0474. I can't call there anymore.

Doing the Laundry

Doing the laundry is not a quandary; it's an opportunity to serve the family.

Doing the laundry is not a quandary; let's do chores and errands cheerfully.

We'll never forget Mrs. Edward McCaskey; she did her work joyfully.

Doing the laundry is not a quandary and let them know when you're out of detergent.

Your family life will be resurgent; doing the laundry is not a quandary.

Second Quarter

"I started going to Bears' training camps when I was seven.

George Blanda taught us how to kick.

Bill George taught us how to play linebacker.

Bill Wade taught us how to play quarterback."

—Patrick McCaskey

Walking to Commemorate Papa Bear

In our third Sports and Faith Series book called *Pilgrimage*, we included a section on the Way of Saint James in Spain. It's one of the oldest Christian pilgrimages. In ancient and medieval times, pilgrimages involved long journeys and hardship that "tested" one's faith. The most popular Saint James route is 500 miles long!

In celebration of the 100th anniversary of the Bears, Chicago Bears Chairman George McCaskey walked from the original site of the Decatur Staleys football team to the team's home turf at Soldier Field. The 196-mile trek was made from July 15–25, 2019. The journey put him in touch symbolically with his grandfather George Halas—his struggle to manage the Chicago Bears from its early days in Decatur throughout its history in Chicago. Although symbolic, the trip involved a strenuous effort to complete.

Halas's "journey" with the Bears tested his faith and his faith gave him the strength to continue. The anniversary journey was a fitting "pilgrimage."

According to Bears Senior Writer, Larry Mayer, McCaskey started in Decatur; traveled to Champaign, home of Halas's college team; and then he moved on to the Bears Bourbonnais training camp at Olivet

Nazarene University. From Bourbonnais, it was on to Midway Airport then through the city to Soldier Field. McCaskey walked by himself. Training since the beginning of the year, McCaskey managed roughly 20 miles a day.

Statues at Soldier Field

Anyone who follows the news can attest to the power of statues and what they commemorate. Sports statues have meaning for fans and when they are placed on stadium campuses they add something powerful to the culture. At the same time, they often mean something personal to the observers.

The Chicago Bears unveiled statues for George Halas and Walter Payton on September 3, 2019, at the south entrance of Soldier Field. The unveiling coincided with the start of celebrations for the 100th NFL season.

It was a cloudy, dreary day. Virginia McCaskey, who spoke at the ceremony, quipped that she had prayed that the morning's rain would pause for the proceedings (and it did), but she went on to confess that she had forgotten to pray about the wind, which was in evidence. She talked about what it meant personally to her:

My brother and I used to ride in a car along the outer drive through the parks and see the statues in the park settings. It seemed like most of them were generals on horses, but we never dreamed that someday, our dad and a Chicago Bears player would be honored in the same way. We are very happy to be here.

Walter Payton's daughter, Brittney Payton, said:
We know that dad is definitely smiling down on all of us. And he would be so proud of this moment and moved beyond words.

The statues were created by sculptor Chad Fischer. The windy conditions along the Chicago Lakefront will not cause any problems for the edifices, they are both 12 feet high and weigh 3,000 pounds.

WALTER PAYTON STATUE, SOLDIER FIELD

GEORGE HALAS STATUE, SOLDIER FIELD

Matt Nagy

Matt Nagy is from Manheim, Pennsylvania, about 11 miles outside of Lancaster where my dad's family settled. Nagy went to Manheim Central High School where he played quarterback. He grew up in a sports family. His dad, Bill Nagy, was a high school coach.

After high school, Nagy went to Delaware University where he played exceptionally well. According to the school website, Nagy was a strong-armed quarterback who led Delaware to NCAA FCS semifinals when he earned third team The Sports Network All-American honors and he was a first team All-Atlantic 10 selection. Nagy set many quarterback records at Delaware, but it was not enough to get him drafted in the NFL. Nagy tried out with the Packers and had a few other contacts with teams, but he was not picked up. He ended up playing in the Arena League. After the arena league halted operations in late 2008, Nagy was out of football.[12]

Nagy learned some tough lessons when he was out of work at 30. Nagy was in the midst of starting a family and the economy was terrible.

Out of work and facing a recession economy, he met with Larry Wisdom about a job with Keystone Custom Homes, a Central Pennsylvania home builder. After starting the job that gave him a lifeline in a sense, he was invited back to football. After a career that began at the very depths of professional football in Philadelphia with the Eagles, Nagy was making an impact. He followed Andy Reid from Philadelphia to Kansas City. After Kansas City, the Bears' opportunity came along.

---

[12] After one year without games, the Arena League came back.

Experiences taught Nagy about overcoming the odds, living through disappointments, and perhaps something about destiny.

Augustus Eugene Staley

On February 25, 1867, Augustus Eugene Staley was born on a farm in Randolph County North Carolina. Staley would establish the A. E. Staley Manufacturing Company in 1906 that would create many uses for corn and soybeans. Staley, his heirs, and his employees would grow his Decatur Company into an international agribusiness.

Staley was a sports fan, but he had not gone to school long enough to participate in the organized variety. The industrialist was also a big-thinker and highly competitive. In an effort to enhance morale and loyalty, he envisioned the creation of a company sports organization that would further spotlight his company. It was said that he was also sensitive to the relationship between sports and sportsmanship. Sports could be a positive force for developing human character and spirited competition among his employees. Sports also helped provide entertainment for workers on the weekends.[13]

The A. E. Staley Manufacturing Company established an industrial baseball team and then asked George Halas to join the company to establish a great football team. Halas and Staley were like-minded men and both achieved tremendous success.[14] Neither of these men could have imagined the incredible twists

---

[13] Dan Forestal, *The Kernel and the Bean: The 75-Year Story of the Staley Company* (New York: Simon and Schuster, 1982) 40.

[14] Through various mergers and acquisitions, the A. E. Staley Manufacturing Company was acquired by Tate and Lyle.

and turns that their enterprises would take over the years.

A. G. Spanos

A.G. Spanos Companies builds multi-family housing and master planned communities. Through the success of this company, its owner, Alex Spanos, was able to acquire the San Diego Chargers. When he became an owner in 1984, he exclaimed: "I always believed in the pursuit of one's dreams. In buying the Chargers, I've been able to realize a dream."[15]

From his early days operating a food truck that served migrant farm workers to his success in real estate and development, Spanos became the patriarch of a tremendous philanthropic family.

The A.G. Spanos organization, including the Chargers, is a family-run operation. In 1994, Alex turned over the Chargers to his oldest son, Dean. Son Michael Spanos and other family members are also involved in the Chargers management today. Spanos died on October 9, 2018, at age 95.

> **Alex Spanos**
> A baker, a soldier, a builder, the best
> He was secretly unhappy because
> A baker, a soldier, a builder, the best
> Got paid for what he did but no applause
> He gladly bid those dreary jobs goodbye
> For the Chargers' Ownership, and why?
>
> There's no owner like Alex Spanos
> He has danced with Bob Hope
> Everything about him is appealing

---

[15] See San Diego Charges website for more information: https://www.chargers.com/team/front-office-roster/alex-g-spanos

Patrick McCaskey

Everything his wife, Faye, will allow
Nowhere could he get that happy feeling
When he is stealing that extra bow

There's no owner like Alex Spanos
He smiles when he has won
He has a franchise that he knows can win
He is more famous than Rin Tin Tin
Chargers' success gives him a happy grin
He has twirled a baton

The jerseys, the stadium, the wake-ups, the
Bolts
The audience that cheers you when you've won
The headaches, the heartaches, the backaches,
the Colts
The agents who would like you out of town
The kickoff when your heart beats like a drum
The ending when you know that you have won

There's no owner like Alex Spanos
He has danced with Bob Hope
You get word before the game has started
That your favorite player is injured
Top of that your three handicap has parted
You're broken hearted, but you endure

There's no owner like Alex Spanos
He won't run out of dough
Chargers come from everywhere with lots of jack
And when you give it there's no attack
Where could you get money that you give right
back
He has twirled a baton

SPORTSMANSHIP

The offense, the defense, the special teams
The police who move the cars at games
The music, the spotlight, the people, the wins
The contracts with incentives pasted on
The laundry and the buses and the smell
The towels you are given from each hotel

There's no owner like Alex Spanos
He has danced with Bob Hope
Traveling around the world was so thrilling
Standing out in front on opening nights
Smiling as you watch the theater filling
And you had billing with Bob Hope

There's no owner like Alex Spanos
He smiles when he has won
Long ago they told you you would not go far
You danced with Bob Hope and there you are
Next day on your office door they hung a star
He has twirled a baton
He has twirled a baton

BENJAMIN FRANKLIN

Press On

Philippians 3:14, "I continue my pursuit toward
the goal, the prize of God's upward calling, in
Christ Jesus."
God created
Electricity, cotton, and many other wonders.
Benjamin Franklin discovered electricity.
Someone might have said to him,
"Go fly a kite."
Eli Whitney invented the cotton gin.
I am allergic to synthetics,
But God, Franklin, and Whitney
Fortify me.
When it comes to ironing cotton handkerchiefs,
I press on.
Take nothing for granted.
Work like a dog
With a cheerful attitude.
Train diligently.
Leave the results to God.
John Cassis says,[16]
"Concentrate on the gold,
Not on all the dirt."
Saint Paul says,
"Press on."
While you press on,
Keep your eyes fixed
Upon the Lord.

---

16 John Cassis was a pre-game inspirational speaker for the Chicago
Bears.

Halftime

"At Indiana University, I was living in a sorority as a houseboy for seventy ladies. I gave that up to work for the Bears."

—Patrick McCaskey

Chuck Pagano

Chuck Pagano is the defensive coordinator of the Chicago Bears under Matt Nagy. Nagy described his new coach immediately after his hiring, "a great teacher with an aggressive mentality that fits our style of football." Pagano is another coach who helps the Bears become champions in sports and spirit.

Pagano spent six seasons as the head coach of the Indianapolis Colts from 2012-2017. He received the George S. Halas Courage Award from the Pro Football Writers Association in 2013. Pagano underwent treatment for leukemia early on in his first season with the Colts. Returning to the team in the final week of the season, Pagano fought cancer with courage and became a great example to those facing the disease all over the country. Pagano and his wife, Tina, credited Christ with getting them through the crisis.

Pagano previously served as secondary coach for the Cleveland Browns, defensive backs coach for the Oakland Raiders, secondary coach and then defensive coordinator for the Baltimore Ravens. He held several college coaching positions prior to the NFL. Pagano graduated from the University of Wyoming where he played strong safety.

Paul Bauer and Father Mike McGovern

Father Mike McGovern is a Chicago Archdiocesan priest who was my pastor at the Church of Saint Mary in Lake Forest. Father McGovern, like other parish priests, prepares parishioners for the sacraments and ministers them, visits the sick, listens to parishioners' worries and concerns, prays for his flock, and says Masses along with many other duties. Perhaps no service better exemplifies Father McGovern's vocation than a Funeral Mass.

On February 13, 2018, Father McGovern's friend and former classmate from Saint Ignatius High School, Chicago Police Commander Paul Bauer, was gunned down in downtown Chicago while pursuing a suspect. Bauer was a faithful Catholic and a much-admired policeman. His wake, funeral Mass, and funeral procession were attended by thousands. People lining the streets gave a particularly painful witness to crime in Chicago and the price that is being paid by those who are called on to serve and protect.

Father McGovern concelebrated the funeral Mass at Nativity of Our Lord Church in Bridgeport, a neighborhood in Chicago with a long Catholic history. The church was packed and many more stood outside in the chilly air. At Communion, Father McGovern went outside the church to serve the Eucharist to the hundreds there. The Church was present for Commander Bauer, his family, and everyone else who needed healing after this great loss. Father McGovern was there to serve.

COMMANDER PAUL BAUER

Goodbye Pastor

St. Mary's parish in Lake Forest began in 1875 when Catholic parishioners met as a committee to talk about building a new church. Bishop Thomas Foley approved the initial wooden building. The current brick structure was approved in 1909 and built in 1910. Coincidently, another McGovern, Father James McGovern, was the first pastor of the parish. Over 100 years later, after serving the Church of Saint Mary, Father Michael McGovern has moved to a new assignment at Saint Raphael the Archangel Parish in Old Mill Creek. Symbolic of our continued life of faith, the new-yet-old structure of Saint Raphael integrates portions of two closed Chicago churches: Saint John of God and Saint Peter Canisius.

Saint Raphael the Archangel Church features the limestone exterior of St. John of God, including its twin one hundred forty foot steeples. The church interior contains elements of St. Peter Canisius: solid oak pews, wall sconces, Italian marble statuary and altars, and stained-glass windows.

Father Mike McGovern

Father Mike McGovern is a native of Chicago, Illinois.

Father Mike McGovern imitates Jesus Christ with a lot of joy.

We'll never forget the way he works hard and gives very good homilies.

Father Mike McGovern lets us know the way to Saint Raphael.

We'll be most welcome anytime with Father Mike McGovern.

BROKEN MARY PROCESSION

Broken Mary

Humorous media personality Kevin Matthews worked in radio on two different networks in Chicago. After a job change, he was commuting to Michigan when he experienced neurological symptoms that suggested a stroke. Diagnosis determined that he had multiple sclerosis. Weakened by the disease, Matthews was making adjustments to his life. He was fearful about his future prospects. He reached back to his Catholic past and began saying the Rosary.

Driving in the Western suburbs of Chicago one day, he felt compelled to stop at a cemetery that he knew and pray at a cross. He was swept over by a feeling of peace and was able to let some of his fears go. Sometime later, he felt compelled to stop and pick up some flowers for his wife. Outside the florist, he saw a statue of Mary that was in great disrepair and broken in half. He was inspired to salvage the statue and had it partially mended back into a whole statue, but otherwise retaining its chips and breaks. The statue spoke to Matthews about the notion that many people are in fact broken and in need. In time, he decided to take "Broken Mary" to interested audiences and tell his story. A devotion has grown out of the statue and Matthew's experiences. Matthews has written a book about his experiences called *Broken Mary: A Journey of Hope.*

On the feast of the Visitation of Mary, Matthews told his story to people at St. John Cantius Church in Chicago. Then, a group of over 1500 people processed many miles to Chicago's Water Tower to pray for peace in the city. First responders, who often have to deal with the worst events in the city, carried the statue of Our Lady of the Broken, as it is now being called.

Paul Brown: Son of a Railroad Man

Many schools and other institutions that serve young people are taking a hard look at their athletic programs. They want a winning program on the field, but one that also reaps long term benefits with their athletes.

One of the most disciplined coaches at any level of football was Paul Brown, one of the "Pillars of the NFL."[17] Brown groomed athletes to be their best— champions in sports and spirit.

Brown played quarterback at Miami University in Oxford, Ohio. Miami University would go on to achieve fame as the "Cradle of Coaches," so called because it produced so many noted football coaches.

Brown was supremely organized and a successful coach in high school, college, the military, and professional football. Brown's father, Lester Brown, a dispatcher for the Wheeling and Lake Erie Railroad, was a "railroad man with a watch"—serious and disciplined. Something his son inherited and crafted to an art form.

Brown developed organized football programs that might remind readers of the sophisticated business organizations of the time. But underneath the organized structure, was Brown's belief in managing human beings and guiding them to be their best. He told his players things that other coaches may have assumed that they would know. He taught them. He tested his athletes for intelligence because he wanted to make sure they were capable of following his program and growing with it. Brown was able to lead his players in confidence, help them develop their skills to the

[17] Patrick McCaskey, *Pillars of the NFL: Coaches Who Have Won Three or More Championships* (Crystal Lake, IL: Sporting Chance Press, 2014) 112-161.

maximum, and then make sure that everything was in place so they could execute. Discipline was fundamental. Execution was key. Results dictated strategy.

For Brown's teams, rules extended to activities outside the football field. Players were expected to take part in offseason activities. Each practice session was choreographed for maximum result. Assistant coaches played an integral role. Scouting was valued. Athletes needed knowledge. Brown provided playbooks.

Brown sought the intelligent, hungry, quick, and hard working. He did not care about race. When he fielded his "best 11 men" on the field, they were the best 11 men. He would teach and promote discipline and dedication to becoming stronger, faster, quicker, leaner, and tougher. As players developed, they were drilled to deliver near perfect execution as members of a team. Many of today's coaches have adopted best practices that began with Brown without knowing their origins.

Riding My Bike
on My Old Running Course

Five miles of streets I ran non-stop.
Now my bike wants to go with me.
It's strange how my interests change;
I used to like to climb a tree.

My bike is tired after a mile.
I stop to watch boys play hockey.
The Park District flooded the park.
I dream: me, a six-one jockey.

The boys' parents think they're funny;
They ask if my bike has snow tires.
Noise from the game is amateur;

Boys think they're Bob Hull; they're liars.

The game's over; I'm left alone,
But the cold makes me yearn to roam,
The mile to ride before I'm home,
The mile to ride before I'm home.

Wheaton College

When I was a high school sophomore, I hitchhiked from Des Plaines to Wheaton to see Louise Raymond. Two men in a pickup truck gave me a ride. As soon as I got in the truck, they shared Bible verses with me and told me about Wheaton College.

When I was a high school junior, I rode my bike twenty-five miles from Des Plaines to Wheaton to see Louise Raymond. She wasn't home.

For my thirty-third birthday, I received permission to date. After nine months of prayer, Mrs. Swider suggested that Gretchen Wagle and I meet. Four months later, we looked at a house that was for sale. After the tour, Gretchen asked me, "Why are you looking for a house?"

I crossed my mouth with the back of my right hand and muttered, "In case you want to get married."

She accepted my invitation. On Saturday, March 3, 1984, we got married at College Church in Wheaton. Wayne Gordon was the minister. Louise Raymond did not attend.

Gretchen & I have a mixed marriage. I did not go to Wheaton College.

I am willing to accept an honorary degree. It doesn't have to be a doctorate.

Our son, Ed, was born exactly nine months after the Bears won Super Bowl XX. He reported two days early. We felt that showed good initiative.

Ed lived the cliché: left-handed relief. He set Wheaton College baseball records for saves.

Gretchen and I have three children. If I had gone to Wheaton College and met Gretchen ten years earlier, we might have had eleven children. God had a different plan. Not my will, but God's.

For Christmas, the Bradleys gave me Leland Ryken books. Here is what I have learned: About a third of the Bible is in poetic form. Psalm 23 is the greatest poem of all time.

I like to drive in the Wheaton College lane, the far right.

Doing the Dishes
To clean the dishes is keen
To bring order out of chaos
To work with a cheerful attitude
To show the cook some gratitude

To stack the dishes quite neatly
To rinse the milk from the glasses
To wipe before loading the dishes
To soak the silverware enough

This is my job
To work like a dog
It is not hopeless
I'll sleep like a log

To call for the right
To do the night dishes
To be able to do it alone
 Is one of my wishes

And I know if I'll only do
The dishes each night
That my wife will be peaceful and calm
And think I'm all right

And this home will be better for this
That one man, so grateful for dinner
Still strove to make the meal a winner
To clean the dishes again

Third Quarter

"When I started working for the Bears, my hair was brown, curly, and thick. Now my hair is white, straight, and thin. God is protecting my marriage. I was too good looking."

—Patrick McCaskey

RED GRANGE

My Ball: Allen Robinson

Allen Robinson is the Chicago Bears' wide receiver who consistently runs excellent routes and makes the catches that win games. He is the kind of receiver that quarterbacks love because when he is anywhere around the ball, he is likely to make it his. Defenders struggle to stay with Robinson and he is often able to outmaneuver them. When the quarterback is under pressure, Robinson adjusts his route and gets open.

Robinson played for the Jacksonville Jaguars for 4 seasons before coming to the Bears in 2018. Robinson is still young at 26-years old, but he is a veteran talent. He is 6-foot-2, 220 pounds. Robinson attended St. Mary's Prep in Orchard Lake northwest of Detroit. He followed with the Nittany Lions at Penn State. Robinson is on highlight reels everywhere he plays. He not only makes the difficult grab, but he can be very difficult to bring down once he has the ball. Robinson is the clutch receiver who always brings his "A-game."

Robinson is an excellent veteran for the Bears as he talks about the need to be patient as the team is growing and improving. And off the field, Robinson brings good news. The Allen Robinson Within Reach Foundation provides education opportunities and resources to low-income and inner-city Chicago-area students.

Payton's Great Mates

Matt Suhey's grandfather, Bob Higgins, was a Penn State alum who played end with the Canton Bulldogs in the first two seasons (1920 and 1921) of the NFL.[18] Matt Suhey's father, Steve Suhey, was a Penn State alum who played guard for the Pittsburgh Steelers for two seasons (1948 and 1949). Matt Suhey was a Penn State alum drafted in the 2nd round in 1980 who played fullback with the Bears for 10 seasons through 1989.

Suhey is remembered as the fullback who played alongside Walter Payton during much of the 1980s, including the 1985 Championship season. Suhey was a team player who blocked for Payton. When Suhey ran with the ball, he gave the offense a "change up." Suhey was also a good friend of Payton. Suhey had a splendid career with 828 career rushes for 2,496 yards for 20 touchdowns. He also had 260 receptions for 2,113 yards and 5 touchdowns.

Roland Harper was the first back who played with Walter Payton on the Bears. Payton was the 1st round selection for the Bears in the 1975 draft and Harper was a 17th round selection—a long shot. Harper was a Louisiana Tech alum like Terry Bradshaw who had been selected in the 1st round in 1970. Harper played for 8 seasons for the Bears from 1975 through 1982.

With Harper and Suhey, Walter Payton had excellent blockers and support for his 13-year Hall of Fame career. Harper was sidelined with a knee injury in 1979 so Dave Williams played fullback that year. Payton tallied 3,833 rushes for 16,726 yards and 110 touchdowns. He had 492 receptions for 4,538 yards and 15 touchdowns.

Harper had 757 rushes for 3,044 yards and 15 touchdowns. He also had 128 receptions for 1,013 yards

---

[18] George Halas played against Bob Higgins in at least one game. See Don Pierson, "Bears Suhey Has a Tradition to Uphold," *Chicago Tribune*, May 11, 1980.

and 3 touchdowns. Payton played at 5-foot-10 and 200 pounds. Harper played at 5-foot-11 and 208 pounds. Suhey was 5-foot-11 and 218 pounds.

NFL Schedules

In the first decade of the NFL, the League was establishing itself and working out some consistency with the member teams and their schedules. At first, the number of games played varied from team-to-team. Teams formed and disbanded quickly. Of the inaugural season teams, only the Decatur Staleys/Chicago Bears and the Chicago/Saint Louis/Arizona Cardinals survived. Stronger markets were added and eventually the schedules were made consistent.

On September 24, 1933, the Bears opened the season with a 14—7 win over the Green Bay Packers. In 1933, the NFL went to a consistent 11-game schedule that would last until the war years.

On September 26, 1943, the Bears and Packers opened the 10-game season in a 21—21 tie. The War was taking its toll on the NFL and there were only eight active teams that year.

On September 29, 1946, the Bears opened the 11-game season with a 30–7 win over the Green Bay Packers. Sid Luckman was the Bears quarterback.

On September 28, 1947, the Bears would open the 12-game season losing to the Green Bay Packers, 29–20. The NFL would stick to a 12-game schedule until 1961.

On September 17, 1961, the Chicago Bears began their season by playing the Minnesota Vikings. The NFL regular schedule began a week earlier than the previous season as teams adjusted to their new 14-game regular season. It was the expansion-team

Vikings first game of their inaugural season. They beat the Bears, 37–13, with Fran Tarkenton's 17 completions on 23 attempts for 250 yards and 4 touchdowns. Beating the Bears in the opener was a good first step for the franchise, but the Vikings would end up 3–13 for the season including a 52–35 loss to the Bears on December 17.

On September 3, 1978, the Chicago Bears began their first 16-game season by playing the Saint Louis Cardinals. The NFL regular schedule began 2 weeks earlier than the previous season as teams adjusted to the longer regular season. The Bears beat the Cardinals, 17–10. Bob Avellini was the Bears starting quarterback and Walter Payton and Roland Harper combined for 194 yards.

Bill Walsh: Son of an Autoworker

Bill Walsh is one of the Pillars of the NFL—one of those great coaches who won three or more championships.[19] Walsh never took success for granted. Once he had success, he used his position to change things for the better.

Walsh was a "fighter" in life both physically and mentally. In fact, Walsh was an excellent boxer. He started out tough. Later, he became known as the "Genius" for his cerebral game plans.

Walsh was also an elegant presence on the sidelines, often looking like he just walked off the golf course. But perhaps more than anything else, Walsh was a great handler of athletes, especially quarterbacks. It wasn't always easy, but he was willing to endure.

---

[19] Patrick McCaskey, *Pillars of the NFL*, (Crystal Lake, IL: Sporting Chance Press, 2019) 277-307.

Like other great coaches, Walsh groomed athletes to be their best—champions in sports and spirit.

Early on, he was an assistant coach of the Bengals and Paul Brown. There he helped Virgil Carter and Ken Anderson develop. Carter was smart, quick on his feet, and accurate, but was not a long-ball thrower. Anderson was pure potential. Coming from Augustana College, he needed a lot of pro training that quarterbacks from larger schools often get. Walsh established achievable game plans for Carter and spent long hours with Anderson.

When Walsh moved on to San Francisco, he snagged Joe Montana in the 3rd round of the draft. Montana had enormous talent, but needed work. For Walsh, a quarterback should play free of any devastating errors. He has to be resourceful. He should be a communicator under the most difficult situations. He should be mechanically efficient—no wasted motion.

Walsh expected all his players to perform and he thought everyone should have a chance to succeed. Walsh also believed his position as an NFL coach came with social responsibilities. He wanted his players from all races to get along well and he brought Sports Sociologist Harry Edwards in to facilitate that. Walsh also created the Minority Coaches Fellowship program with Edwards.[20]

---

[20] Patrick McCaskey, *Pillars of the NFL* (Crystal Lake, IL: Sporting Chance Press, 2014) 302-303.

Father James Mallon and Healthy Faith-Life

Father James Mallon is a priest from the Halifax-Yarmouth Diocese in Canada. He was born in Scotland and moved to Halifax with his family in 1982 when he was 13 years old. Originally interested in Medicine, Mallon studied Biochemistry at Dalhousie University before entering the Seminary of Christ the King where he completed a B.A. in Philosophy. After studying Theology at St. Augustine's Seminary and the Toronto School of Theology, Mallon was ordained to the Catholic priesthood in 1997. Father Mallon splits his time between parish work and the Divine Renovation Ministry—a parish renewal program that is obviously near and dear to his heart.

Father James is the author of the bestselling book *Divine Renovation: From a Maintenance to a Missional Parish*, a guide for parishes seeking to cultivate faith communities centered on missionary discipleship. He has created several works on the Divine Renovation ministry. He speaks on the Divine Renovation movement all over the world. Father Mallon spoke at our archdiocese.

Here's to an Evening with Father James Mallon

We are grateful for Father James Mallon.
He's like holy water by the gallon.

He wants to revitalize our parish.
He's a holy man; he is not garish.

He is here to engage in discussion.
What he says will not cause a concussion.

He will help renew the Archdiocese.
Let us all work together, won't you please?

Father Mallon's "Divine Renovation"
Focuses on parish transformation.

We'll have dynamic faith cultivation.
God's Kingdom will be a great sensation.

We'll have missionary discipleship.
This will lead to a faith championship.

My Own "Temperance Movement"

Surrounded by conditioned athletes all my life, I decided at an early age to refrain from drinking alcohol, to never smoke, and to eat healthy.

Taking care of yourself also has a spiritual component. This is born out in our own experiences and others around us. Yet, even athletes who take good care of themselves understand that they are at the mercy of God. We all need God's help and mercy regardless of our circumstances.

In *Sports and Faith: More Stories of the Devoted and the Devout,* I wrote about my determination to follow up a successful high school quarterback experience that I had at Notre Dame High School in Niles where the Dons went 9–0 in my senior year. Like many Catholic athletes, I had my sights set on playing football at the University of Notre Dame. To make it happen, I accelerated my training and I enrolled at Cheshire Academy in Connecticut to further my education and allow me to play another year of football. But just as I was packing my bags for Cheshire, I found that I had developed serious eye trouble. Playing any more football would jeopardize my sight. I decided to make the best of it. At Cheshire, I was able to pursue cross country where I was able to meet many good people including Alan Swanson of Stony Brook who is one of those featured in my book *Worthwhile Struggle*.[21]

The Chicago Bears have had players of all faiths and religious backgrounds. We certainly do not force religion on anyone. At the same time, we have followed a long standing practice of having Mass and chapel services before games. Our players have also followed the practice of having Bible study. A professional athletic career can come to a close in a heartbeat. God is in charge.

Learning from Father Maczkiewicz

Bellarmine Jesuit Retreat House is located on 80 acres 40 miles northwest of Chicago. The Bellarmine grounds are described on their website as a peaceful setting for reflection and spiritual contemplation. Indoors, the chapels, conference center, lounges, library, and individual private rooms maintain a comfortable and tranquil environment for retreatants.[22]

From Friday, February 8 through Sunday, February 10, 2019, Father Keith Maczkiewicz, S.J., gave a series of eight talks at Bellarmine Jesuit Retreat House in Barrington. It was a men's silent retreat.

---

[21] Patrick McCaskey, *Worthwhile Struggle* (Crystal Lake, IL: Sporting Chance Press, 2019) 129-132.

[22] See the Retreat Center's website at https://jesuitsmidwest.org/Retreat-Center-Detail?TN=CODE-20130409084923

Here are ten thoughts from his talks that I want to share with you:

1. *Gifts are unmerited and unearned. They are freely offered without any expectation of being repaid. God gives freely of Himself.*

2. *Don't dismiss the miracles right in front of you with the hope of finding something better somewhere else.*

3. *God will not be outdone in generosity. We are limited; God is not.*

4. *People are more important than ideas. Don't let the dream overtake the reality.*

5. *The sacrament of reconciliation helps us make everything new. God does not get tired of forgiving us.*

6. *You don't save yourself. Get to know your Savior. Follow Him. Watch Him.*

7. *Work takes up most of your time and identity. The labor you do makes up what you are.*

8. *Work to live; don't live to work. Look to the Life of Christ. His work was miracles and healing.*

9. *The way in which we work reveals who we are. Everyone wants to change the world and no one wants to do the dishes.*

10. *The apostles were useless to Jesus in the Garden of Gethsemane. True compassion is always about the other. Let go; keep watch; stay awake.*

Fourth Quarter

"In 1981, the Bears had a half mile run to start training camp. One player, Kris Haines, finished ahead of me. He was later cut."

—Patrick McCaskey

McGarry in the Ring

We live in an age of video games, home theaters, and smart phones. Fast food tempts us as we drive down the street. Unhealthy options are at our doorstep. But to develop good habits with our youth, people have reached out to help kids with sports.

Sports require active participation, training, and practice. Sports require discipline at every turn. Sports help prepare kids for their future that includes hard work. Luckily, all over the country, adults help kids with sports—many after work and on weekends. Chicago's Martin "Marty" McGarry was one of the best.

Losing his own father at age 14 in Ireland, McGarry was the youngest of eight born in County Mayo, home to the "Quiet Man" and Our Lady of Knock Shrine. After their father died, the McGarrys left home for more opportunities here in the states in 1969. Marty also followed five of his brothers into the boxing ring.

A talented pugilist, McGarry was a Golden Gloves champion, a state champion, and a Catholic Youth Organization (CYO) champion. The *Beverly Review* quotes McGarry: "Boxing made me tough...fighting was in my blood."

If You Build It, They Will Come

McGarry earned a living as a pipefitter, but he "prized" the ring. He began to work with kids, training them for

97

the sport he loved so much. Behind his house, he built a building that included a boxing ring. There, he trained young athletes at McGarry's Boxing Club and continued as long as he could—building character along the way.

Despite the boxer's tough exterior, McGarry had a big heart that looked out for others. Whenever he could, he offered a helping hand to those in need. He was active in his church, Saint Barnabas. He was known for his boundless energy. McGarry's gym offered boxing exhibitions that helped out parishes and schools. Thousands of quiet hours in the gym were followed by exuberant matches. He was someone you could always count on when the chips were down.

Despite taking exceptional care of himself physically, McGarry was diagnosed with familial amyloidosis, a hereditary disease that took the lives of other McGarry family members. As everyone who knew him expected, the fighter took on the disease with courage and determination. Eventually, the magnificent athlete became bound to a wheelchair. The "fight" grew expensive. A fundraiser was given for his care. No miracle followed. McGarry died on January 24, 2018. His son, Morgan McGarry, runs McGarry's Boxing Club today.

In 2014, we honored Marty McGarry with induction into the Sports Faith International Hall of Fame. It was a privilege.

Manual Academy Grant

From humble beginnings, the NFL and the Bears have grown so much that we are able to work with various civic organizations and their partners to improve stadiums and other facilities to promote health and fitness. The building of the (Peoria) Manual Academy football field is an example of these efforts. In 2018, we were thrilled to celebrate this tremendous resource for deserving families and children. The football stadium is our largest classroom. Let sportsmanship prevail.

There are many things about which we can worry and even more about which we should be grateful. God has been very, very good to us.

We promise to be good stewards of our finances and our resources and our blessings. There is much about which we can fret. Better yet to thank God for all things.

Israel Idonije

Israel Idonije played for the Bears from 2004 through 2012. He was a force on the kickoff coverage team and a gunner on the punt coverage team.[23] In 2018, Israel created a "Monsters of the Midway" comic universe to promote the Bears' schedule.[24]

> Whenever we needed to help other people
> Or needed a fine defensive lineman
> We got Idonije; he knew how to play
> Israel is named for a Biblical wrestler
>
> Before the games got out of hand
> Before a win was just a bright thought in the playbook

---

[23] A "gunner" is a fearless player with great speed who runs down the sideline to be one of the first players to tackle the returner on kickoffs and punts.

[24] See the Bears Monster of the Midway pages at https://www.chicagobears.com/fan-zone/monsters-of-the-midway-2019 .

Out on the field he liked to run
Bears play together and give something worth
remembering

Dale Haase

In the eighth-grade variety show, on May 29, 1963, my
friend Dale Haase was in the Mitch Miller singing
group.[25] From the eighth-grade year book, we know
that Dale was born on February 12. His pet peeve was
school. His ambition was to be a doctor of dentistry
and a surgeon. He willed his height to Lorette Gates.
It was predicted that Dale and I would be prominent
ditch diggers for the Therese Snow Sewer Lines
Company.

Dale was a forward on the Saint Mary's basketball
team. In the championship game of the Maryville Don
Bosco tournament, Dale scored nine points in the 46–
45 overtime victory. For the season, Dale scored 106
points. The ideal boy would be as friendly as Dale.

From the 25-year class reunion yearbook, we know
that Dale was the owner and president of Northern
Environmental Systems. He had a B.S. from Quincy
College and an Engineering degree from the University
of Illinois Graduate Extension. He was married to
Jeanne M. Eppers Haase. They had two children–
Matthew and Meredith.

His worst job was stacking books for a book factory.
His best job was president at his company. His favorite
grade school memory was basketball games and parties
after those games (not necessarily in that order). His

---

[25] This grade school skit was based on a popular TV show called "Sing
Along with Mitch," featuring musician, recording artist, and record
producer, Mitch Miller, conducting an all-male chorus performing
popular hits with lyrics appearing at the bottom of the screen.

best experience since grade school was actually breaking some of the Ten Commandments. His message or thought to share was, "I probably won't realize how much I miss St. Mary's until the night of the reunion and seeing our former classmates."

We had speeches in alphabetical order. Cathy Green said, "I always lined up in front of Dale Haase."

Dale said, "You always looked good from behind Cathy."

From Dale's obituary, we know that he "passed away on June 3, 2019, surrounded by family. For over 25 years, Dale taught physical education at Lincoln Middle School in Park Ridge, Illinois. He was the consummate sports fanatic."

Dale played football, basketball, and baseball at Maine West. He earned a baseball scholarship at Quincy College. "He played semipro baseball and as a father became involved in Libertyville Little League as a coach and a Board Member. He coached Greater Libertyville Soccer Association (GLSA) youth soccer for his daughter Meredith and was instrumental in bringing and starting lacrosse with Matt in Libertyville where he coached varsity lacrosse at the high school for many years. Golf was another of Dale's passions...he enjoyed fishing and snowmobiling."

Dale was a powerful rebounder and a great friend.

Overtime

"If you know some people who are not Bear fans, don't be discouraged. Some of the greatest Christians started out as atheists. Jesus forgave the good thief. All they have to do is repent."

—Patrick McCaskey

Fair play is something that we need to support beyond the playing fields. America's sense of acceptable behavior has taken some strange twists and turns lately. While most people suggest that certain outrageous behavior is not something their own families would practice, there has been a movement to lower the bar for others. However, the challenge is that we are all in this life together. In Catholic circles, we say that we are part of the Mystical Body of Christ.

People talked about how all mothers would fight to protect their children—both born and unborn. People believed that the life of a child was precious. Yet, while we might believe life is precious, we also know that young life needs protection. When a society lets its guard down on protecting life, something fills that void and the results can be catastrophic.

As human beings, we are often overwhelmed by such problems. While we need to act to do what we can, we also need to put the worry in God's hands. Traditionally, many pray for God to look over our young and we also teach our young to ask for God's help.

Ken Kavanaugh

Ken Kavanaugh played baseball and football at Louisiana State University (LSU). He received the Touchdown Club's first Knute Rockne Memorial

Trophy in 1939; this award recognizes exceptional performance by a lineman. He finished seventh in the voting for the Heisman Trophy that same year.

Kavanaugh was the Bears 2nd round draft choice in 1940. Football historian Bob Carroll of the Professional Football Researchers Association (PFRA) called him a quality receiver in that his value could not be measured in the number of catches he made, but by what he did after he caught them.[26] The 6-foot-3 205-pound end had 162 receptions for 3,626 yards and 50 touchdowns. Kavanaugh's 50 receiving TDs is still a Bears record. His 13 receiving touchdowns in a single season is tied with Dick Gordon's top spot with the Bears.

Kavanaugh played with the Bears in 1940 and 1941. He then went off to War for 3 ½ years with the U.S. Army Air Forces. He eventually became a Captain. Kavanaugh was a consummate all-American soldier and citizen. Like many of the "greatest generation," he had a war-time romance that led to marriage. Kavanaugh's son, Ken Kavanaugh, Jr., wrote an excellent book on his dad's life called *The Humility of Greatness*.[27]

Extensive training led Kavanaugh to becoming a pilot while many other candidates would "wash out." In October of 1942, Kavanaugh got his wings from the Army Air Force flight program in a San Antonio ceremony. On his way to marry his girlfriend, Ann Porter, and take on his new assignment at Westover

---

[26] Bob Carroll, "Ken Kavanaugh: The Bears Home Run Hitter," *The Coffin Corner*: Vol. 8, No. 2 (1986) viewed at http://profootballresearchers.com/archives/Website_Files/Coffin_Cor ner/08-02-254.pdf on August 16, 2019.
[27] Ken Kavanaugh, Jr., *The Humility of Greatness* (Bloomington, IN: Xlibris, 2002).

Field in Springfield, Massachusetts, he listened to the Bears beat the Cardinals, 41–14, on a car radio on October 11. Further along on his journey east, he stopped by Wrigley Field after a Bears' practice.[28]

Kavanaugh was assigned to the 7th Anti-Submarine Group. At first he flew as a co-pilot on short-range daylight bombing exercises off the East Coast. He was then sent down to Trinidad where he used radar to help him search for submarines. It was not very dangerous work, but it helped him improve his piloting skills. Later pilot recruits would be sent out on dangerous missions right after training with devastating consequences.

On August 17th, the 7th Group was sent to Langley Air Base in Northern Virginia. Kavanaugh knew something was brewing. There at Langley, he received training on the state of the art B-24 Liberator. Next stop was Mountain Home Idaho, where the 7th was being reorganized into the 851st Bomb Squadron of the 490th Bomb Group. He received more training as a pilot and his own crew. Finally he was sent to a base at Eye England.[29]

Flying a bomber with targets in France, Germany, and other parts of Europe was one of the most dangerous jobs in the military. Kavanaugh and his crew flew 30 nerve-racking missions in the European Theater. The courage and steady hand Kavanaugh displayed was exceptional. On one mission, he lost engines and had severe damage to his plane, but he was able to bring it home safely. Several other times his

---

[28] Ken Kavanaugh, Jr., *The Humility of Greatness* (Bloomington, IN: Xlibris, 2002).113-114

[29] Ken Kavanaugh, Jr., *The Humility of Greatness* (Bloomington, IN: Xlibris, 2002).135.

plane was damaged. Flying both the B-24 and B-17, he and his men witnessed many crashes and catastrophes. No small feat, he was able to bring his men back safely and perform the work assigned. Kavanaugh was awarded the Distinguished Flying Cross and the Air Medal with four oak clusters.

Naturally, Kavanaugh returned to the Bears in 1946 upon his discharge. He remained through 1950. The War required many sacrifices, but he still had a great career. He played on the Bears' 1940, 1941, and 1946 Championship teams. He was first-team All-Pro two times. He made the NFL 1940s All-Decade Team. He was a Bears' assistant coach in 1951. In 1954, he joined the New York Giants organization as an assistant coach. He stayed with the Giants organization as a coach and then as a scout until his retirement in 1999. Kavanaugh died on January 25, 2007.

Matt Forte
On the brink of distinction stood Matt Forte, Chicago Bear
On the other side of the football stood opponents with fierce stares
Scoring touchdowns was his goal, such a thrilling sight to see
Since his blockers played together, the Bears obtained victory

Matt Forte loved playing football
With a love as big as the sky
Matt Forte loved playing football
With a love that didn't die

He could reach the end zone often because he worked out every day

He could help the Bears win often because
running was his forte
In the daylight we could see his practice habits
on the field
He sure gained much total yardage and we know
he would not yield

Matt Forte loved playing football
With a love as big as the sky
Matt Forte loved playing football
With a love that didn't die

Investigative Reporter Lila Rose

Child's Prayer

Angel of God,
my guardian dear,
To whom God's love
commits me here,
Ever this day,
be at my side,
To light and guard,
Rule and guide.

Lila Rose is a speaker, writer, and human rights activist who has been on national news programs and social media. Rose founded Live Action, a media and news nonprofit dedicated to ending abortion and inspiring a culture that respects all human life. Live Action's groundbreaking news coverage and compelling videos reach millions.

Rose's investigative reporting on the abortion industry has been featured in most major news outlets. Rose's outreach has expanded internationally. She has addressed members of the European Parliament and spoken at the United Nation's Commission on the Status of Women.

Lila Rose

Lila Rose, we're grateful to you
Planned Parenthood is on the run
Lila Rose, we're grateful to you
Doing God's work is lots of fun
Ding dong ding
We can hear the angels sing rhymes
Ding dong ding
At the least suggestion, we asked some questions

Lila Rose, we're grateful to you
Planned Parenthood now has shame
Lila Rose, now everyone knows
Marching for Life is our best game
So here is our love song, not fancy or a line
Lila Rose, we think you're quite fine
Lila Rose, oh Lila Rose oh Lila Rose

Unique from Day One
To help the Court Supreme
We keep marching towards a dream
March for life, march for life
Instead of drinking wine
We keep marching to feel fine
March for life, march for life

We are unique from day one
Here there's hope for everyone
Here our warm pro-life hearts will have won
We're unique from day one
And before our lives are done
We can show we're unique from day one

On the Chicago streets
We think marching is quite neat
March for life, march for life
Like this cold, winter earth
We are marching for rebirth
March for life, march for life

We're unique from day one
Here there's hope for everyone
Here our warm pro-life hearts will have won
We're unique from day one
And before our lives are done
We can show we're unique from day one

When the weather is cold
And you're feeling old
You are not old, you are quite mature

Shakespeare at Halftime

(Based on Henry the Fifth, Act III, Scene 1.)
One more half to play for the victory,
And end the game with our best effort!
In church there's nothing so becoming
As modest stillness and humility,
But when the whistle blows to restart the game,
Then imitate the action of Bears:
Stiffen the sinews, summon up the blood,
Disguise fair nature with hard-favored rage;
Then lend the eye a terrible aspect:
Let it pry through the portage of the head
Like the brass cannon; let the brow overwhelm it
As fearfully as does a galled rock
Overhang and jutty his confounded base,
Swilled with the wild and wasteful ocean.
Now set the teeth and stretch the nostril wide,
Hold hard the breath and bend up every spirit
To its full height! Go, go you great Bears,
Whose blood is full from fathers of game-proof,
Fathers that like so many Coaches
Have in these parts from morn till even played
And then stopped playing for lack of games.
Dishonor not your mothers; now play hard
That those whom you called fathers did beget you!
Be copy now to men of grosser blood
And teach them how to play! And you, good coaches,
Whose limbs were made quite near here, show us here
The mettle of your coaching. Let us pledge

That you are worth your breeding; which I doubt not,
For there is none of you so mean and base
That has not noble luster in your eyes.
I see you, Bears, ready to play,
Straining for the kickoff. The game's today!
Follow your spirit; and upon this charge
Cry "God for Coaches and the Chicago Bears!"

Jerry Angelo

Jerry Angelo was the Bears' general manager from 2001 through 2011. Two of the highlights during his tenure were the winning of the Halas trophy and the hiring of Cliff Stein.

Mister Jerry got great players
They were like dragon slayers
We won the games like roses in clover
We could tell that our losing games were over

Mister Jerry, we thank you
He rebuilt the orange and blue
He turned on his magic beam
Mister Jerry gave us a dream

Mister Jerry we had a dream
To be the champs would be real keen
He gave us his word he was not a rover
We could tell that our losing games were over

Mister Jerry, we thank you
He rebuilt the orange and blue
He turned on his magic beam
Mister Jerry, we had a dream

Mister Jerry, Halas trophy to hold
Was really great before we were too old
We thank him for his magic beam
Mister Jerry brought us a dream

Yes...

Giving Thanks

"Several hours after the Chicago Bears drafted Walter Payton in the 1ˢᵗ round of the 1975 NFL Draft, I drove to O'Hare Airport to meet him. However, he ended up not making the flight. Instead of nursing a grudge, I married a nurse."

—Patrick McCaskey

Matt Cullen

Matthew Cullen is a former professional ice hockey center who played an incredible 21 seasons in the National Hockey League (NHL). He played for three Stanley Cup Champions: the 2006 Carolina Hurricanes and the 2016 and 2017 Pittsburgh Penguins. Like many kids growing up with hockey, his father iced the backyard down and created a rink for his sons to play on. Matt, Mark, and Joe Cullen loved playing in the backyard with their dad.[30] Cullen's hockey dreams were shaped at Moorhead High School where his father, Terry Cullen, was the school's varsity ice hockey coach.

Cullen was named Minnesota's Player of the Year (high school) by the Associated Press after scoring 47 goals and adding 42 assists in 28 games. Cullen went on to play at St. Cloud State University from 1995 to 1997.

The young skater was drafted in 1996 in the 2ⁿᵈ round by the Mighty Ducks of Anaheim. He played in Anaheim from 1997 until 2003. He played for many other teams in his long career including the Florida Panthers, Carolina Hurricanes, New York Rangers,

[30] Official site of Pittsburgh Penguins, A Hockey Life, viewed at https://www.nhl.com/penguins/team/a-hockey-life on August 19, 2019.

Ottawa Senators, Minnesota Wild, Nashville Predators and Pittsburgh Penguins. Cullen retired from the NHL after 21 seasons in the summer of 2019. He played 1,516 games, scored 266 goals with 465 assists, and 731 points.[31] Cullen was also a bronze medal winner in the 2004 Ice Hockey World Championships as a member of the U.S. Team.

Raised in a Catholic family, Cullen regularly attended Mass at St. Joseph's Catholic Church in Moorhead.[32] He read the Bible at an early age. His NFL teammates helped rekindle his faith on the professional hockey circuit. He got into the habit of going to chapel at the rink and going to church as a family. Fellowship of Christian Athletes Hockey helped him play with courage and fight fear.[33]

Cullen shares Bible stories with his children. Prayer has helped him in life including his hockey career. In fact, Cullen has seen an increase in the faith of professional hockey players during his career.

According to Cullen…"the biggest lesson I've learned from my 21 years and 1,500-plus games in the NHL is that you have to take a risk…I think you're given certain opportunities in life and if you're willing to take a risk and throw yourself in all the way then special

---

[31] "A CSJ Conversation with Matt Cullen," *Christian Sports Journal*, October 1, 2016, viewed at http://christiansportsjournal.com/a-csj-conversation-with-matt-cullen/ on August 19, 2019.

[32] Roxane Salonen, "Faith Conversations: Matt Cullen Lives Faith on and Now Off the Ice," *Inforum*, August 9, 2019, viewed at https://www.inforum.com/lifestyle/faith/4565385-Faith-Conversations-Matt-Cullen-lives-faith-on-—-and-now-off-—-the-ice on August 19. 2019.

[33] "A CSJ Conversation with Matt Cullen," *Christian Sports Journal*, October 1, 2016, viewed at http://christiansportsjournal.com/a-csj-conversation-with-matt-cullen/ on August 19, 2019.

things can happen. For me, that was the case. We leaned on our faith a lot and took leaps of faith. Thank God we took those chances and opportunities where He was sending us."34

Wanting to give back after having such good fortune, Matt and his wife Bridget founded the Cullen Children's Foundation, also known as "Cully's Kids," in 2003. The foundation provides financial resources to organizations that support children's healthcare needs. After retirement, Cullen joined the Pittsburgh Penguins' hockey operations department in a player development role.

Cullen looks back on his career in an NHL.com Video and shares this special message: "There is no way to know what is ahead of me, but no matter what it is, I'll always be able to look over my shoulder at what's behind me and see the love and support that's pushing me forward for the rest of my life."35

34 Official site of Pittsburgh Penguins, *A Hockey Life*, viewed at https://www.nhl.com/penguins/team/a-hockey-life on August 19, 2019.
35 From NHL.com video, "Matt Cullen: My Story (07.10.19)," viewed at https://www.nhl.com/video/matt-cullen-my-story-071019/t-277350912/c-68631203?q=matt+cullen

SPORTSMANSHIP

MATT CULLEN

MARK TWAIN

Monsignor Dempsey

Mark Twain said that *Joan of Arc* was his best book. He did 12 years of research. He rewrote it six times in 2 years. Here is an excerpt.

"Whatever the parish priest believes, his flock believes; they love him, they revere him; he is their unfailing friend, their dauntless protector, their comforter in sorrow, their helper in their day of need; he has their whole confidence; what he tells them to do, that they will do, with a blind and affectionate obedience, let it cost what it may. Add these facts thoughtfully together, and what is the sum? This: The parish priest governs the nation...."

Mark Twain had a sense of humor.

Monsignor Dempsey was born and raised in Chicago. Pope John Paul II ordained him in 1980. He is the pastor of Saint Patrick Church in Lake Forest. He serves with distinction on the Sports Faith International Committee.

True or false: In 2012, Monsignor Dempsey and the Saint Philip the Apostle Parishioners received the Mary Ellen Nolan Guardian Angel Award from Amate House?[36] True

I have made many mistakes with Monsignor Dempsey. I have often called him Father. Not once did he stomp his foot and exclaim, "I am a Monsignor."

Monsignor reminds me of Cardinal George. Monsignor Dempsey is very intelligent. He is an

---

[36] Amate House is a program that offers a year of intensive leadership development in Chicago. Fellows are young adults ages 21-29 who commit to living in intentional community and serving under-resourced communities in Chicago through full time community service.

excellent homilist; he is very supportive of Sports Faith; and he has a sense of humor.

Teammates in Christ

Philippians 1:3-6, "I give thanks to my God at every remembrance of you, praying always with joy in my every prayer for all of you, because of your partnership for the gospel from the first day until now. I am confident of this, that the one who began a good work in you will continue to complete it until the day of Christ Jesus."
As the 2,000-year old man,
Mel Brooks said,
"Philip was the leader
Of our tribe,
Very big, very strong,
A big chest and big arms.
He could walk on you
And you could die.
We prayed to him.
'O Philip,
Please don't take our eyes out
And don't pinch us
And don't hurt us.'
One day Philip was hurt by lightning.
And we looked up.
We said,
'There's something bigger than Phil.'"
Thanks to Paul,
The Philippians knew
That someone was God.
Athletes and athletes
Who have gone to seed
(sometimes known as coaches)
Are in need
Of Christ and each other.

The Year of Growth
2 Peter 3:18
"But grow in the grace and knowledge of our
Lord and Savior Jesus Christ. To him be
glory both now and forever! Amen."
Christ's divinity was acknowledged here.

The Lawndale Christian Community Church
LC3 forty first anniversary.

Brian Piccolo number forty-one
When a white player was between two black
players, he said, "a human oreo."

Let us keep this church going forever.
Let us be a halfway house to heaven.

Coach and Anne Gordon will not grow taller.
I need for my stomach to grow smaller.

Grace and knowledge of Christ help us to grow.

Love & Marriage

Friends of the family, Joey and Sarah, asked me to do a
prayer at their wedding rehearsal dinner. Here it is.
A reading from Paul's First Letter to the Corinthians,
which I have rewritten a little.

Now I shall show you the way which surpasses all
the others. If I speak in human and angelic tongues as
well, but do not have love, I am a noisy gong, a clanging
cymbal. If I have the gift of prophecy and, with full
knowledge, comprehend all mysteries, if I have faith
great enough to move mountains, but have not love, I
am nothing. If I give everything I have to feed the poor

119

and hand over my body to be burned, but have not love, I gain nothing.

Even if I were the greatest blocker, the greatest tackler, the greatest runner, the greatest passer, the greatest receiver, the greatest interceptor, the greatest placekicker, the greatest punter, a combination of some or all of these, I would be nothing, if I did not love.

Love is patient; love is kind. Love is not jealous, it does not put on airs, it is not snobbish. Love is never rude, it is not self-seeking. It is not prone to anger; neither does it brood over injuries. Love does not rejoice in what is wrong but rejoices with the truth. There is no limit to love's forbearance, to its trust, its hope, its power to endure.

Love never fails.

Paul McCartney wrote and sang, "Love doesn't come in a minute."

Joey and Sarah dated each other for 6 years before they became engaged.

When Joey was in junior high, I was one of his football coaches. I only had to discipline him once. I don't remember what he did wrong and he is still talking to me.

Anthony was a fine example for his brother Joey. The H in Hrusovsky is silent, but it stands for the heart that Joey will bring to his marriage.

In the name of the Father and of the Son and of the Holy Spirit. Bless us O Lord and these thy gifts which we are about to receive from thy bounty through Christ Our Lord Amen. God bless the cook and the servers and all who partake. May we be satisfied with this excellent sufficiency. Thank you for your many, many blessings and lessons. In the name of the Father and of the Son and of the Holy Spirit.

2019 Sports Faith Awards Ceremony

The Sports Faith Awards Ceremony was on Pentecost Vigil, Saturday, June 8, at Mundelein Seminary. Father Dwight Campbell serves with distinction on the Sports Faith International Committee. He grew up in Chicago. Now, he is doing Bears' missionary work in Wisconsin. He got us started in the right way with the opening prayer.

The Honorable Mark Curran has often led us in the Pledge of Allegiance. He nominated the Honorable Jim Ryan for a Sports Faith Award. So, Mark Curran is like John the Baptist; Jim Ryan is like Jesus Christ. Jim Ryan led us in the Pledge of Allegiance.

The Saint Catherine's High School football team of Racine, Wisconsin, won the state championship in a direct manner; they won every game. Mike Arendt is the athletic director. Dan Miller is the head football coach. Defensive Line Coach Mike DeGuire was there to receive the Sports Faith High School Team of the Year Award.

The honorable Jim Ryan was a Golden Gloves boxing champion. He fights for the Catholic faith and Pro-life. He is a strong advocate for abused women, children, and crime victims. He was there to accept the Sports Faith Virtue of Saint Paul Award.

Father John Smyth gave up professional basketball to become a priest. Father Martin Luboyera was a great soccer player who gave it up to become a priest. He was a priest of the Archdiocese of Kampala in Uganda. He studied theology at Mundelein Seminary. He is an associate pastor at Saint Joseph Parish in Libertyville. He was there to accept the Sports Faith Father Smyth Award.

John Shinsky grew up as an orphan. He played football for Saint Joseph High School in Cleveland. He was an Academic All–American at Michigan State where he earned a bachelor's degree, a master's degree, and a doctorate degree in general and special education. He and his wife, Cindy, started the City of Children orphanage in Metamoros, Mexico. He was there to accept the Sports Faith All-Star College Lifetime Achievement Award.

The Benedictine College football team of Atchison, Kansas, attended the school president's Wednesday morning Rosary through the entire season. They made it to the NAIA national championship game. Steve Minnis is the school president. Charlie Gartenmayer is the athletic director and the defensive coordinator. Larry Wilcox is the head football coach. Wilcox is a NAIA Hall of Fame Coach. He was there to receive the Sports Faith Collegiate Team of the Year Award.

Elvis Grbac played football and basketball for Saint Joseph High School in Cleveland. He played football for the University of Michigan, the San Francisco 49ers, the Kansas City Chiefs, and the Baltimore Ravens. He was on the National Football League Championship 1994 San Francisco 49ers. He played in a Pro Bowl. He is studying to become a deacon for the Diocese of Cleveland. He was there to receive a professional Sports Faith Award.

Joe DeLameilleure played football, basketball, and baseball for Saint Clement High School in Center Line, Michigan. He was an All-American offensive lineman at Michigan State. He played offensive guard for the Buffalo Bills and the Cleveland Browns. In Buffalo, DeLameilleure was a member of the famed offensive line nicknamed "Electric Company" that was credited with opening running lanes for Hall of Fame running back O. J. Simpson. He played for 13 seasons in the National Football League. He played in six Pro Bowls. He was first-team All-Pro six times. He is a Pro Football Hall of Famer. DeLameilleure was named to the NFL's 1970s All-Decade Team. He was there to receive a professional Sports Faith Award.

Jesus had the wedding feast at Cana. We had dinner with Matt & Angela Tomlinson, the Honeymooners. Jesus cooked for his disciples. Mundelein Seminary cooked for us.

Bishop Tom Paprocki plays hockey and he runs marathons. He is a Sports Faith Hall of Famer. He is doing missionary work in Springfield. He speaks English, Polish, Spanish, and Italian. When he led us in the closing prayer and the blessing of the athletes, he did it in English.

More than Coincidences
There are ten commandments
My football number was ten.

There were twelve Old Testament prophets.
There were twelve New Testament apostles.

There are twelve Chicago Bears Pro Football
Hall of Famers whose numbers are retired.

In honor of the Trinity,
we have a three-step handshake.

There are eight beatitudes.
We have an eight-step handshake.

There are seven sacraments.
George Halas was number seven.

PART THREE: PRAISEWORTHY

CELEBRATING THE GREAT ONES

Heroes

"In Seventh Grade on the Des Plaines Saint Mary's basketball team, we lost to Arlington Heights Saint James, 46-1. I led the team in scoring that game."

—Patrick McCaskey

Harold Abrahams and Eric Liddell

I have seen the movie "Chariots of Fire" many times and I could easily see it again. The story examines the struggles of athletes Harold Abrahams and Eric Liddell as they prepare and compete in the 1924 Olympics.

When I was in high school, my sports motivation was similar to Harold Abrahams's. I didn't realize it at the time, but I felt like Abrahams who said, "They'll lead you to the water, but they won't let you drink."

Abrahams was constantly humiliated by the anti-Semitism of his day. I felt like Abrahams who raced to get back at the world, to take his tormenters on "one by one and run them off their feet."

We didn't have a Fellowship of Christian Athletes (FCA) group at my high school and I wish we had. We didn't know about FCA summer conferences for high school athletes and we missed a great deal.

After college and a 10-year layoff from athletic competition because of eye and allergy problems, I became associated with the Fellowship of Christian Athletes. I attended summer conferences in 1978 and 1979. The experiences there reminded me of a line from the Hebrew poet Yehuda Amichai. "The passing years have calmed me, and brought healing to my heart, and rest to my eyes."

At the FCA summer conferences that I attended, athletes played with exemplary, gentlemanly sportsmanship and actually prayed for the referees. Everyone had a great deal of good, clean fun. It was very much like the competition in "Chariots of Fire."

Eric Liddell was a "muscular Christian." His missionary father told him, "you can praise the Lord by peeling a spud if you peel it to perfection. Run in the Lord's name and let the world stand back in wonder."

Now my sports motivation is similar to Eric Liddell's. He said, "God made me for a purpose, but He also made me fast. When I run I feel His pleasure. To give that up would be to hold Him in contempt."

The Biblical principles on which Eric Liddell based his life can be learned at the FCA summer conferences. His widow said, "He always spent the first hour of the day in Bible reading, prayer, and planning the day's concerns. He was never shocked or judgmental about other people's conduct or problems. He could be very naughty himself and had a remarkable sense of humor. His greatest gift was his understanding of people. They felt it and came to him constantly for help."

Thanks to Liddell, I know where the power comes "from to see a race to its end: from within." And here is what Abrahams said about Liddell. "I've never seen such desire, commitment in a runner. He runs like a wild animal. It unnerves me."

George Halas

It won't surprise readers that George Halas is one of my heroes. Grandpa was frequently recognized for his achievements and the help he gave others. Likewise, Halas always had an appreciation for Bears' fans.

Sometimes I was there to witness the gratitude of others and how Grandpa accepted it.

In the winter of 1967, my grandfather, George Halas, published a series of 21 articles about the Chicago Bears in the *Chicago Tribune*. The articles were later collected in a booklet entitled, *That's How the Ball Bounces.*

In the summer of 1968, Grandpa received an award from the National Football League Players Association commemorating his lifetime of service to pro football. The banquet was in downtown Chicago.

My brother, Mike, and I drove there. It was around the time of the Democratic National Convention. When a protester saw us, he shot a cap gun at us and yelled, "Keep your hands off the Dominican Republic."

When my grandfather received the award, he told a story from Chapter Ten of *That's How the Ball Bounces.*

"Thank you for this award. I feel like Bull Lipski who played linebacker for the Philadelphia Eagles. He once attempted to tackle Bronko Nagurski and he was knocked unconscious by a churning knee. But Bull had great recuperative powers and—after being revived—he again attempted to tackle Nagurski on the next play and again was rendered unconscious.

"Since it now appeared improbable that Lipski could be revived quickly enough to remain in the game, two of the Philadelphia substitutes came off the bench and started to drag Bull off the field. Bull came to as they neared the sideline and muttered something about getting back to the huddle in a hurry. Apparently, he was concerned about incurring a penalty for delaying the game.

"Lipski need not have worried about this possibility because play already had been resumed—and the Bears were headed in his direction on a sweep with Nagurski leading the interference.

"Bronko overtook Lipski and the two subs about five yards from the sideline and—WHAM—Bronk threw a block that sent all three of them flying into the Eagles' bench.

"Poor Lipski was knocked out for the third time...

"Thank you for this award. Like Bull Lipski, I am overwhelmed."

There were three comedians at the banquet: Johnny Carson, Buddy Hackett, and George Halas.

George Halas's Military Service

Freshman George Halas was out on summer vacation from the University of Illinois in 1915. Between high school and college, he worked at Western Electric's famed Hawthorne Works in Cicero, Illinois.[37] He was back again that summer at Hawthorne. He was about to head out to the Western Electric Summer picnic in Michigan City on July 24th when his brother Frank stopped him and asked him to hit the scales. The older Halas brothers, Walter and Frank, like others, saw much potential in George. The brothers were coaching him on gaining weight and muscle for college football. The delay meant that Grandpa arrived late for the excursion ship, the Eastland, which was scheduled to head over to Michigan City for the picnic. The Eastland capsized on the Chicago River as it was filling up with Western Electric passengers. Halas could have been one of those passengers had he arrived earlier. This life-saving event spoke volumes to Grandpa about his

---

[37] The Hawthorne Studies began in 1924 and studied workers' conditions, attitudes, and the social organization of people at work.

future prospects. Halas sensed that he was destined for achievement. He said a Rosary in thanksgiving.

In his senior year at the University of Illinois, Halas was in the midst of his final stretch of his academic career when the United States entered World War I. He joined the Navy to destroy German submarines—a relatively new weapon at the time. He was assigned to Great Lakes Naval Training Station and entered Officer Training School. He played on the Great Lakes football team. Halas was chosen MVP in the 1919 Rose Bowl when his Great Lakes team beat the Mare Island Marines, 17–0. Orders never came for duty overseas. The sports program was not the duty he wanted, but it was what he was told to do and it turned out providential. Grandpa got extra exposure to many of the stars of the day.

Duty Calls Again

When Pearl Harbor was bombed and World War II began for the United States, the Bears were in their final regular season game. Halas went to Great Lakes and asked an old friend, Captain T. DeWitt Carr, for a new Navy Assignment that would allow him to fight the Japanese. The Navy was slow to respond. Grandpa was 46 years old and many discouraged his pursuing another stint in the service for the middle-aged engineer. The Navy was building a new base in Normal Oklahoma where Halas was sent as a Lieutenant Commander. Grandpa awaited his fate and wrote letters for combat action. When Captain Carr was assigned to MacArthur's Seventh Fleet in Brisbane, Halas was reassigned Welfare and Recreation Officer to what was the staging area for the Fleet's operation in the Pacific. By this time in his life, Grandpa had proven himself to be a great organizer. If he could keep the unwieldly NFL on its feet through The Great Depression, he could accomplish great things for the Navy during the war.

Halas expanded services, had sports facilities built, and helped tens of thousands become better, healthier sailors. When "red tape" was in the way, Grandpa hopped on a plane and negotiated his case with his superior officers for better equipment and supplies. He was good at his job.

At the same time, the military was never shy about using men like Halas to bolster their PR efforts. General MacArthur sent for Grandpa and had him escort Bob Hope and his entourage on their Pacific tour of forward military operations. Halas was then made Commander. After Douglas MacArthur's famous return to the Philippines, Grandpa was moved to Pearl Harbor with a new assignment for the American invasion of Japan. But again, no direct combat duty. More appeals for military duty followed and then the War ended.

Halas Addendum

George Halas had a focus on the future—he had a focus on next week's game rather than ruminate on the game that was lost or won a few days ago.

At the same time we study the past for many good reasons. Several great thinkers have written in some form or another that those who do not know their history will repeat their mistakes.

In football, there are always new trends and seemingly new ways of doing things. Halas was keenly aware of this. He was confident, but sought help when he needed it. He often tapped former players and coaches he knew. One of those was Hunk Anderson. Anderson played for Knute Rockne at the University of Notre Dame and then played with Halas in the first decade of the Bears' existence. Anderson also coached at Notre Dame—some years at the same time he played for the Bears! He also coached for the Bears. Anderson was an industrious man, maintaining a super-human schedule all the while making his mark in football. At 5-foot-11 and 191 pounds he was an undersized lineman with a lot of guts and near-perfect technique. As a coach, some would consider him the finest line coach of his time. He was on the Bears staff in the 1940s during the Bears awesome decade of trials and triumphs.

Halas and his staff had reconstituted the old T Formation starting in the late 1930s and 1940s. Defenses had learned to focus on the center of the field for the standard T Formation, but developments like the "man-in-motion" added new complexity and made the modified T Formation formidable. Grandpa tapped coaches like Clark Shaughnessy and Ralph Jones to help renew the T Formation for the Bears. Halas also added players who would excel under the T Formation especially his quarterback from Columbia, Sid Luckman. But success had been limited until 1940 when Anderson was hired and he changed the blocking schemes to use all the weapons that the Bears had been building. Much has been written about the 73–0 annihilation of the Washington Redskins administered by Halas and his Bears in the championship game in 1940. Moreover, the results sold many other teams on the power of the new T Formation. Yet, Hunk Anderson would add a little inside information:

"Our 73–0 annihilation of the Washington Redskins was generally credited to the T Formation's explosiveness. Nonsense! We would have done the same with any of the formations in vogue at the time. George Halas had our guys psychologically keyed up to such a point that our relentless assault forced the Washington Redskins to lose their poise and fall apart."[38]

William Spencer McCaskey

The Chicago Bears celebrate and honor our fighting men and women. My family is well represented in that number from the early days of the nation to the present.

The McCaskeys arrived in the era of the birth of our nation in 1793. William McCaskey was the first American born McCaskey in the line. He married Margaret Piersol whose father fought in the War of 1812. Her grandfathers were also officers in the army.

William's eldest son, John Piersol McCaskey, was an educator, printer, publisher, musician, scholar, and mayor of Lancaster, Pennsylvania. J. P. was born in Lancaster County Pennsylvania the first of seven children of a farm family. I have written about J. P. in *Sports and Faith: More Stories of the Devoted and the Devout*. J.P. is my great-great grandfather.

The third son of William and Margaret McCaskey was William Spencer McCaskey. William had a long distinguished career in the military. He joined the local militia, the "Lancaster Fencibles," which began his long military career.

In 1861, McCaskey joined the 79th Pennsylvania Infantry as the first sergeant of his company. He was promoted to captain. He and his unit fought

---

[38] Heartley W. "Hunk" Anderson with Emil Klosinki, *Notre Dame Chicago Bears and Hunk* (Oviedo, Florida: Florida Sun-Gator Publishing, 1976) 129.

throughout the Civil War in Kentucky, Tennessee, Georgia, and North Carolina.

When the war ended, McCaskey was commissioned as a second lieutenant in the U.S. Infantry out west in 1866. He would spend many years out west—taking on a soldier's duty in often primitive conditions, yet establishing a family. Hostilities were common between the troops and Native Americans. After he was promoted to captain of the 20th Infantry, he was ordered to command Fort Abraham Lincoln in the Dakota Territory in 1876. At that time, Lieutenant Colonel George Armstrong Custer and the 7th Cavalry had departed the fort as part of an effort to crush the Sioux. Custer located a Sioux encampment (in what is now Montana) and attacked on June 25, 1876. Custer and 264 of his men were slaughtered in the Battle of Little Bighorn by a force that has been estimated to be about 2,000. It was McCaskey who informed Elizabeth Custer of the death of her husband. Despite the great number of military battles and skirmishes he fought, McCaskey would remember this duty as his most difficult.

McCaskey remained in the Army. After spending 2 years out east, he returned to the West and attained the rank of major in the 20th Infantry. McCaskey also served with distinction in the Spanish-American War and the Philippines. He was promoted to lieutenant colonel, colonel of his regiment, and brigadier general. Retiring as a major general in 1907, William Spencer McCaskey had a long and meritorious career.

John Perkins

John Perkins grew up just outside New Hebron, Mississippi, where his parents were sharecroppers.[39] After experiencing family tragedies from bigotry, Perkins left for California in 1947, where he went on a spiritual quest that led him to Christianity. He was ordained a Baptist minister.

His faith drew him back home to Mississippi where he began to orchestrate social and religious programs to counter racial hatred and the debased conditions of minorities. His ministries developed affordable housing and helped people develop a more worldly vision of their faith. Perkins's dedication to building up the entire social network would later earn him the nickname, "Father of Christian Community Development."

The late 1960s and early 1970s was an especially active period for civil rights. Perkins was severely beaten when he went to check on two of his associates who had been imprisoned. After moving to Pasadena, California, Perkins and his wife founded another Christian community center. In 1983, Perkins established the John M. Perkins Foundation for Reconciliation & Development, Inc. to advance the principles of Christian community development and racial reconciliation throughout the world. Perkins returned to Mississippi in retirement in 1996, where he remains active in his ministries.

John Perkins
Grandpa Perkins
You're a brother to me

---

[39] Perkins's life is covered in greater detail in *Sports and Faith: Stories of the Devoted and the Devout* (p. 118-121), published by Sporting Chance Press in 2011.

Grandpa Perkins
How we love you
You are always a brother to me
And together we will see how joyous heaven will be

Grandpa Perkins
How we love you
We're so glad that God has blessed your work
And along with Vera Mae
Your duty you won't shirk

In our meetings
We get carried away
We dream of when we'll see
No racial bigotry
Grandpa Perkins
Tries to love every one
He is like God's own Son, he does not weigh a ton

Not Grandpa Perkins
And we love you
And we're so glad that you love the Lord
And together we will see how joyous heaven will be

Grandpa Perkins
You're a brother to me

John Perkins, great Christian
Lord, he is quite like You
All of his days
We want to praise
The wonders of his forgiveness

Our mentor, our hero

Accepts God's mercy and love
Let every breath, all that we are
Never cease to say thank you

Hall of Famer, John Perkins, let us sing
Poor and vulnerable under your wing
Youngsters bow down and the crowds all roar
At your empowerment
We sing for joy about your ministry
You help so many overcome poverty
Nothing compares to the great work that you have done

Father Smyth, a Remembrance

I knew Father Smyth since he became a priest. His first assignment was at Maryville. I played basketball for Saint Mary's School in Des Plaines. We played in a league at Maryville (children's home) on Saturday afternoons.

There was a buzz in the stands. "See that priest over there. He gave up professional basketball to become a priest. That's Father Smyth."

I grew up about two miles from Maryville. When my parents' children were children, we had a mandate each year to give one of our Christmas gifts to Maryville.

One year I received a new baseball glove. I said to my parents that I wanted to give it to Maryville. My parents asked me if I was sure. I was. The next spring, Art Contreras was wearing that glove when he struck me out.

I wanted my parents to adopt Art Contreras. I thought he would make Saint Mary's stronger athletically. I guess my parents thought that eleven children were enough.

Father Smyth coached Maryville's teams. Saint Mary's never beat Maryville's A teams. At Father Smyth's funeral, Art Contreras told me how Father Smyth coached.

Father Smyth said, "You get five fouls in basketball. Make sure your first one is a good one. Let your opponents know that you came to play."

In the winter of 1963, when I was in eighth grade, Saint Mary's won the Maryville Don Bosco basketball tournament. Maryville's A team was busy in another tournament.

Father Smyth was very, very good to me and to my family. My father's funeral was at Maryville. Father Smyth was the celebrant.

When I applied to be on the governance board of Notre Dame College Prep, my opening statement was, "Father Smyth was a great friend of mine."

Father Smyth taught me, "Never refuse help."

Father Smyth helped build Maryville. He helped save Notre Dame College Prep. He helped the Standing Tall Foundation stand tall.

Father Smyth was wonderful. He was a combination of Davy Crockett, Big Bad John, and Johnny Angel.

Father John Smyth

Father Smyth, Father Smyth
He was a great priest
Father Smyth, Father Smyth
He gave to the least
Faith, Family, Education
Father Smyth, Father Smyth

Born in Chicago in 1934
He grew up doing many a chore
When he needed food he went to the store

SPORTSMANSHIP

He grew into a legend forever more

Father John Smyth helped a lot of people

He graduated from DePaul Academy
Then he went to a university
Notre Dame was the place for him to be
He played basketball and made history

Father John Smyth was a servant leader

After a year of pro basketball
He decided to give God his all
He went to the seminary
There were times when he was contrary

Father John Smyth was a visionary

For over forty years he built Maryville
If he had his way, he'd be building there still
Then he helped save Notre Dame College Prep
The Standing Tall Foundation was his next step

Father John Smyth was a great builder

Every Standing Tall function you could see him
arrive
He stood six foot six and weighed two forty-five
Kind of broad at the shoulder and narrow at the
hip
And everybody knew, that you didn't give lip to
Father

Everyone knew that Chicago was his home
When he had trouble with his sight he felt alone

He never complained because he was a tough
guy
When we spoke to him, we said more than "Hi"
to Father

Somebody said that he played quarterback
But a shoulder injury ended that attack
And crashing fouls from a huge left hand
Sent Notre Dame opponents to the Promised
Land

Then came the day when the high school might
have closed
And Father came up with a lot of great dough
Alumni were praying and hearts beat fast
And many people thought that the school
wouldn't last, except Father

Through the debt and the smoke of a man made
school
Walked a giant of a man who was nobody's fool
Grabbed the moaning donors, no longer school
thorns
And like a giant oak tree, he just planted acorns

And with all his strength he built a great grotto
His new parking lot helped every auto
The high school was no longer a would be grave
Like Murray Bannerman, Father made a great
save

The Shamrock Shindig was a great event
It was indoors, so no need for a tent
The Standing Tall luncheons were a great feast

SPORTSMANSHIP

Father John Smyth helped those who had the
least

He was a legend and all of us know
His great example was the way we should go
No need for excuses. Don't waste time.
We needed more scholarships. That was our
mountain to climb

Father John Smyth
How he stood tall
He had something we could not resist
He let everyone know that God exists

Father John Smyth
Raised money
How we tingled when he passed by
Every time he said hello money began to fly

We were in heaven
We got carried away
We dreamt of when we'd be
Out of purgatory
Other causes
Wanted our every dime
We worked on God's own time
With the Spirit we were sublime
With Father John Smyth
Because he stood tall

My Favorite Writers

"As soon as my sons got out of their cribs, I had them switching hands on the dribble."

—Patrick McCaskey

Sports journalists' memoirs often include a chapter that discusses their favorite people—athletes, coaches, and other sports personalities that they have covered in their writing career. As a writer and speaker, I have included this chapter on my favorite writers.

What people write about says a great deal about them. And in return, what we read about says something about us. Many of the people whose writing I enjoy have lived difficult lives, but they wrote with abundant humor. Some had connections with Chicago or sports. Others were a source of inspiration and faith that I picked up while in college or from family members and friends. As a life-long fan of *The New Yorker*, some of the best modern writers were frequent contributors who became favorites of mine. Here's a "rundown" of my favorite authors.

James Agee

James Agee was born on November 27, 1909, in Knoxville, Tennessee. He went to Saint Andrews Seminary and Phillips Exeter Academy. He graduated from Harvard in 1932. Agee was an American novelist, journalist, poet, screenwriter and film critic. His novel, *A Death in the Family*, was published in 1957 after his death. It won the Pulitzer Prize for Fiction in 1958.[40]

---

[40] Pulitzer Prizes Columbia University website at:
https://www.pulitzer.org/prize-winners-by-year/1958 .

Let Us Now Praise Famous Men written by Agee with photographs by Walker Evans reports on the real lives of poor tenant farmers during The Great Depression. Agee labored with this effort to bring the sharecroppers' story to life with dignity. Agee's reviews and stories were widely read during his life, but much of his writing has come to light after his death. He died on May 16, 1955, of a heart attack on his way to a doctor's appointment.

Sholom Aleichem

Sholom Aleichem was born on March 2, 1859, in the Ukraine. He fell in love with Olga Loyeff who was the daughter of a patron. Olga's father refused to allow Aleichem to marry his daughter. Then Aleichem wrote a heartbreaking story about their love that convinced Olga's father to permit the marriage in 1883. After a pogrom in 1905, Aleichem moved to New York in 1906. He was known as the Jewish Mark Twain. When he met Twain, Twain said people always referred to him as "The American Sholom Aleichem." Aleichem died of a nervous breakdown on May 13, 1916, in New York City. A collection of his stories led to the musical comedy "Fiddler on the Roof" in 1964.

FRED ALLEN

Fred Allen

Fred Allen was born on May 31, 1894, as John Florence Sullivan in Cambridge, Massachusetts.[41] He graduated from the High School of Commerce in Boston in 1911. He was a book-runner at the Boston Public Library. He read about comedy and practiced juggling. He was a comic juggler. He met dancer Portland Hoffa in 1922. He began courting her in 1924. They married each other in May 1927. They broke into radio with "Portland serving up the bubbly straight lines for Fred's witty rejoinders."[42] She appeared on his radio program from 1932 to 1949. His autobiography is entitled *Treadmill to Oblivion*.[43] Two years before Fred Allen died, James Thurber wrote, "You can count on a thumb of one hand the American who is at once a comedian, a humorist, a wit, and a satirist, and his name is Fred Allen." Thanks to Harrison Kinney's 1,238 page biography of Thurber, we know that "Thurber's favorite of Allen's radio stories was the one about the scarecrow that so frightened the crows that they brought back some corn they had stolen two days before."[44] Fred Allen died on March 17, 1956, in New York City.

---

[41] Fred Allen, *Much Ado About Me* (Boston: Little Brown and Company, 1956).

[42] Old Time Radio catalogue description viewed at https://www.otrcat.com/p/fred-allen on October 7, 2019.

[43] Fred Allen, *Treadmill to Oblivion* (Boston: Little Brown and Company, 1954).

[44] Harrison Kinney, *James Thurber: His Life and Times* (New York: Henry Holt and Company, 1995).

Yehuda Amichai

Yehuda Amichai was born on May 3, 1924, in Germany. He immigrated to Palestine with his family and moved on to Jerusalem in 1936. He was in the British Army during World War II and fought in the 1948 Arab-Israeli war with an underground force. Then he attended Hebrew University to study Biblical texts and Hebrew literature. He was a teacher and a leading contemporary Hebrew poet.[45] In his poem, "Once a Great Love," he wrote:

"The passing years have calmed me

and brought healing to my heart and rest to my eyes."

Amichai traveled to the United States to teach and speak. He lived in Jerusalem until he died on September 22, 2000.

Roger Angell

Roger Angell was born September 19, 1920, in New York City. He graduated from Harvard in 1942. From 1942-1946, he was in the U. S. Army Air Forces and he served in the Pacific Theater. He has been a contributor to *The New Yorker* magazine since 1944 and a fiction editor since 1956. He is a great baseball writer who reports not only what goes on down on the field, but captures the feel of the game from those in the stands. His model for writing was his stepfather, E. B. White.

---

[45] See more general information on the poet at the Poetry Foundation: https://www.poetryfoundation.org/foundation/people and Encyclopedia Britannica: https://www.britannica.com/biography/Yehuda-Amichai .

SPORTSMANSHIP

"You ought to be ashamed of yourself!"

WIZARD OF OZ ILLUSTRATION

Frank Baum

Frank Baum was born on May 15, 1856, in Chittenango, New York. He and Maud Gage married each other on November 9, 1882. Their home in Chicago at 1667 North Humboldt Boulevard has a marker of distinction. They lived there from 1891 through 1910. His book *The Wonderful Wizard of Oz* was published in 1900. Baum wrote other books on Oz as well. Baum died on May 6, 1919, in Hollywood. The book became the movie in 1939. Because of its many television showings between 1956 and 1974, the movie has been seen by more viewers than any other movie.[46]

Clair Bee

Clair Bee was born on March 2, 1896, in Grafton, West Virginia. He was in the U.S. Army 1917-1919. He has degrees from Waynesburg College (1925), Rider College (1929), and Rutgers University (1931). He married Mary Margaret "Peg" Miller, on December 31, 1940.[47] He was in the U.S. Maritime Service, 1943-1946, and became a commander. He coached basketball at Rider College 1926-31 and Long Island University 1931-52. His winning percentage (.827) is the best ever. He wrote the 24 volume Chip Hilton Sports Series. Like his father before him, Chip was all-

---

[46] See the Library of Congress online exhibit: "The Wizard of Oz: An American Fairy Tale," at https://www.loc.gov/exhibits/oz/ozsect2.html .
[47] Dennis Gildea, *Hoop Crazy*, (Fayetteville: University of Arkansas Press, 2013) 194. Bee's wife is shown on the Bee gravestone as Mary M. and listed on the Clair Francis Bee Jr. entry on Find-A-Grave website as Mary Margaret Miller Bee. In Hoop Crazy she is listed as Margaret Miller Bee.

state in football, basketball, and baseball for Valley Falls High School. Like his father before him, Chip was All-American in football, basketball, and baseball at State University.

The Chip Hilton series offered exciting and inspirational books for young men while promoting good behavior and character development. The series started in the late 1940s and continued through the mid-1960s. Efforts have been made to resurrect and update the series for today's youth. Having amassed an incredible coaching record, when Bee was asked about his greatest accomplishments, he pointed to his Chip Hilton series. Clair Bee died on May 20, 1983, in Cleveland, Ohio.

Robert Benchley

Robert Benchley was born on September 15, 1889, in Worcester, Massachusetts. He graduated from Harvard. He married Gertrude Darling on June 6, 1914. He was a writer, a filmmaker, and an actor. Benchley worked for several prominent periodicals in New York. He contributed articles and then worked for *The New Yorker* magazine for over a decade.[48] When he was in Venice, he sent a telegram to *New Yorker* editor Harold Ross. "Streets full of water. Please advise." He died on November 21, 1945, in New York City.

Ira Berkow

Ira Berkow was born on January 7, 1940, in Chicago, Illinois. He received a Bachelor of Arts degree from

---

[48] Steven Gale, *Encyclopedia of American Humorists* (New York: Routledge, 2016) 36-44.

Miami University in Oxford, Ohio, in 1963 and a master's degree from the Medill School of Journalism, Northwestern University 1965. He has been a sportswriter for the *New York Times* since 1981.[49] Among his 25 books published is *Red Smith: A Biography of Red Smith*. His articles routinely appeared in popular sports anthologies.

Jim Brosnan

Jim Brosnan was born October 24, 1929, in Cincinnati, Ohio. He attended Xavier University for a brief time when he was interested in becoming a doctor. He was a major league pitcher from 1954 through 1963. He married Anne Pitcher on June 23, 1952. They lived in Morton Grove, Illinois. He wrote *The Long Season* a chronicle of his 1959 major league season. Brosnan's book broke new ground as a completely honest portrayal of the day-to-day existence of a major league player.[50] Brosnan wrote a second book called *Pennant Race*. He published articles in *The Atlantic*, *Esquire*, *Look*, *Life*, *Sports Illustrated*, *Sport*, and *Saturday Evening Post*. He went on to write several sports books for kids. Brosnan died on June 28, 2014.

Hoagy Carmichael

Hoagy Carmichael was born on November 22, 1899, in Bloomington, Indiana. He earned undergraduate and law degrees from Indiana University. His first memoir,

[49] *New York Times* biography viewed at
https://archive.nytimes.com/www.nytimes.com/ref/sports/bio-
berkow.html on September 25, 2019.
[50] Mark Armour, "Jim Brosnan," Society for American Baseball Research (SABR) viewed at https://sabr.org/bioproj/person/b15e9d74#_ednref6 on September 25, 2019.

The Stardust Road, was published in 1946. He won an Academy Award for composing the song "In the Cool, Cool, Cool, of the Evening" in 1951. Among his other song compositions were "How Little We Know," "I Get Along Without You Very Well," "Skylark," "Stardust," "The Nearness of You," and "Two Sleepy People." He recorded an album, "Hoagy Sings Carmichael" in 1956. His second memoir, *Sometimes I Wonder*, was published in 1965. He received an honorary doctorate from Indiana University in 1972. He was an actor, a composer, a lawyer, a lyricist, and a singer. He died on December 27, 1981, in Rancho Mirage, California. His biography, *Stardust Melody: The Life and Music of Hoagy Carmichael*, by Richard Sudhalter, was published in 2002.

Oswald Chambers

Oswald Chambers was born on July 24, 1874, in Aberdeen, Scotland. He was a missionary to Egypt during World War I. From David McCasland's biography *Abandoned to God*, we know that Chambers had to learn to soften his style of preaching, but not his content. He did not want to water down the Bible. He also learned not to defend himself. His faith helped him to keep silent. He felt that God would defend him.

Chambers also believed that prayer helped him get in step with God. Prayer wasn't for God to bless his plans. Prayer was work and battle, asking and receiving.

Christ died for Chambers so he felt obliged to do something for Him. Chambers felt that the world was his parish. Chambers and his wife felt called to serve God and then each other. He did not hold anything back. He never despaired of anyone because of the way

God changed him. He let mistakes correct themselves and he did not criticize. He was a very deep person because he drew his strength from God.

Chambers read many other books beside the Bible. He enjoyed classical music and nature. He wrote poetry and newspaper articles. He was graceful and unhurried. He sought the company of children.

Before his sermons, he had quiet time to prepare himself. He was almost 36 when he got married, and his wife was almost 27. His approach to the future was, "Trust God and do the next thing."

Chambers was consistent in how he lived and in what he said. He trusted God patiently. When someone was doing something wrong, Chambers prayed for God to convict him.

Chambers urged his congregations to give up their rights to themselves to God and do His will. When we follow God's will, we will be joyful and blessed. Once, when Chambers was on a ship, he had difficulty finding a place to pray. Then he crawled into a lifeboat for some time with God.

Chambers had a great sense of humor which he used to plow the land. Then he planted the seeds of faith. He even asked for God's blessing on a boxing match. Instead of relying on common sense, he waited for God to fulfill His purpose. He trusted God every day.

Chambers and his wife never discussed money matters in front of other people. He died on November 15, 1917, in Cairo, Egypt from appendicitis at the age of 43. Her mission, after he died, was not to sell books, but to help people. She wrote books from his sermons which she had taken down shorthand. The daily devotional, *My Utmost for His Highest*, has this entry for October 12th. "The worth of a man is revealed in his attitude to ordinary things when he is not before the footlights."

During World War II, 40,000 copies of Chambers' books were burned. His wife calmly waited on the Lord for an answer. Now millions of people all around the world read his devotional every day.

Geoffrey Chaucer

Geoffrey Chaucer was born in 1343 in London. He was an ambassador from England to Italy and France. He knew their languages and their literatures. He had the courage to write humor after the Black Death (1348-1349) and during the Hundred Years War (1346-1446). He wrote as an avocation and gave readings at court. *Canterbury Tales* and other works were not published during his lifetime because the printing press had not been invented.[51] Chaucer became more religious in his later life, but perhaps as a youth he was an altar boy who goofed around a little during Mass. More research is needed in this area. He wrote "pitee renneth soone in gentil herte." He died on October 25, 1400.

Pat Conroy

Pat Conroy was born on October 26, 1945, in Atlanta, Georgia. He played basketball at the Citadel in Charleston, South Carolina. He taught English in Beaufort, South Carolina, and on Daufuskie Island off the South Carolina shore. My favorite book of his is *The Great Santini*. His novels were based on his difficult family life. Four of his books were made into popular

---

[51] Chaucer lived from about 1340 to 1400; Gutenberg was born about the time of Chaucer's death and his printing press was in operation about 1450.

movies. Conroy is considered by some to be one of the best writers from the south in the late 20th century. Pat Conroy died on March 4, 2016.

Jim Croce

Jim Croce was born on January 10, 1943, in Philadelphia, Pennsylvania. He was a psychology major at Villanova University and he graduated in 1965. He worked at the Villanova University radio station. He met his wife, Ingrid, at a singing contest. She was a competitor and he was a judge. They married each other in 1966. He was a songwriter and a performer. For years, they struggled for money. He was giving a lot of concerts, but they had trouble paying their bills. After he had returned from a road trip, they had an argument about money. Then she went upstairs to bed and he went to the basement to write "I'll Have to Say I Love You in a Song." The next morning, he woke her by singing that song. He died in a plane crash in Natchitoches, Louisiana, on September 20, 1973. He is buried in the community of Frazer, which is 25 miles west of Philadelphia.

Will Cuppy

Will Cuppy was born on August 23, 1884, in Auburn, Indiana. He earned an undergraduate and a master's degree from the University of Chicago. He lived in Greenwich Village, New York. He wrote for *The New Yorker* magazine. He began writing what many consider to be his masterpiece, *The Decline and Fall of Practically Everybody*, in 1933. He died on September 19, 1949, in Greenwich Village. *The Decline and Fall of Practically Everybody* is a collection of humorous, but well-researched biographies of historical figures that was published after his death in 1950. His other books include: *Maroon Tales* (1910), *How to Be a Hermit* (1929), *How to Tell Your Friends from Apes* (1931), *How to Become Extinct* (1941), *How to Attract the Wombat* (1949), and *How to Get from January to December* (1951). *How to Get from January to December* was compiled after his death, but includes a wide range of his comic topics.

Bill Dana

Bill Dana was born William Szathmary on October 5, 1924, in Quincy, Massachusetts. He is best known as Jose Jimenez, the reluctant astronaut. His father came from Hungary at the age of 14. He did real estate work until the stock market crash in 1929. Bill never knew any luxury. When he went into the service, he couldn't believe the free food.

When Bill was a student at Daniel Webster Grammar School, a teacher said to him, "Szathmary, you're a buffoon."

Bill replied, "Let's keep religion out of this."

The Szathmary family was fairly ecumenical. They were Jewish, but they were brought up with Catholics. Bill knew the Stations of the Cross. He also knew the following joke.

During the ceremony where novitiates become Brides of Christ, the Bishop noticed an Orthodox Jewish man praying loudly. Not being able to conquer his curiosity, the Bishop had to stop the ceremony long enough to ask the man, "Sir, I realize you are not a Catholic. I must ask you why you are here at this marriage of our Lord to these novitiates?"

The old man answered with a lovely, Jewish accent, "I'm on the groom's side."

After graduation from Quincy High School, Bill went into the Army Air Corps and then the Infantry. He served a little over three years, 1942-1945. He described World War II as "the late unpleasantness against the Huns." He was decorated for "extreme precaution under cover."

Bill went to Emerson College in Boston on the GI Bill. He graduated with high honors in speech and drama and had a minor in English. He and a friend built the campus radio station, WERS. He described himself as a Jewish dropout because he doesn't have a PhD.

After college, he couldn't get a job. By a fluke, he became employed with the Douglas Testing Division in Santa Monica, California, on the Nike Project. A friend of his was a page at NBC in New York. Bill took a leave from Douglas.

Bill never did blue material because he broke in on television. He wrote the material that got Don Adams on "The Steve Allen Show." Then Bill was a writer for "The Steve Allen Show." Jose Jimenez, the reluctant astronaut, was born on that show in 1959.

"The Bill Dana Show" was on the air in the early sixties. It can now be seen on the Christian Broadcasting Network (CBN) in glorious black and white.

Bill took a Don Adams character and made the "Get Smart" character. He wrote the only half-hour episode to be nominated best show of the year in the history of the Emmys, "Sammy Davis Visits the Bunkers" for "All in the Family." The show that won that year was "Brian's Song." Bill entertained at the 1986 Brian Piccolo Golf Tournament Banquet: "to get revenge." He asked for and received a standing ovation. He had performed at my parents' 40th anniversary party in 1983.

Bill did a lot of work on the healing power of laughter. His book on that topic is called, *The Laughter Prescription.* He wrote, "Stress is connected with all of man's physical problems. If you have cancer, just tell it a good joke: titters for the terminal. Anybody in a survival mode has to have humor or it's over and out. After a long wonderful career that brought great joy to his audiences, Bill Dana died on June 15, 2017.

Clarence Day

Clarence Day Junior was born on November 18, 1874, in New York City. He was secretary of his class at Yale. He and his father were partners on Wall Street. During the Spanish-American War, Day served in the Navy.

After the war, Day went back into business. When he was confined to bed with arthritis, he became a freelance writer and a book reviewer. He also wrote poems and drew cartoons. He enjoyed visiting with friends. He was courageous and he had no bitterness or self-pity.

During The Great Depression, he wrote about his childhood in a series of short pieces. His editor at *The New Yorker* magazine was E. B. White's wife, Katherine. The short pieces became a book entitled *Life with Father.*

Life with Father was originally published in August 1935. Day died on December 28, 1935. The story was popular as a play, a movie, and a television series.

Emily Dickinson

Emily Dickinson was born on December 10, 1830, in Amherst, Massachusetts. She lived in Amherst in her parents' home. After she finished her education, she spent her time reading, writing, and looking after others in her home. She wrote many poems that were unconventional in punctuation and meter. Her social life was her letter-writing. She died on May 15, 1886, in Amherst, Massachusetts. Most of her poems were unpublished during her lifetime, but eventually were appreciated by publishers and readers. Her work is said to be enigmatic and modern.

John Gardner

John Gardner was born on July 21, 1933, in Batavia, New York. He went to Batavia High School, DePauw University, Washington University in Saint Louis, and the University of Iowa. He earned a master's and a doctorate. He was a teacher and a writer. He taught at Oberlin College, Chico State College, San Francisco State College, Southern Illinois University in Carbondale, University of Detroit, Northwestern University, Skidmore College, Williams College, George Mason University, and State University of New York at Binghampton. His book *Grendel*, the story of Beowulf written from the monster's perspective, brought attention to his work. My favorite book of his is *In the Suicide Mountains*. It's a modern fairy tale that is "a new twist on suicide." "You don't really throw away your life at all; instead you kill, as St. Paul says, the 'old' man–the carnal man, the self-regarding man– to give abundant life to the 'new.'" John Gardner died on September 14, 1982, near Susquehanna, Pennsylvania, in a motorcycle accident.

God

God wrote the Bible through 35 writers over 1,500 years. There are 1,328 chapters in the Bible. If we read 26 chapters a week, we can read the Bible in 51 weeks and have a week off for Christmas break. When we need to know the truth, we need to read the Bible.

Oscar Hammerstein II

Oscar Hammerstein II was born on July 12, 1895, in New York City. He went to Columbia University as an undergraduate and graduated from Columbia Law School.[52] He was 6-foot-3. He wrote the books and lyrics for "Show Boat," "Oklahoma," "Carousel," "South Pacific," "State Fair," "The King and I," and "The Sound of Music." The last song he wrote was "Edelweiss" from "The Sound of Music." He died on August 23, 1960, at Highland Farms, Doylestown, Pennsylvania, of cancer.

Earl Hamner

Earl Hamner Junior was born on July 10, 1923, in Schuyler, Virginia. He went to the University of Richmond, Northwestern University, and the University of Cincinnati. He married Jane Martin on October 16, 1954. He wrote the novel *Spenser's Mountain* which led to the movie of the same name. He also wrote the novel *The Homecoming* which led to the television series "The Waltons." He wrote the screenplays for "Heidi" and "Charlotte's Web." Hamner died in Los Angeles on March 24, 2016, after a long successful life. He is buried in the Hamner Family Cemetery in Schuyler, Virginia.

---

[52] Songwriters Hall of Fame biography at
https://www.songhall.org/profile/Oscar_Hammerstein.

Mark Harris

Mark Harris was born on November 19, 1922, in Mount Vernon, New York. He was in the military from 1943-1944. After his service, he was a journalist, a novelist, and a professor. He did his undergraduate work at the University of Denver. He also earned a master's degree in English from Denver and a doctorate in American Studies from the University of Minnesota. He was in the Peace Corps in Sierra Leone. He taught at San Francisco State College, Purdue University, California Institute of the Arts, the University of Southern California, the University of Pittsburgh, and Arizona State University-Tempe. Harris was best known for a series of four novels about baseball players: *The Southpaw* (1953), *Bang the Drum Slowly* (1956), *A Ticket for a Seamstitch* (1957), and *It Looked Like For Ever* (1979). *The Southpaw* is a novel about a character named Henry Wiggen who was a baseball player and writer. The sequel novel *Bang the Drum Slowly* was also a movie about a catcher who died of cancer. From his autobiography *Best Father Ever*, we know that Mark Harris was a baseball player and used his own experiences in his books. Mark Harris died on May 30, 2007, at the age of 84.

Seamus Heaney

Seamus Heaney was born on April 13, 1939, near Castledawson, Northern Ireland. He was a teacher and a writer. When he was away from his home, he wrote love poems to his wife. In his essay, "The Government of the Tongue," he wrote about John 8:1-11. The essay refers to the Biblical passage about a woman who was caught in adultery. Jesus wrote something in the dirt. No one knows what it was. Then he invited anyone who was without sin to cast the first stone. No one was qualified. Jesus didn't throw any stones at her either. He told her not to sin anymore. Seamus Heaney compares the writing of Jesus in the dirt to poetry.

"The drawing of those characters is like poetry, a break with the usual life but not an absconding from it. Poetry, like the writing, is arbitrary and marks time in every possible sense of that phrase. It does not say to the accusing crowd or to the helpless accused, 'Now a solution will take place,' it does not propose to be instrumental or effective. Instead, the rift between what is going to happen and whatever we would wish to happen, poetry holds attention for a space, functions not as a distraction but as pure concentration, a focus where our power to concentrate is concentrated back to ourselves."

When he was on a working vacation in Greece in 1995, he called home to see if anything was new. "Yes," his son replied, "You won the Nobel Prize."

After he had given a reading at the Art Institute of Chicago on September 11, 1996, I was able to meet him at a dinner. Seamus Heaney died on August 30, 2013.

Gerard Manley Hopkins

Gerard Manley Hopkins was born on July 28, 1844, in Stratford, England. He was 5-foot-2. He studied Classics at Balliol College University of Oxford in 1863. He entered a Jesuit novitiate in 1867. He was ordained in 1877. It was customary to become a Jesuit at the age of 33 because that was the age of Jesus when He ended His ministry. Hopkins wrote nine sonnets that year including "God's Grandeur" and "The Windhover." In "God's Grandeur," he wrote:

...the Holy Ghost over the bent

World broods with warm breast and with ah! bright wings."

He was a preacher, a priest, and a professor of Greek and Latin. He died on June 8, 1889, of typhoid fever. His poems were never published during his lifetime.

Garrison Keillor

Garrison Keillor was born August 7, 1942, in Anoka, Minnesota. He graduated from the University of Minnesota where he started his radio career. He began his public radio show "A Prairie Home Companion" on July 6, 1974, in Saint Paul, Minnesota. He is 6-foot-4. He writes essays, poems, and novels. He has done recordings of his writings. He lives in Saint Paul, Minnesota, and New York City. I've been to about a dozen of his shows and I've talked with him after about half of those shows. James Thurber's grandsons are Bear fans. After one of Keillor's shows, one of my literary thrills was to introduce a Thurber grandson to Keillor.

Ring Lardner

Ring Lardner was born on March 6, 1885, in Niles, Michigan. He married Ellis Abbott on June 28, 1911. He wrote for the *Chicago Tribune* and *The New Yorker* magazine. For the *Tribune*, he wrote a newspaper column called "In the Wake of the News" that allowed him to expand his writing into a variety of subjects. He has been called the originator of the modern American newspaper column. He wrote on sports, theater, the war, and marriage. He also wrote short stories, plays, and songs. He wrote a series of baseball stories for *The Saturday Evening Post*—later to be published as a book: *You Know Me Al. You Know Me Al* also became a syndicated comic strip. Other books followed.[53] He died of a heart attack on September 25, 1933, in East Hampton, Long Island.

C. S. Lewis

C. S. Lewis was born on November 29, 1898, in Belfast, Ireland (now Northern Ireland). He graduated from Oxford and he was a literature professor there. From George Sayer's biography *Jack: A Life of C. S. Lewis*, we know that "Jack was incapable of doing simple household chores, and, in spite of his many attempts, he never succeeded in learning to drive a car....He never bought a newspaper."

One thing Lewis could do was write. He published books on literary criticism, science fiction and fantasy, Christian apologetics, and more. Although his books were all written over 60 years ago, much of it is fresh and contemporary today. Lewis is also very popular with young Christians.

Lewis wrote, "In reading great literature I become a thousand men and yet remain myself. Like the night sky in a Greek poem, I see with a thousand eyes, but it is still I who see. Here, as in worship, in love, in moral action, and in knowing, I transcend myself: and am never more myself than when I do."[54]

He also wrote, "There is no use in talking as if forgiveness were easy. We all know the old joke, 'You've given up smoking once; I've given it up a dozen

---

[53] Chicago Literary Hall of Fame viewed at https://chicagoliteraryhof.org/inductees/profile/ring-lardner on September 27, 2019.

[54] C. S. Lewis, *An Experiment in Criticism* (London: Cambridge University Press, 1961)141.

times.' In the same way I could say of a certain man, 'Have I forgiven him for what he did that day? I've forgiven him more times than I can count.' For we find that the work of forgiveness has to be done over and over again.[55]

"The demand that God should forgive such a man (bent on evil) while he remains what he is, is based on a confusion between condoning and forgiving. To condone an evil is simply to ignore it, to treat it as if it were good. But forgiveness needs to be accepted as well as offered if it is to be complete: and a man who admits no guilt can accept no forgiveness.[56]

"Christianity does not want us to reduce by one atom the hatred we feel for cruelty and treachery. We ought to hate them. Not one word of what we have said about them needs to be unsaid. But it does want us to hate them in the same way in which we hate things in ourselves: being sorry that the man should have done such things, and hoping, if it is anyway possible, that somehow, sometime, somewhere, he can be cured and made human again."[57]

C. S. Lewis died on November 22, 1963, in Oxford, England.

Abraham Lincoln

Abraham Lincoln was born on February 12, 1809, on Sinking Spring Farm near Hodgenville, Kentucky. Lincoln was a magnificent writer. The Gettysburg Address was a three-minute speech. The man who spoke before Lincoln talked for two hours and nobody

---

[55] C. S. Lewis, *Reflections on the Psalms* (NY: Harper Collins, 2017)24-25.
[56] C. S. Lewis, *The Problem of Pain* (NY: Harper Collins, 2000) 125.
[57] C. S. Lewis, *Mere Christianity* (NY: Harper Collins, 2001) 117.

remembers what he said.[58] In his biography of Lincoln, Carl Sandburg pointed out that Lincoln wrote more words than are in the Bible or in the works of William Shakespeare. Lincoln was shot on April 14, 1865, at Ford's Theater in Washington, D.C. He died the next day.

Michael Lindvall

Michael Lindvall was born in 1947 in Minnesota. He studied at the University of Wisconsin, the University of Michigan, and Princeton Theological Seminary. He was most recently the pastor of the First Presbyterian Church of Northport, New York, before he retired in 2017. He is an excellent speaker and writer. In summer 2017, he was asked to lead services at Crathie Kirk, the church where the Queen and the royal family worships when they are at Balmoral Castle in Scotland.[59] In his book of short stories, *The Good News from North Haven*, he wrote, "God accepts our fumbling attempts at performance, at love and fairness, and then covers them with grace."

Richard Llewellyn

Richard Llewellyn was of Welsh ancestry. He was born on December 8, 1906, in Herndon (in greater London) in the United Kingdom. Llewellyn lived a nomadic existence and had a number of diverse jobs. His father was a hotelier. Richard Llewellyn wrote the 1940 novel

---

[58] American statesman and orator, Edward Everett was the speaker before Lincoln.

[59] Jamie Duffy, "Local Man Prepping to Preach for Royal Family," *The Journal Gazette*, July 29, 2017, viewed at https://journalgazette.net/news/local/20170729/local-man-prepping-to-preach-for-royal-family on October 8, 2019.

How Green Was My Valley that became an international bestseller. *How Green Was My Valley* was made into a movie that won best picture in 1941. Llewellyn wrote 23 more novels based on divergent settings. During World War II, Llewellyn served in the Welsh Guards. He also worked as a journalist after the war and wrote spy novels. Llewellyn died on November 30, 1983, in Dublin, Ireland.

Norman Maclean

Norman Maclean was born on December 23, 1902, in Clarinda, Iowa. He grew up in Missoula, Montana. He graduated from Dartmouth in 1924 and taught there until 1926. He began graduate studies in English at the University of Chicago in 1928. He was a literature professor there. He retired from the University of Chicago in 1973. His book, *A River Runs through It and Other Stories*, was published in 1976. He died on August 2, 1990, in Chicago, Illinois. *A River Runs through It* was made into a movie in 1992. Maclean said, "a great teacher is a tough guy who cares deeply about something that is hard to understand."

Don Marquis

Don Marquis was born on July 29, 1878, in Walnut, Illinois. He attended Knox College. He was 5-feet-10½. He married Reina Melcher on June 8, 1909. She died December 2, 1923. He married Marjorie Potts Vonnegut on February 2, 1926. She died October 25, 1936. He was a humorist, journalist, and playwright who experienced a great number of tragedies in his life, but he expressed himself with great humor. He surrounded himself with fictional characters in his work. His character Archy was a cockroach who jumped on typewriter keys and wrote "expression is the need of my soul." One of his plays became a silent film called the "Old Soak" and later was made into a talkie with Wallace Berry called the "Good Old Soak." Marquis died blind, broke, and disabled on December 29, 1937.

J. P. McCaskey

J. P. McCaskey was born on October 9, 1837. He married Ellen Chase on August 8, 1860, in Bath, New York. Two mules pulled their canal boat to Albany, New York for their honeymoon. He was wearing a plug hat that she didn't like. So he threw it into the canal. After their honeymoon, they returned to his home in Lancaster, Pennsylvania.

He was principal of the high school from 1865 to 1906. He wrote the song "Jolly Old Saint Nicholas" in 1867. To each graduate of the high school he gave a portrait of himself with this inscription, "The best of men that ever wore earth about him was a patient sufferer, a soft, meek, tranquil Spirit, the first true gentleman that ever breathed." J. P. McCaskey died on September 19, 1935. A few years later, the high school was renamed after him: McCaskey High School.

James Michener

James Michener was born on February 3, 1907, in Doylestown, Pennsylvania. He was an English and History major at Swarthmore College. His first of many books was *Tales of the South Pacific* which won a Pulitzer Prize for fiction in 1948. *Tales of the South Pacific* was the source for Rodgers and Hammerstein's musical "South Pacific." Michener's well-researched books often included historical, geographical, and anthropological details. Michener wrote dozens of fiction and non-fiction titles including ones that were made into movies and mini-series.

He died on October 16, 1997, in Austin, Texas.

Ogden Nash

Ogden Nash was born on August 19, 1902, in Rye, New York. He grew up there and in Savannah, Georgia. He went to Harvard University. He wrote and worked for *The New Yorker* magazine. He married Frances Rider Leonard on June 6, 1933. He lived in New York and Baltimore, Maryland. From Garrison Keillor we know that Ogden Nash wrote, "Oh, what a tangled web do parents weave/ When they think that their children are naïve." He died on May 19, 1971, in Baltimore.

Bob Newhart

Bob Newhart was born on September 5, 1929, in Oak Park, Illinois. He went to Saint Ignatius High School and Loyola University Chicago. He served in the U. S. Army. He was an accountant. Then he became a comedian and an actor. He married Virginia Quinn in 1963. Buddy Hackett was their matchmaker. When Bob Newhart received the 2002 Mark Twain Prize, Tom Poston said, "Bob is very unusual... He's still on his first marriage and none of his children are in rehab."

John Powers

John Powers was born on November 30, 1945, in Chicago. He has diplomas from Brother Rice High School and Loyola and Northwestern Universities. I saw him the first time he was ever on a stage at a comedy club in Chicago. He did material from his book

The Last Catholic in America about the differences between Catholics and Publics.

On Saturday, January 8, 1994, I heard John speak at a men's ecumenical breakfast in Lake Forest. Among many other worthwhile things, he said, "Each of us in this room, every morning when we awake, we have before us this gift which we call life. Through our love of living, and the love of ourselves, the love of the people in our lives, we learn to unwrap that gift so that we can discover all the beauty and the challenge and the excitement that that gift holds for each of us. Only then can we give it to those around us. Because you cannot give what you have not got."

John and his family lived in Lake Geneva, Wisconsin. My wife and children and I were guests in their home. He died on January 17, 2013.[60]

Ernie Pyle

Ernie Pyle was born on August 3, 1900, near Dana, Indiana. He studied journalism at Indiana University. He was a travel writer for newspapers. During World War II, he wrote about the infantrymen. His human interest stories that focused on the common soldier were popular on the front lines and back home. Pyle reported from the European Theater and then from the Pacific Theater. He was killed on the Pacific island of Ie Shima on April 18, 1945. The journalism building at Indiana University is named Ernie Pyle Hall.

---

[60] A brief biography of John Powers can be found in *Pilgrimage* by Patrick McCaskey at pages 129-130.

Edwin Arlington Robinson

Edwin Arlington Robinson was born on December 22, 1869, in Head Tide, Maine. He went to Harvard and lived in New York. My favorite poem of his is "A Christmas Sonnet: For One in Doubt." Here are the last two lines.

"Something is here that was not here before,

And strangely has not yet been crucified."

He died on April 6, 1935, in New York.

Will Rogers

Will Rogers was born on November 4, 1879, near Oologah, Oklahoma. He was a journalist, film star, political wit, vaudeville performer, comedian, and writer who did rope tricks and was an expert horseback rider. After an eight-year courtship, he married Betty Blake in November 1908. He said, "I never met a man I didn't like until two or more of them got together on a committee." He died in a plane crash on August 15, 1935, in Point Barrow, Alaska.

J. D. Salinger

J. D. Salinger was born on January 1, 1919, in Manhattan, New York. He attended New York University, Ursinus College, and Columbia University. His father wanted him to come into the family business of importing meat and cheese from Eastern Europe. During World War II, he did counterintelligence work for the U. S. Army. He wrote for *The New Yorker* magazine. His most famous work is *Catcher in the Rye*, which was reported to have sold as many as 60 million copies at the time of Salinger's death by the Associated

Press.[61] My favorite book of his is *Franny & Zooey*, a collection of his work from the *The New Yorker*. Salinger lived on a small farm in Cornish, New Hampshire. Salinger died on January 27, 2010.

Carl Sandburg

Carl Sandburg was born on January 6, 1878, in Galesburg, Illinois. During the Spanish-American War, he served in the U. S. Army. He played basketball for Lombard College which is now Knox College. He married Lillian Steichen in 1908. His nickname for her was Paula. Their home at 4646 North Hermitage Avenue in Chicago has a marker of distinction. They lived at 331 South York Street in Elmhurst in the fall of 1919. He was a writer and a performer. From his biography of Abraham Lincoln, we know that when Abraham Lincoln was mad at someone, he wrote that person a letter. Then he never mailed it. The Sandburgs lived on a goat farm in Flat Rock, North Carolina from 1945 through 1967. Carl Sandburg was the Illinois poet laureate until he died on July 22, 1967. He is buried in Galesburg. The home in Flat Rock is a National Park. I have been there a few times.[62]

Scott Sanders

Scott Sanders was born on October 26, 1945. When he was 16, he met Ruth Ann McClure at a summer science camp. For five years, they wrote to each other. They saw each other maybe a dozen times. He went to

---

[61] Salinger obituary from Associated Press viewed at http://www.legacy.com/ns/j.d.-salinger-obituary/139034135 on October 3, 2019.

[62] A brief biography of Carl Sandburg can be found in *Pilgrimage* by Patrick McCaskey at pages 130-133.

Brown University on a physics scholarship. They married each other in 1967. He earned a doctorate in literature at Cambridge University on another scholarship. He has been a teacher at Indiana University since 1971. I was in his writing class in the fall of 1973. He is a great teacher and a wonderful writer. He also gives readings from his writings. My family and I have been guests in his home. He and his family have been guests in my home. In his essay "Letter to a Reader," he wrote, "My steady desire has been to wake up, not to sleepwalk through this brief miraculous life. I wish to go about with mind and senses alert to the splendor of the world. I wish to see the burning bush."

Bob Schul

Bob Schul was born on September 28, 1937, in West Milton, Ohio. He ran for Miami University in Oxford, Ohio. He won the gold medal in the 5000 meter run in the 1964 Tokyo Olympics. From his book, *In the Long Run*, we know that he has "always believed runners should run the way they feel and how their strengths measure up against their opponents." He coached cross-country for Wright State University.

William Shakespeare

William Shakespeare was born on April 23, 1564, in Stratford-upon-Avon. He was baptized on April 26 at Holy Trinity Church. He married Anne Hathaway on November 27, 1582, at Temple Grafton. He was an actor and a writer. When the theaters were closed because of the Plague from 1592 to 1594, he wrote poetry. He died on April 23, 1616. He was buried at Stratford's Holy Trinity Church on April 25.

When I was a high school freshman, Mister Wicklund taught us that swear words were clichés. He encouraged us to use creative language like Shakespeare.

Bishop Sheen

Bishop Fulton J. Sheen was born on May 8, 1895, in El Paso, Illinois, 20 miles north of Bloomington. He was 5-foot-7. He graduated from Saint Viator College in Bourbonnais, Illinois. He went to Saint Paul's Seminary in Saint Paul, Minnesota. He went to the Catholic University of America in Washington, D.C. to earn a doctorate in philosophy. He was ordained in 1919. He received two degrees from CUA in 1920. He earned from Louvain University in Belgium a Ph.D. in philosophy and then earned the University's "super doctorate," the *agrege en Philosophie*.[63]

Sheen was assigned briefly to Saint Patrick's parish in Peoria.[64] He returned to Catholic University of America where the popular professor taught philosophy and theology from 1926 to 1950. In Washington, D.C., the bishop began writing books, both scholarly and popular titles. He was on the "Catholic Hour" radio program.

Sheen started working with Cardinal Spellman of New York. He became head of the American branch of

---

[63] Thomas C. Reeves, "Fulton J. Sheen, Catholic Champion," viewed on Catholic Education Resource Center website at https://www.catholiceducation.org/en/faith-and-character/faith-and-character/fulton-j-sheen-catholic-champion.html on October 8, 2019. Reeves is the author of *America's Bishop: The Life and Times of Fulton J. Sheen.*

[64] This parish has been closed.

the Society for the Propagation of the Faith.[65] He was consecrated a bishop in Rome in 1951. He was a talented writer and a performer. In New York, he began a television show called "Life Is Worth Living" that attracted millions of viewers.

In Sheen's *Guide to Contentment*, he wrote, "Joy is not the same as pleasure or happiness. A wicked and evil man may have pleasure, while any ordinary mortal is capable of being happy. Pleasure generally comes from things, and always through the senses; happiness comes from humans through fellowship. Joy comes from loving God and neighbor. Pleasure is quick and violent, like a flash of lightning. Joy is steady and abiding, like a fixed star. Pleasure depends on external circumstances, such as money, food, travel, etc. Joy is independent of them, for it comes from a good conscience and love of God."

Sheen became the Bishop of Rochester in 1966. He resigned and returned to New York in 1969. He met Pope John Paul II in October 1979. Bishop Sheen died on December 9, 1979. The tomb of Archbishop Fulton J. Sheen resides at St. Mary's Cathedral in Peoria.

L. E. Sissman

L. E. Sissman was born on January 1, 1928, in Detroit, Michigan. He was 6-foot-4 and he graduated from Harvard University. He was an advertising executive and a writer. He wrote for *The Atlantic Monthly* and

---

[65] Thomas C. Reeves, "Fulton J. Sheen, Catholic Champion," viewed on Catholic Education Resource Center website at https://www.catholiceducation.org/en/faith-and-character/faith-and-character/fulton-j-sheen-catholic-champion.html on October 8, 2019. Reeves is the author of *America's Bishop: The Life and Times of Fulton J. Sheen.*

The New Yorker magazines. In his essay, "What I Gave at the Office," he wrote, "All this is satisfying and fulfilling: even if you live for your family, for an avocation, or for some other goal, a sense of belonging at-and to-the office helps to round out and validate our lives...Whatever I gave at the office, I took far more away." He died on March 10, 1976, of Hodgkin's disease a form of cancer of the lymph glands at the age of 48.

Red Smith

Red Smith was born on September 25, 1905, in Green Bay, Wisconsin. He graduated from the University of Notre Dame. In "The Quiet Olympics," he wrote, "...it was pleasure enough to see [Mal] Whitfield run. Seeing this luggage-tan young man in action is like peering over Rembrandt's shoulder, hearing Toscanini drain music from a string section, watching the almost evil grace of Ray Robinson in the ring. The guy flows over the track as a mountain brook bubbles across a meadow..." Red Smith died on January 15, 1982, in Stamford, Connecticut.

Nicholas Sparks

Nicholas Sparks was born on December 31, 1965, in Omaha, Nebraska. He grew up in Fair Oaks, California. He went to the University of Notre Dame on a track scholarship. He majored in Business Finance and graduated in 1988. He moved from California to North Carolina in 1992. He's 5-10, 180. He goes to church, he runs, and he reads. His novel, *The Notebook*, is about the 60-year marriage of his wife's grandparents.

Jimmy Stewart

Jimmy Stewart was born on May 20, 1908, in Indiana, Pennsylvania where his father owned a hardware store. Jimmy studied architecture at Princeton University. During his junior year, he was a cheerleader. He played the accordion for the Triangle Club, a student acting group. He graduated with a B.A. degree in 1932. He won an Oscar for his performance in "The Philadelphia Story." He kept the award in the window of his father's hardware store. During World War II, he was a bomber pilot and a squadron commander in the Army Air Corps. He married Gloria Hatrick McLean in 1949. *Jimmy Stewart and His Poems* was published in 1989. He died on July 2, 1997, in Los Angeles, California.

Paul Stookey

Paul Stookey was born on December 30, 1937, in Baltimore, Maryland. He graduated from Michigan State University. He was a singer and a songwriter with Peter, Paul & Mary beginning in 1960. After the death of Mary Travers in 2009, Stookey has occasionally performed with Peter Yarrow. He and his wife, Elizabeth, married each other in 1963. They moved to Blue Hill Falls, Maine in 1974. He often sang at the Northfield Mount Hermon Chapel in northwestern Massachusetts. In his song "For the Love of It All" are these lyrics.

"Long ago on a hilltop where now the curious crawl

A man on a cross paid the ultimate cost

For the Love of it all."

Frank Sullivan

Frank Sullivan was born in 1892. He graduated from Cornell University. He wrote for *The New Yorker* magazine. In his book *Well, There's No Harm In Laughing*, he wrote, "In another time that tried men's souls, Abraham Lincoln was fond of opening Cabinet meetings by reading Artemus Ward's latest.[66] Politicians like [Edwin] Stanton and [Salmon] Chase were shocked at this because they did not think Ward was as important as a battle. Lincoln suspected Ward 'was' as important as a battle." Frank Sullivan died in 1976.

Henry Thoreau

Henry Thoreau was born on July 12, 1817 in Concord, Massachusetts. He graduated from Harvard in 1837. He was a teacher and a writer. When he needed a break from the family business of making pencils, he built a home on the shores of Walden Pond and wrote *Walden: or, Life in the Woods*. He wrote, "Books are the treasured wealth of the world and the fit inheritance of generations and nations." He died on May 6, 1862, of tuberculosis at Concord.

---

[66] Ward was the pseudonym of humorist Charles Farrar Browne.

JAMES THURBER HOUSE

James Thurber

James Thurber was born on December 8, 1894, in Columbus, Ohio. He went to Ohio State University. He wrote and worked for *The New Yorker* magazine. Thurber was a humorous author, essayist, cartoonist, and journalist. His short stories such as "The Secret Life of Walter Mitty" and "The Catbird Seat" would be read by millions of students in textbooks and anthologies. He would publish two dozen books and a couple plays. His works would also be the source for movie and television shows.

Thurber had severe eye problems and eventually went blind. My favorite Thurber fable is "The Little Girl and the Wolf." At the end, "the little girl took an automatic out of her basket and shot the wolf dead. Moral: It's not so easy to fool little girls nowadays as it used to be." He performed a revue of his works on Broadway. He died on November 2, 1961.

Mark Twain

Mark Twain was born Samuel Clemons on November 30, 1835, in Florida, Missouri. He kept pouring money into a typesetting machine and his publishing company. He went bankrupt and felt honor-bound to repay his creditors. So he went on a world-wide lecture tour that he did not enjoy. He paid his debts and he went a little goofy because of family tragedies. I know Twain as a performer because of the Hal Holbrook recordings. When I am forced into hearing a person talk incessantly, I remember a Twain line. "It's a terrible death to be talked to death." He died on April 21, 1910, in Redding, Connecticut.

Arturo Vivante

Arturo Vivante was born in Rome on October 17, 1923. He graduated from McGill University in Montreal. He earned a medical degree from the University of Rome in 1949. He practiced medicine in Rome until 1958. Then he moved to America to be a writer. He had been a college teacher and then he retired. He lived in Wellfleet, Massachusetts. My favorite book of his is a collection of short stories, *Run to the Waterfall*. He died on April 1, 2008, at the age of 84.

Robert Penn Warren

Robert Penn Warren was born on April 24, 1905, in Guthrie, Kentucky. He graduated from Vanderbilt University in 1925. He received a master's degree in English from the University of California, Berkeley in 1927. He studied at Yale and earned a degree from Oxford in 1930. He was a teacher and a writer. He taught at Southwestern College, Vanderbilt, the University of Minnesota, Louisiana State University, and Yale. He became the first U. S. poet laureate in 1986. In his poem, "Waiting," he wrote,

"You will have to wait.../until you/remember surprisingly, that common men have done good deeds. Until it/grows on you that, at least, God/has allowed us the grandeur of certain utterances."

Warren wrote books of poems, novels, children's books, books on writing, and textbooks. His best-known work is *All the King's Men*, a novel that won the Pulitzer Prize in 1947. The book was made into a movie in 1949 and it won three Academy Awards including Best Picture. Robert Penn Warren died on September 15, 1989.

E. B. White

E. B. White was born on July 11, 1899, in Mount Vernon, New York. He graduated from Cornell University. He wrote and worked for *The New Yorker* magazine. He had an aversion to public speaking. He never accepted his many awards in person. Two performances that White did give were the readings of two of his children's novels *Charlotte's Web* and *The Trumpet of the Swan*.

When I was a student at Indiana University, I was an English major, but I really majored in James Thurber and E. B. White. I bought and read the books that they had written. I also read a lot of articles about them in the IU Library.

In the early days of *The New Yorker*, they shared an office. They wrote a book together called *Is Sex Necessary*. Thurber had eye problems; so did I. White had allergy problems; so did I. They had problems with women; so did I.

I talked with White on his birthday in 1977 and 1985. I simply called directory assistance in North Brooklin, Maine. I thanked him for his wonderful writing. He chuckled that someone would call him from Chicago.

My favorite White essay is "Freedom." In it is this sentence. "Or to an older youth, encountering for the first time a great teacher who by some chance word or mood awakens something and the youth beginning to breathe as an individual and conscious of strength in his vitals."

E. B. White died on October 1, 1985, in North Brooklin, Maine. On Saturday, August 1, 1998, I visited the farm and the town in Maine where he lived. People at the General Store told me how to get there. The folks who now own the farm were not home. So I walked the place on my own.

I saw the barn that inspired *Charlotte's Web*. There is still a rope swing in the doorway. I walked through the pastures to the shore of the cove. I looked in the window of the boathouse where White did a lot of writing. I walked on the road that led back to the house through the garden.

Then I went back to the General Store and bought a tape of what White's son, Joel, had read to his father during the last year of his life. It was several of White's essays, poems, and stories.

I walked across the street to the Library. The courtyard garden is dedicated to the memory of White and his wife, Katherine. I bought a copy of one of White's essay collections, *One Man's Meat*. White's daughter-in-law, Allene, had donated several publisher's copies for sale at the Library.

The librarian let me study the file of articles on White. She also made copies for me. I was particularly pleased to get a copy of a picture of White, in his eighties, swinging on the barn doorway rope swing. It had been part of the memorial service program.

Richard Wilbur

Richard Wilbur was born on March 1, 1921, in New York City. He grew up on a farm in North Caldwell, New Jersey. He graduated with a B.A. from Amherst College in 1942. During World War II, he served in the U.S. Army in France, Germany, and Italy. He earned a M.A. from Harvard in 1947. He taught at Harvard, Wesleyan, Wellesley, and Smith. He was the United States poet laureate from 1987 to 1988. He was also a literary translator of several plays written in French. He said, "Poems have to be based on autobiography; how else should they come about? But if they are to be of any use, they must end by being about everybody." Wilbur died on October 14, 2017, at aged 96.

Thornton Wilder

Thornton Wilder was born on April 17, 1897, in Madison, Wisconsin. He studied at Oberlin College, spent a year in the Coast Guard, and graduated from Yale in 1920. He taught French for several years. He earned a master's degree from Princeton University in 1926. He was a teacher and a writer. He taught at the University of Chicago from 1930 to 1936. My favorite work of his is the play "Our Town," which won him a Pulitzer Prize for Drama in 1938. He won another Pulitzer for "By the Skin of Our Teeth" in 1943. His book, *The Bridge of San Luis Rey*, won the Pulitzer Prize for the Novel in 1928. During World War II, he served with the U.S. Army Air Corps Intelligence in North Africa. He died on December 7, 1975, in Hamden, Connecticut.

Pat Williams

Pat Williams was born May 3, 1940, and grew up in Wilmington, Delaware, where he went to the Tower Hill School. At the age of seven, he decided that he wanted to become a catcher. He went to Wake Forest University on a baseball scholarship. After he had graduated with a degree in physical education, he played for the Class A Miami Marlins. He also earned a master's degree in physical education from Indiana University.

Williams has worked for the Marlins, the Spartanburg Phillies of South Carolina, the

Philadelphia 76ers, the Chicago Bulls, the Atlanta Hawks, and the Orlando Magic.

Williams and his wife, Ruth, have 19 children and 18 grandchildren. He is the author of 114 books.

Williams was the original chairman of the Chicago Fellowship of Christian Athletes. He started the Chicago group in 1973.

Williams was the speaker for Bears chapel services prior to the game in Tampa with the Buccaneers on October 25, 1987. He talked about how he pursued monuments to man for the first 28 years of his life. He sought fortune, fame, power, and pleasure. He wanted to get rich, be famous, take control, and indulge himself.

Then he learned that Jesus Christ pardons sins. From the Bible, he found that the "peace of God passeth all understanding." He discovered a purpose for his life. He had a platform for witnessing through athletics. Regardless of what happened in the world, he could be triumphant. God's love is unconditional. Until our life is right with God, we cannot love.

Williams also talked about the three ingredients for a successful life. One, you have to have a self fit to live with. Two, you have to have a faith to live by. You have to keep on growing through a Bible Study and a strong church. Start in the Book of James. There the rubber of life hits the road of reality. Let people build you up and hold you accountable. Three, you have to have work to live for. Let God use you.

Williams was the main speaker at the Chicago Fellowship of Christian Athletes 1988 Spring Banquet. FCA has meant a great deal in Williams's life. He was with a Philadelphia Phillies farm team for his first exposure. As a result of getting involved, he became interested in FCA. FCA has impacted many lives.

For his talk, Williams discussed Acts 18:24-28. "Meanwhile a Jew named Apollos, a native of Alexandria, came to Ephesus. He was a learned man, with a thorough knowledge of the Scriptures. He had been instructed in the way of the Lord, and he spoke with a great fervor and taught about Jesus accurately, though he knew only the baptism of John. He began to speak boldly in the synagogue. When Priscilla and Aquila heard, they invited him to their home and explained to him the way of God more adequately.

"When Apollos wanted to go to Achaia, the brothers encouraged him and wrote to the disciples there to welcome him. On arriving, he was a great help to those who by grace had believed."

Williams offered Apollos as a significant role model. Paul was on a missionary journey and he met a young man by the name of Apollos. He was born in Alexandria. He was an eloquent man. He was a learned man. Williams challenged young people in the audience to become readers. "Read devotionals and biographies and newspapers."

Apollos dedicated his learning to the Lord. He was mighty in the Scriptures. The New Testament hadn't been written yet. Williams said, "You should read the Bible every day. It was written over 1500 years. We have to do the work. We have to read."

The 25th verse pointed out that Apollos was instructed in the way of the Lord. He was a man of strong convictions. He sought out diligently, the things of the Lord. Williams said, "Young people need sound teachers. Be careful who you listen to."

The 26th verse says that Apollos began to speak boldly in the synagogue. He was willing to take a public stand. His knowledge was incomplete. Two godly people began to teach him. He was willing to learn. He was not a know-it-all. Williams said, "Have a teachable spirit."

In verse 27, we learn that Apollos's support group encouraged him. Williams said, "Lone wolf believers are not very effective. You need a support group.

"Apollos was an encourager. He had the heart of a servant. The world is not a playground. It is a battleground. Be a Christian encourager like Apollos. Tame your tongue. Use it for encouragement and uplifting. Encourage each other and stay behind for the injured until they are healed. The Scripture was Apollos's only authority."

John Wooden

John Wooden was born on October 14, 1910, in Hall, Indiana. He was an All-American basketball player at Purdue. When my grandfather, George Halas, owned the Chicago Bruins basketball team, Wooden played three games for them. When Wooden was the head basketball coach at UCLA, they won ten national championships in 12 years. He could be the best coach of any sport at any level. In his book, *Wooden: A Lifetime of Observations and Reflections On and Off the Court*, he wrote, "My favorite American hero is Abraham Lincoln. He had alertness. He once said that he never met a person from whom he did not learn something, although most of the time it was something not to do. That also is learning, and it comes from your alertness." John Wooden died on June 4, 2010.

Herman Wouk

Herman Wouk was born on May 27, 1915, in New York City. He edited the humor magazine at Columbia University and he earned a B.A. degree there. Then he became a radio scriptwriter for Fred Allen in 1936. During World War II, he served in the U.S. Navy in the Pacific. He married Betty Sarah Brown in 1945. His novel, *The Caine Mutiny*, won the Pulitzer Prize for fiction in 1952. It was made into a brilliant movie starring Humphrey Bogart. Two of his books became popular TV miniseries: *The Winds of War* and *War and Remembrance*. Wouk died on May 17, 2019, at age 103.

Philip Yancey

Philip Yancey was born in 1949 in Atlanta, Georgia. He has earned degrees from Columbia Bible College, Wheaton Graduate School, and the University of Chicago Graduate School. He is editor-at-large for *Christianity Today* magazine. About the only disagreement between my wife, Gretchen, and me is who gets to read his column first. In a column about his high school reunion, he wrote, "Instinctually, animals mark the weak (the nerds?) for quick destruction; we are commanded to value them. We are also told that fulfillment comes not in the pursuit of happiness, but rather in the pursuit of service. We are asked to respond to our most grievous failures not by covering them up, but by repenting of them openly. When you are wronged, says the gospel, extend forgiveness, not vengeance. And don't hoard material things, but trade them all for the kingdom of heaven, a pearl of great price..."

Lines from My Favorite Comedians

"If I die before my wife does, I hope that she gets married again. But I don't want my successor to wear my Super Bowl ring."

—Patrick McCaskey

Jimmy Aleck started his act by saying, "Hi; I hope I'm funny."

He said, "We knew my sister was going to be a mortician because she used to read the newspaper obituaries and cross out the names in the phone book."

He said, "Now that I'm out on my own, I'm glad I know how to bunt."

Woody Allen said, "Why does a man kill? He kills for food, and not only for food. Frequently, there must be a beverage."

Jack Benny said, "If there's one thing that doesn't have to go on, it's the show."

He said this about his glasses, "I only need these to see."

Mel Brooks served in the Army during World War II and wrote a song parody of Cole Porter's "Begin the Beguine" called "When We Clean the Latrine"?

He said, "Keep a smile on your face and a nectarine in your pocket."

He said, "As long as the world keeps spinning on its axis, people are going to get dizzy, and they're going to make mistakes."

John Bynner did an impersonation of John Wayne as a surgeon. The line was, "We're gonna have ta yank it outta there."

George Carlin said, "When Thomas Edison worked late into the night on the electric light, he had to do it by gas lamp or candle. I'm sure it made the work seem that much more urgent."

Chuckles the Clown on "The Mary Tyler Moore Show" said, "A little song; a little dance; a little seltzer down your pants."

When Lou Grant (**Ed Asner**) visited Ted Baxter (**Ted Knight**) in his office and saw a bunch of board games like Monopoly and Clue, here's what Ted said in his own defense. "I work hard and I play hard."

Howard Cosell said at his roast, "What these people have said about me is like throwing spit balls at a battle ship."

Rodney Dangerfield said, "I haven't spoken to my wife in years. I didn't want to interrupt her."

Tom Dreesen said, "I grew up in Harvey, Illlinois, where the veterinarian was also the taxidermist. His slogan was, 'either way you get your dog back.'"

Finley Peter Dunn said, "Trust everyone, but cut the cards."[67]

Shecky Green said, "Frank Sinatra saved my life. Some guys were beating me up. Then Frank rolled down the window of his car and said, 'He's had enough.'"

Bob Newhart said, "Jack Benny was, without a doubt, the bravest comedian I have ever seen work. He wasn't afraid of silence. He would take as long as it took to tell a story." On the Bob Newhart television show where Bob played a psychologist, **Suzanne Pleshette** played his wife, Emily. Emily was a schoolteacher. One of her students answered questions in class with songs. He was in detention. At 2:45 he and Emily were the only ones in detention. So he sang, "It's quarter to three. There's no one in the place, 'cept you and me."

---

[67] Dunn was a journalist and author from Chicago who lived from 1867-1936. His popular syndicated newspaper column featured a fictional Irish barkeeper, Mr. Dooley, of the south side of Chicago.

Bob Newhart said this about Don Rickles, "Someone has to be his friend."

Pat Paulsen said, "All the problems that we face in the United States today can be traced to an unenlightened immigration policy on the part of the American Indian."

He said, "A good many people feel that our present draft laws are unjust. These people are called soldiers."

Don Rickles said to Frank Sinatra, "Make yourself at home Frank. Hit somebody."

Before he was married, Don Rickles said to Frank Sinatra, "Frank, I have a dinner date tonight with a lady. If you could come over to my table and pretend that we are friends it would really help me." Then when Frank Sinatra came over to the table Don Rickles said, "Not now, Frank. Can't you see I'm with somebody?"

Don Rickles came into his bedroom on his wedding night with an Olympic torch and said, "Let the games begin."

James Thurber said, "Love is what you've been through with somebody."

Mark Twain said, "It's a terrible death to be talked to death."

Jackie Vernon said, "My grandfather was an old Indian fighter. My grandmother was an old Indian."

He said, "When I was born my father spent three weeks trying to find a loophole in my birth certificate."

He said, "This might be hard for you to believe, but I used to be a dull guy. You're probably wondering what changed me from the prosaic deadbeat I was to the effervescent gay blade I am today."

He said, "Never spit in another man's face unless his mustache is on fire."

He said, "Do unto others; then cut out."

He said, "The meek shall inherit the earth. They'd be too scared to refuse it."

Flip Wilson said, "Don't order a drink for the road because the road is already laid out."[68]

As the character Geraldine, he said, "Love is a feeling you feel when you're about to feel a feeling that you've never felt before."

As the character Reverend Leroy, he said, "I'm sure that everyone wants this church to progress. Before this church can progress, it has to crawl."

The congregation replied, "Let it crawl, Rev, let it crawl."

Reverend Leroy said, "After this church has crawled, it has to stand up and walk."

The congregation replied, "Make it walk, Rev, make it walk."

Reverend Leroy said, "After this church has walked, it has to run."

The congregation replied, "Make it run, Rev, make it run."

Reverend Leroy said, "For this church to run, it's gonna take money."

The congregation replied, "Let it crawl, Rev, let it crawl."

Steven Wright said, "It's a small world but I wouldn't want to paint it."

He said, "The earth is bi-polar."

He said, "You can't have everything. Where would you put it?"

Henny Youngman said, "Laugh it up folks; these are the jokes. I know you're out there because I can hear you breathing."

---

[68] Comedian popular in 1960s and 1970s. Appearing on Time Magazine's January 1. 1972, cover, referred to as TV's First Black Superstar.

PART FOUR: BIBLICAL POEMS

TAKING TIME TO PRAISE

"Just finished reading the Bible. The Christians won."
—Patrick McCaskey

Matthew

The Adoration of the Three Magi

Matthew 2:1-12
After Jesus was born in Bethlehem,
Three wise men, magi, came to pay homage.
The three wise men were not the three stooges.
The three magi let the great star lead them.

They brought gifts: gold and frankincense and myrrh.
These were not white elephant or gag gifts.

From Saint Hilary of Poitiers, we know,
Jesus received gold because He is king.
He received frankincense because He is God.
Jesus was given myrrh since he is man.

The magi did not expect thank you notes.
Mary and Joseph were not registered.

Jesus Christ was full of humility.
His Father gave Him His authority.

The Flight into Egypt; the Massacre

Matthew 2:13-18
From the Navarre Bible commentary,
We know that, Jesus is "like Jacob who
Went down to Egypt." Christ is also like
The Israeli people who left Egypt.

Jesus and Moses were saved as babies.
They were later called to save God's people.

Rachel would not be consoled for the dead.

Matthew saw the flight into Egypt and
The massacre of the Innocents as
"The fulfilment of God's plan to establish
A new" covenant through Jesus Christ.

The massacre of the holy innocents
Reminds me of abortion. I am
Pro-life and so is my beloved wife.

Jesus Christ Went Fishing for Disciples

Matthew 4:18-22
From the Navarre Bible commentary,
We know that, Christ called "his first disciples
To follow him and leave everything behind."

If the Apostles had played football, they
Would have been a great team. Jesus would have
Been the coach like George Halas. Peter would
Have been the quarterback like Bill Wade.
Andrew was Peter's brother. They would have
Been used to playing catch in the yard. Let's
Put Andrew at tight end like Mike Ditka.

James and John, the sons of Zebedee, were
Known as the sons of thunder. They would have
Been the running backs like Payton and Suhey.

Jesus Christ Taught the Fullness of the Law

Matthew 5:20-26
Christ wants us to be more than compliant.
You cannot be angry at your brother.
You can't utter insults at your brother.
You cannot complain about your brother.

I have seven brothers: Mike, Tim, Ned, George,
Rich, Brian, and Joseph. Jesus had none.

This passage says no thanks to resentment,
Hatred, gossip, backbiting, and slander.

The Navarre Bible notes are instructive.
Saint Augustine noted there is a
Gradation in sin and in punishment.

If my brothers have something against me,
I have to get reconciliation.
Then I'm eligible to give money.

Trusting in God's Fatherly Providence
Matthew 6:19-23
The Navarre Bible notes are instructive.
"Jesus teaches that the true treasure trove
Is made of good works done with an upright
Intention; these will obtain for us an
Eternal reward from God in heaven."

Jesus said, "Do not lay up for yourselves
Treasure on earth." Here is sound stewardship.
Save enough money for estate taxes.

Jesus Christ wisely taught that the eye is
"A lamp that provides the body with light."

Aquinas wrote, "The eye refers to mo-
tive...if your intention is sound...direct-
ed towards God...all your actions, will be
Sound, sincerely directed towards good."

Doing the Will of God; Building on Rock

Matthew 7:21-29
We're here to do the will of God on earth.
We're here to live the Gospel and to put
The Words of Christ into daily practice.
Then we will be doing the will of God.

Praying and fasting and going to Church
Are not enough. We must be faithful like
Job and Abraham in tribulation.

Practice the teachings of Jesus daily.
Our houses built on rock will sustain storms.
Our faith keeps us firm through trials and errors.

Jesus teaches us with authority.
May Legatus become majority.

Even God took a day off. After God
Had a day of rest, He wrote the Bible.

The Call of Matthew and Many Others

Matthew 9:9-13
Peter, Andrew, James, John were fishermen.
Matthew was a sinning tax collector.
Paul was eagerly destroying Christians.
Jesus Christ called them and many others.

The Navarre Bible notes are instructive.
"When God calls us, he does not expect us
To have great qualities; he wants us to
Listen carefully," and respond promptly.

Matthew gave up "collaboration with
The oppressive Roman regime." He took
Up cooperation with Jesus Christ.
The Apostle Matthew wrote the first Gospel.

Jesus associated with sinners.
Thank you for associating with me.

Good News: Fasting Is Not Everlasting
Matthew 9:14-15
Disciples of John and the Pharisees
Griped because the apostles did not fast.
Jesus wanted the apostles to eat
While He was with them. They could fast later.

Saint Augustine said fast to be humble.
Cry out in prayer. Mortify the body.
Turn your back on the pleasures of the flesh.
Hunger and thirst lead to truth and wisdom.

Johnny Carson asked fat Jackie Vernon,
"Is it true that fat people are jolly?"
Jackie Vernon was portly. He replied,
"I don't know. Why don't you ask some fat guy?"

After I fast all night, my stomach's in flight.
I break my fast with a healthy breakfast.

Christ Is the Long Awaited Messiah
Matthew 9:27-31
Two blind men asked Jesus Christ for a cure.
They addressed Jesus as the Son of David.
He confirmed that He was the Messiah.
But he told the blind men not to say so.

Jesus was not a great politician.
He was a humble servant for mankind.
The cured blind men were disobedient.
They spread His fame because they were joyful.

I had eye problems for quite a long time.
Then I had helpful corneal transplants.

My eyes are fine now. Here are some lines from
The Hebrew poet Yehuda Amic-
hai. "The passing years have calmed me and brought
Healing to my heart and rest to my eyes."

Jesus Reproached His Contemporaries
Matthew 11:16-19
From the Navarre Bible commentary,
We know that, Jesus Christ was accused "of
Being a glutton and a drunkard, (and)
A friend of tax collectors and sinners."

The deeds of Jesus Christ "bear clear witness
To who he is and what his mission is."

Jesus Christ made reference to a song.
The group Mercy Me had not started yet.

When Pat Paulsen ran for president, he
Countered his opponents' criticisms
Of himself with "picky, picky, picky."

The sin that I have to confess the most
Is gluttony. If I am not careful,
I may have to take up sumo wrestling.

The Very Purpose of Love and Marriage
Matthew 19:3-12
The Navarre Bible notes are instructive.
"Mutual self-giving of the spouses,
Together with the procreation and
Education of children calls for
Indissolubility" of marriage.

From Vatican II, we also know that,
"Thus a man and a woman, who by their
Compact of conjugal love 'are no long-
er two, but one flesh' render mutual
Help and service to each other through an
Intimate union of their persons and
Their actions...the good of the children
Impose total fidelity on the
Spouses and...an unbreakable oneness..."

The Parable of the Wicked Tenants

Matthew 21:33-43, 45-46
From the Navarre Bible notes, we know that
This is about salvation history.

"Israel is compared to a vineyard."
God lavished a lot of great care on it.
Instead of good grapes, it produced wild grapes.

The tenants are like Israel's rulers.
God charged them to look after his people.
"God sent prophets...but they found no fruit."
The prophets were treated poorly or killed.

Finally, God sent his son Jesus Christ.
The tenants are ready to kill the son.
They expect to inherit the vineyard.
They are mistaken. The vineyard went to
"A nation producing the fruits of it."

Greatest Commandment, Greatest Gift of All

Matthew 22:34-40
Christ teaches the two commandments of love.
Our mandate is to love God and neighbor.

The Navarre Bible notes are instructive.
Saint Bede wrote, "you cannot truly love God
If you do not love your neighbor, (nor) truly
Love your neighbor if you do not love God."

"The only true proof of our love for God:
We love and help and care for our brothers."

Saint Thomas Aquinas wrote, "when man is loved,
God is loved, because man is the image
Of God." Saint Bernard wrote, "the reason to
Love God is God; the method and means are
To love Him without methods or means." No
Other saints were quoted for this passage.

Mark

Four Friends Help a Paralyzed Man Get Cured

Mark 2:1-12

Jesus came to town; the news spread quickly.
Quite soon there was a large crowd around Him.
Four clever friends made a hole in the roof.
They were men of faith, not vigilantes.

They lowered their friend, a paralyzed man,
On a stretcher, through the hole in the roof.
Jesus forgave the paralyzed man's sins.
Then the man was no longer paralyzed.

Max Swiatek is number one on the Bears'
Longevity list: sixty-seven years.
His wife, Irene, shaved him while he slept so
He could get right to work in the morning.
When someone returned to work after sur-
gery, he asked, "How was your vacation?"

The Seed and the Mustard Seed Parables

Mark 4:26-34
From the Navarre Bible commentary,
We know that, "The parables of the seed
And the mustard seed...are based on the
idea of growth; that of the seed speaks of
The Kingdom's...gradual development;
That of the mustard seed..." tremendous growth.

I had to plant corn. The garden in the
North side yard was eighty feet by six feet.
It had to be rototilled, horse manured,
Rototilled again, and then raked smoothly.

Two eighty-foot rows two feet apart down
The length or thirty-nine rows two feet a-
part across the width? I decided to go
With two eighty-foot rows down the length.

The Martyrdom of Saint John the Baptist

Mark 6:14-29
The Navarre Bible notes are instructive.
Saint John the Baptist was the Precursor.
He prepared the way of the Messiah.
People regarded John as a prophet.
They travelled great distances to see him.

"Herod had a certain respect for John
And liked to hear him speak, and yet ended
Up beheading him." The birthday feast was
Wild. The young woman's dance was seductive.
The king made a terrible oath. These are
Examples of how not to behave. Lust
Led King Herod into a greater sin.

Jim Finks said of my dancing, "It looks like
You would rather be taking a beating.

Jesus Cured a Man Who Was Deaf and Dumb

Mark 7:31-37

The Navarre Bible notes are instructive.
Jesus worked a miracle to show "the
Saving power of his human nature."
Christ opens our ears to hear His Father.
We get salvation through the sacraments.

According to Mark, Jesus told people
To be silent about three miracles:
The curing of a man with leprosy,
The raising of a little girl from death,
And the curing of a deaf and dumb man.

"Jesus wanted people to come to His
Mission...in light of his death on the cross."

The people were like Edith Bunker. They
Could not stifle themselves or dummy up.

Jesus Warns Us to Avoid Scandal

Mark 9:41-50
Jesus said accept water in my name.
Do not cause little ones to be ashamed.
If one of your hands causes you to sin,
You should cut it off and be more thin.

Just avoiding sin is not quite enough.
The occasions of sin are not good stuff.
More earthly goods are not our destiny.
Let's have souls ready for eternity.

From the Navarre Bible commentary,
We know that Isaiah 66:24
Is Mark 9:48, "where their worm does not
Die, and the fire is not quenched," that is hell.

"Anything that might lead us to commit
Sin must be cut short..." Enjoy your dinner.

The Sons of Zebedee Make a Request
Mark 10:35-45

James and John were the sons of Zebedee.
They were well known as the sons of thunder.
They would have been like Payton and Suhey.

Christ asked, "Are you able to drink the cup?"
They wanted to be at the right and left
Of Jesus. Instead, Jesus had two thieves.

The Passion of Jesus was Baptism.
His sufferings purified the whole world.

Christ said, "I am here to serve not be served."
Let us go out therefore and do likewise.

Let us see who can be the most humble.
Let us not be proud of humility.

When I started working for the Bears, I
Was everyone's assistant. I still am.

Jesus Censures the Scribes; the Widow's Mite

Mark 12:38-44
From the Navarre Bible commentary,
We know that, "Jesus denounces any
Disordered desire for human honours."

When Bishop Sheen accepted an award,
He thanked his writers: Matthew, Mark, Luke, John.
We also have Bishop Barron, Archbishop
Chaput, Anthony Esolen, Scott Hahn.

From the Workbook for Lectors, we know that,
The widow has the "right intention and
Generous spirit. As she gives the little
which is her all, she becomes the model of one who entrusts herself to God."

A mite is a small coin formerly current.
We can give even when it is not Lent.

Jesus Gave the Apostles a Mission

Mark 16:15-18
From the Navarre Bible commentary,
We know that, "Jesus summarizes the
Apostles' mission...to preach salvation
To the whole world..." baptize everyone.

Let the record show, I have been baptized.
Father Bird presided at Saint Mary's.
George Stanley Halas was my godfather.
Flossie McCaskey was my godmother.

Like the apostles, I have a mission.
I am a lector; I am a speaker.
My themes are Chicago Bears' history,
Faith based education, and sports and faith:

Football has commandments and beatitudes
And if the apostles had played football.

Luke

Mary Went to Visit Elizabeth
Luke 1:39-45

Abraham was the father of nations
Because he believed what God had told him.
Mary became the mother of God be-
cause she accepted the challenge on faith.

God gave Mary intense preparation.
The angel gave Mary revelation.
Mary traveled far for visitation.
Her Son became all our incarnation.

Mary's cousin Elizabeth was pregnant.
Elizabeth's son, John, leapt in her womb.
What Elizabeth said became a prayer.
We have "The Hail Mary" because of her.

From Saint Ambrose, we know, "both women began to prophesy, inspired by their sons."

The Finding of Jesus in the Temple
Luke 2:41-52
Jesus Christ was full of wisdom and grace.
Jesus referred to God as his Father.

From the "Catechism of the Catholic
Church," we know that, "The finding of Jesus
in the temple is the only event
that breaks the silence of the Gospels
About the hidden years of Jesus" Christ.

When I was a student at Saint Mary's
School in Des Plaines, City of Destiny,
We put J.M.J. at the top of our
Papers for Jesus, Mary, and Joseph.

Call letters for Catholic Radio
In Hartford, CT are WJMJ.

Let us listen to God's word and live it.

John the Baptist Preached in the Wilderness

Luke 3:10-18
From the Navarre Bible commentary,
We know "John is the last of the prophets."

Because the Messiah will soon be here,
We should get ready and do penance for
Our sins, mend our ways, and "be able to
Receive the grace that the Messiah brings."

Ancestry does not secure salvation.
We get salvation through true repentance.

John the Baptist was very transparent.
If you have two cloaks, give one to the poor.
Just collect a just amount of taxes.
Don't extort, falsely accuse, or complain.

The message was preached in the wilderness.
God's grace brought it to the best-selling book.

Jesus Makes Us Acceptable to God

Luke 4:21-30

The Garden of Eden was heavenly.
Jesus Christ will help us get to heaven.

Christ lived in Nazareth for thirty years.
Jesus was an indigenous leader.
He does not need a doctor; He's the cure.
Instead of envious, let's be grateful.

We receive God's love through the sacraments.
Jesus wants us humble and confident.
He will purify and sanctify us.

The people of Nazareth were fickle.
Jesus did not passively accept their
Fury. He went away to pray alone.

No poet is accepted in his own
Parish, except of course Seamus Heaney.

Jesus Christ Went Fishing for Disciples II

Luke 5:1-11

When Peter, James, and John fished on their own,
Without Jesus, they were unsuccessful.
With Christ as their guide, the fish did not hide.
They jumped into the boat; they did not float.

My favorite sandwich is tuna on rye,
Without the contamination of celery.

From the Navarre Bible commentary,
Here is what I learned from the passage.
Remember the past with gratitude; live
The present with enthusiasm; look
Forward to the future with confidence.

"Like all those chosen by God for a mission,"
Jesus said to Peter, "Do not be afraid."

Pray with Humility and Confidence

Luke 5:12-16
From the Navarre Bible commentary,
We know that, "The man's disease made him very
(Very) ugly, and people shunned him for fear
Of contagion. Sin has the same effects."

We sin. We need forgiveness and God's grace.
"With humility and confidence, we
Will often borrow the leper's words and
Pray, 'Lord if you will, you can make me clean.'"

And "the Gospel shows us Jesus going
Off alone, to pray. We too need to set aside
Time for frequent, personal prayer in
The midst of our daily activities."

Now let's review. If we ask Jesus to
Cure our ugliness, He will make us clean.

Jesus Has a Discussion on Fasting

Luke 5:33-39
The Navarre Bible notes are instructive.
Jesus fasted before He ministered.

Penitential fasting is important.
During ministry Christ ate joyfully.
The teaching of Christ "calls for new wineskins—
Deeper repentance, profound renewal."

Receiving teaching with a sincere heart,
Helps us prevent the sport of backsliding.

Saint Leo the Great emphasized three things.
It is important to abstain from food.
The soul should give up iniquity
And the tongue should cease to bear false witness.

Let's smile when self-denial is in style.
Thank God fasting is not everlasting.

Jesus Prayerfully Chose the Twelve Apostles

Luke 6:12-16

Before important events, Jesus prayed.
He prayed before He chose the Apostles.
He extended His work through the Church which
Was to last until the end of the world.

Perry Como sang "'Til the End of Time."
My goal is to keep the Bears in the
Family until The Second Coming.

The choosing of the twelve was the first draft.
Later, the first National Football League
Player draft was in 1936.
Joe Stydahar was the Bears' first draftee.

As the two-thousand-year old man Mel Brooks
Said, "Jesus and His twelve friends came into
My store, but they didn't buy anything."

Luke Has Four Beatitudes and Four Woes

Luke 6:17, 20-26
The Navarre Bible notes are instructive.
Saint Luke recorded that Jesus Christ preached
In open spaces to show how "open
Our Lord was to all people and how his
Message was directed to everyone."

Those without an iPad can read God's Word.
Those who are hungry don't have to eat kale.
Those who weep can still hear Jim Gaffigan.
Those Christians who are scorned are like prophets.

Those who are rich are already consoled.
Those who are quite full may need to downsize.
Those who are laughing might soon be crying.
Those who receive praise may soon get a raise.
While they're alive, they're required to tithe.

The Teachings about Love of Enemies
Luke 6:27-38
Jesus said, "love your enemies, do good
To those who hate you, bless those who curse you."

The Navarre Bible notes are instructive.
"Divine mercy is the forgiveness of sins."

Bishop Bob Barron said, "When you turn the
Other cheek hold your ground." The second slap
Will be less powerful; it's a back hand.

George Halas and Vince Lombardi had great
Respect for each other. I never won
Against Art Contreras of Maryville.
I wanted my parents to adopt him.

Alan Swanson of Stony Brook and I
tied for first in a fall cross-country race.
Together, we finished ahead of Choate.[69]

---

[69] These references are to Patrick McCaskey's prep school experiences at
Cheshire Academy.

A Parable about Integrity

Luke 6:39-42
If you have a log in your eye, you are
Not the guy to remove another's speck.

Credibility needs integrity.
Purity is an opportunity.
Salvation is a possibility.

George Bernard Shaw said, "All great truths begin
As blasphemy." And Young Frankenstein said,
"Destiny, no escaping that for me."

The Navarre Bible notes are instructive.
Saint Theophilus of Antioch, loved
By God, said, "Show me that the eyes of your
Mind see and that the ears of your heart hear."

After a conflict resolution, Chip
Hilton's heart sang with a great confidence.[70]

---

[70] Chip Hilton is the fictional character in the Clair Bee sports series. See
the Clair Bee entry in the My Favorite Writers chapter.

The Holy Women Provide for Jesus
        Luke 8:1-3
Jesus preached the good news of salvation.
The twelve Apostles were Hall of Famers.
Christ helped many women become holy.
They gave Him devotion and assistance.
There was cooperation with Jesus.

Mary Magdalene was the first witness
To the Resurrection. Joanna was
Also witness to the Resurrection.
Susanna was also helpful to Christ.

Saint Monica prayed for Saint Augustine.

Saint John Paul II interpreted Scripture.
Men are adequate because of women.

My mother, Virginia, my wife, Gretchen,
And my daughters-in-law provide for me.

Herod Is Curious about Jesus

Luke 9:7-9

From the book "Who's Who in the Bible," we
Know that Herod "had John the Baptist imprisoned and...ordered John's execution."
John had criticized Herod for marry-
ing the wife of Philip his half-brother.

From the Navarre Bible commentary,
We know that, "Jesus' doings provoke the
Key question: 'Who is He?' The Gospel points
Out that the people were unsure as to
The answer and that Herod was perplexed."

Saint John Paul II wrote, "Only the faith pro-
claimed by Peter, and with him by the Church
In every age, truly goes to the heart
And touches the depth of the mystery."

Peter's Faith and the
Passion Announcement

Luke 9:18-22
Jesus prayed. Then He asked the disciples,
"Who do the people say that I am?" The
Disciples answered John the Baptist or
Elijah or one of the old prophets.

Christ asked, "But who do you say that I am?"
Peter professed his faith that Christ was God.
Christ said the disciples should tell no one.
He was not eager to be crucified.

From the Navarre Bible notes we know that
Saint John Vianney wrote, "a person who
Loves pleasure, who seeks comfort, who flies from
Anything that might spell suffering, who
Is over anxious, who complains, who blames
—a person like that is" not living right.

The Transfiguration of Jesus Christ
        Luke 9:28b-36
After Peter confessed his faith in Christ,
Jesus took Peter, John, and James to pray
On the top of a mountain. Then Jesus
Was transfigured into quite dazzling white.
Peter's confession of faith was confirmed.

Jesus revealed that the way of the cross
Would lead to his entry into glory.

The Navarre Bible notes on this passage
Lead to Catechism 555 and
Saint Thomas Aquinas. "The whole Trinity
Appeared: the Father in the voice; the Son
In the man; (the) Spirit in the shining cloud."

"Christ's Passion is the will of the Father."
Jesus Christ died and rose as God's Servant.

Seventy Disciples Have a Mission
Luke 10:1-19
Jesus Christ sent seventy disciples,
Two by two, to places where He would preach.
They were chosen to be the advance men.
They were taught to say, "Peace be to this house."

The Navarre Bible notes are instructive.
"Our Lord...requires of them detachment and
Abandonment to divine providence."

"The actions and words of the disciples
Are, like those of Jesus, a call from God
To repentance, which must come from the heart."

Saint Josemaria Escriva wrote,
"Don't doubt it: your vocation is the greatest
Grace our Lord could have given you. Thank Him
For it." I thank God for my vocation. [71]

---

[71] Saint Josemaria Escriva is the founder of Opus Dei.

The Seventy Return;
Jesus Gives Thanks

Luke 10:17-24

The disciples were thrilled to be a part
Of Christ's mission since they saw its power.
Jesus asked them to look deeper. The real
Celebration was God had chosen them.

Jesus expressed His joy because humble
People understood Him and accepted
The word of God. It was like this school all
Class reunion. Everyone was helpful.

Jesus declared that He knew God the Father.
Christ had a dual role. He revealed God.
He was God. He played offense and defense.
God made Himself accessible to us.

The school bore us without being boring.
The priests and nuns gave us our destiny.

The Kingdom of God Overruled Satan

Luke 11:14-23

Critics said Jesus worked with the devil.
Christ denied the charge and warned the critics.
They saw people had been freed from Satan.
Their stubbornness gave him a place to work.

This passage is blunt and polemical.
The devil is strong; he enslaved mankind.
Christ is stronger; He defeated Satan.
We need to make room for God's Kingdom.

The Navarre Bible notes are instructive.
Saint Caesarius of Arles said that,
"At our Baptism, we were made into
Temples of the Holy Spirit." Don't sin.

When we are at home, when we are away,
The Holy Spirit helps us every day.

The Unclean Spirit and Seven Others
Luke 11:25-26
The house of the unclean spirit was swept
And put in order. So he recruited
Seven other unclean spirits who were
More evil than he. They lived together.
Snow White and the seven dwarfs were better.

From the Navarre Bible notes, we know that,
Saint Caesarius of Arles said that,
"Since Christ at his coming cast the devil
Out of our hearts to make his temple and
Dwelling-place there, we should do everything
In our power, with the help of his grace,
To ensure that" we don't dishonor Christ.

The unclean spirit had seven others.
Jesus had twelve apostles and the Church.

Responding to the Word of Jesus Christ

Luke 11:27-28
From the "Navarre Bible" commentary,
We know that, "The Tradition of the Church
Has always read these words as great praise for
The Blessed Virgin." She believed God's word.

From the "Catechism of the Catho-
lic Church," 149, we know that "Throughout
Her life and until her last ordeal when
Jesus her son died on the cross, Mary's
Faith never wavered. She never ceased to
Believe in the fulfillment of God's word.
And so the Church venerates in Mary
The purest realization of faith."

Mary was not the least bit contrary.
She helped everyone, even the most wary.

Jonah and Saint Teresa of Avila

Luke 11:29-32
From the Navarre Bible commentary,
We know that, "The Ninevites did penance
Because they acknowledged the prophet
Jonah and accepted his message.
Jesus is greater than Jonah...Christ's life
And preaching are a call to conversion."

From the Magnificat, we know that
Saint Teresa of Avila advised,
"Let nothing disturb you, let nothing
Frighten you, all things are passing away:
God never changes. Patience obtains all
Things. Whoever has God lacks nothing; God
Alone suffices." This is holy advice.

My sister Anne's middle name is Terese.

Interpretation of the Present Time

Luke 12:54-59

Talk about weather is superficial.
Salvation talk is supernatural.

Christ gave us miracles, his life, and his
Teachings to show He is the Messiah.

Now is the time for our correct conduct.
Get ready for judgment; don't be condemned.
The Trinity is the most Supreme Court.
Their decision is the ultimate one.
On Judgment day, we either pass or fail.

Hardened hearts lead to incorrect judgments.
With Christ, we can live with humility.

Here is a quote from writer James Thurber.
"Let us not look back in anger or forward in fear, but around in awareness."

Jesus Cures a Woman on the Sabbath

Luke 13:10-17
From the Navarre Bible commentary,
We know that, "By performing this cure on
A Sabbath, Jesus shows his divine mag-
nanimity...the Sabbath is a day
For praise of God and a day of joy. That
Is why it made sense to cure the woman...?"

Jesus Christ had mercy and tenderness.
Persistent compassion imitates God.
Let us stand up straight and glorify God.
If you cannot stand up straight, do your best.

On the day of rest, we are God's guest.
It does not have to be on a Sunday.
Monday through Friday, I ride ten miles each
day on a stationary bike. On most
Saturdays, I run four hundred meters.

Obtain Salvation through the Narrow Door

Luke 13:22-30
The Navarre Bible notes are instructive.

From Vatican II, we know that we should
Use the strength of Christ's gift to follow
In His footsteps; conform to His image;
And do the will of God in everything;
Devote ourselves to the glory of God
And to the service of every neighbor.

"God will judge us...on our response to grace."
Christ said eternal life is a banquet.
Let all banquets be previews of heaven.

Let there be Caesar salad and skim milk,
And loaves and fishes. I'll do the dishes.
I am the loader; I have a system.
I am trying to be the most humble.

Parables: The Lost Sheep and the Lost Coin

Luke 15:1-10
God Almighty desires everybody:
Incarnation for civilization.

The shepherd found the lost sheep and rejoiced.
The woman found the lost coin and rejoiced.
The shepherd and the woman are like God.
When a sinner repents, there is much joy.

From the Navarre Bible commentary,
We know that, "In the face of our weakness,
God does not stand idly by: he goes out
In search of what is lost and makes every
Effort to find it...But, above all, he
Rejoices—as he does when we seek him."

Christ received sinners and ate with them. Thank
You for receiving and eating with me.

The Parable of the Prodigal Son

Luke 15:1-3, 11-32
The younger son offended his father.
Both of them need reconciliation.
There is forgiveness and a fatted calf.
The older son is selfish and jealous.
He also needs reconciliation.

The Navarre Bible notes are instructive.
"Meditation on this passage will help
Us to be optimistic (and) confident."

In relation to the parable of
The prodigal son, I've been the younger
Son. I have been rebellious. I have been
The older son. I have been resentful.

Now my goal is to be the father. Forgive others as I have been forgiven.

SPORTSMANSHIP

The Parable of the Unjust Steward
        Luke 16:1-13
Parables helped Jesus convey teachings.
He taught the Apostles to be clever.

Saint Josemaria Escriva wrote,
"What zeal people put into their earthly
Affairs...When you and I put the same zeal
Into the affairs of our souls, we will
Have a living and working faith. And there
Will be no obstacle that we cannot
Overcome in our apostolic works."

The Navarre Bible notes are instructive.
"At all times, in little things and big things,
In wealth or poverty our focus should
Be on God." Christ said, "And I tell you,"
God alone is the source of every good.

The Revelation about God's Kingdom

Luke 17:26-27
Jesus reminded his disciples about
The days of Noah and the days of Lot.
The ark saved Noah and his family.
Fire and brimstone destroyed Sodom. Jesus
Encouraged the disciples to obey.

Here is David Steinberg's routine about
Lot and his wife. As they were leaving Sod-
om and Gomorrah, the twin cities, Lot's
Wife said, "Lot, what's the matter with you? That
Was fun back there. How come you always do
What God tells you to do?" Lot responded,
"Dear, God told me to tell you to look back."

Dick Smothers asked his brother Tommy, "If
Someone told you to jump off a bridge, would
You do it?" Tommy replied, "Not again."

Jesus Told the Unjust Judge Parable

Luke 18:1-8
The Navarre Bible notes are instructive.
"The parable of the unjust judge is
A very eloquent lesson about the
Effectiveness of" prayer perseverance.

Our mandate is to pray without ceasing.
Let us overcome laziness and pray.
If we are a praying delegation,
Then we will be a great sensation.

In the public square, we can say a prayer.
During a quiet walk, let us not squawk.
At your work station, pray for our nation.
As we do a task, don't forget to ask.

"Prayer nourishes faith, but faith, in turn, grows
When it is enlivened by prayer." Amen.

Jesus Christ Wept Over Jerusalem

Luke 19:41-44
The Navarre Bible notes are instructive.
"When the procession reaches a place that
Looks out on a good view of the city,"
The disciples were surprised when Jesus wept.

Christ worked many signs in Jerusalem.
The Covenant will be sealed on the Cross.

Jesus visits each of us. He teaches
Us through the preachings of the Holy Church.

"He grants us forgiveness and grace through the
Sacraments. If we are faithful and at-
tentive to his word, we can ensure that
Our Lord has not come in vain." So be it.

The Bears have never played in Jerusalem.
That sounds like a prayer request. So be it.

Jesus Drove the Robbers from the Temple

Luke 19:45-48
From the Navarre Bible commentary,
We know that, the "cleansing of the temple
Is a reminder of the respect due
To the House of the Lord. Christian temples
That house the Blessed Eucharist are
Worthy of even greater reverence."

Halas Hall is a place of work and not
A den of thieves. It is a halfway house
To heaven. Instead of saying, "Please be
Quiet," we say, "Please become a mime."

Thank you for listening. This is better
Than talking to myself. It is great to
Be with you. Have a Hall of Fame day.

Tribulation and the Second Coming

Luke 21:20-28
Armies circle cities and people flee.
Nations in distress will be quite a mess.
Christ's victory is a great sign for me.
Bear trials patiently; get eternity.

While we work on sod, we endure for God.
Do good works with patience and persevere.
If we give up halfway along the path,
Then we will get what we deserve: God's wrath.

The Navarre Bible notes are instructive.
From Saint Cyprian, let us remember,
"He would lose the fruit of what he had done
...he did not finish what he had begun."

Jesus will be with us on Earth again.
He will be here for both women and men.

The Fig Tree Shows Us
the Kingdom of God

Luke 21:29-33
Jesus Christ told a fig tree parable.
When trees come out in leaf, summer is near.
He also said that God's Kingdom is near.
First, the Apostles had to rake the leaves.

From the Navarre Bible notes, we know that
All that Jesus "has said will come to pass."

Figs on trees create a heavenly breeze.
When you eat Fig Newtons, think of heaven.

Alan Lerner wrote "I Talk to the Trees."
It's from the musical "Paint Your Wagon."
Tommy Smothers thought that it was goofy.
"Oh, hello stage. You used to be a tree."

At a roast, what did Foster Brooks say to
Billy Graham? "I really like your crackers."

Patrick McCaskey

Jesus Christ Had a Hall of Fame Thursday

Luke 22:14-23:56
On Holy Thursday, Christ instituted
The Eucharist, foretold the treachery
Of Judas and the denial of Pete,
Appealed to the apostles, prayed and
Agonized in the garden, arrested.

The apostles became priests who offered
Communion when they celebrated Mass.
The apostles shared in the trials of Christ.
They also shared in the triumph of Christ.

The bishops are legates of Jesus Christ.
They are leaders as foot-washers for God.
The devil was successful with Judas.
Jesus prayed for Peter who was later
Restored. Peter gave his life for the Lord.

The Episode of the Good
Repentant Thief
Luke 23:35-43
The good thief repented. He also said
Jesus didn't do anything wrong; Jesus
Was innocent. The good thief said that he
Believed in Jesus. Christ gave him heaven.

Saint Augustine gave up dissipation.
Then he became a Doctor of the Church.
Confession of crimes leads to punishment.
Confession to God leads to salvation.

From John Paul II, we know that forgiveness
Is more powerful than sin. Forgiveness
Leads to reconciliation to God
And in relationships between people.

I used to be in high school detention.
Now I'm on my high school governance board.

Jesus Christ Appeared in the Upper Room

Luke 24:35-48

Jesus Christ showed that He was flesh and bones.
He was not just a guy named Smith or Jones.

Jesus was very hungry because He
Had not eaten since Holy Thursday night.
After He had asked for something to eat,
The apostles gave Him something quite light.

"They gave Him a piece of baked fish." It was
A secular communion. When they served
Loaves and fishes, there were a few dishes.
Then there was time for Jesus in His prime.

They did not have dessert even though it
Was the end of the original Lent.

The apostles went to every nation.
They brought the humble news of salvation.

SPORTSMANSHIP

John

From a Den of Thieves
to a House of Prayer

John 2:13-22

When Jesus saw animals and money-
Changers in the temple area, He
Was upset. So He cleared them out of there.
Once again the area had clean air.

Jesus could raise the temple in three days.
He was told that it took forty-six years.
Jesus said His body was a temple.
The disciples understood later on.

This passage is sometimes wrongly used to
Justify a loss of temper. Here is
One of my father's impersonations
Of me. "What do you mean I have a bad
Temper? I haven't hit anyone since
Nineteen seventy-five." I rest his case.

Patrick McCaskey

Christ Is the One Who Reveals the Father

John 6:37-40
Jesus Christ is our gateway to heaven.
He gives us our noble aspirations.

When I was a student at Saint Mary's
In Des Plaines, the City of Destiny,
We had Mass on First Fridays. After Mass,
We consumed sweet rolls and hot chocolate
For ten cents that went to the missions.

When I was a child, at the end of grace
Before meals, my father used to pray, "Dear
Lord, please convert the Russians. Our Lady
Help of the sick pray for them. May the souls
Of the faithful departed, through the mer-
cy of God, rest in peace, Amen." Later,
He said, "In your prayers, remember the Bears."

Jesus Went from God to Jerusalem

John 7:1-2, 10, 25-30
Those who accept Christ are His family.
Some people do not see Christ as Savior.
Jesus has power to bring salvation.
Listen to His words; they are obvious.

Christ waited for the right time to be born.
He allowed Himself to be put to death.
Let us acknowledge Him for what He did.
This requires conversion of heart and mind.

The Navarre Bible notes are instructive.
To understand and appreciate Christ
Let us strive and thrive to be like Jesus.
What would Christ do is good for me and you.

Every day is Christmas; each day is Lent.
Preparing for heaven is time well spent.

The Writing of Jesus Christ in the Dirt

John 8:1-11

Early in the morning, Jesus Christ was
In the temple area. When people
Came to Jesus, He sat down and taught them.

A woman was caught in adultery.
She was brought to Jesus for a ruling.
Jesus wrote something unknown in the dirt.

He invited the sinless to stone her.
No one was qualified, except Jesus.
Jesus told her not to sin anymore.

Seamus Heaney compared the writing of
Jesus Christ in the dirt to poetry.

Poetry, like the dirt writing, marks time.
"Poetry holds attention for a space."
Poetry functions as concentration.

Jesus Cured a Man Who Had Been Born Blind

John 9:1-41
Jesus spat on the ground and made spittle.
Then he anointed the man's eyes with clay.

Christ said, "Go, wash in the pool of Siloam."
"So, he went and washed and came back seeing."

Jesus Christ gave light to the blind man's eyes.
Christ also enlightened the blind man's mind.
The blind man believed in Jesus as Christ.
We also have that opportunity.

This miracle is like our Baptism.
Our soul is cleansed. We have the light of faith.

I had eye problems thirty-seven years.
From "The Quiet Man," "Those were the bad days."
Doctor Rubenstein restored my vision
Through two successful corneal transplants.

The Attempt to Stone Jesus Was Postponed

John 10:31-42
Jesus and the Father are unified.
Divine Revelation is quite a guide.
Christ became human to sanctify man.
Salvation is a most wonderful plan.

To avoid getting stoned Jesus withdrew.
You can follow Christ. Won't you come, too?
The Navarre Bible notes are instructive.
They help us to cope with the destructive.

John the Baptist prepared us for Jesus.
Followers of John drew near to Jesus.
John said that Jesus is the Messiah.
Christ quoted Scripture and did miracles.

Work in the name of God is not wasted.
The fruit of Christians is always tasted.

Christ Reacts to the Death of Lazarus

John 11:1-45

Lazarus was ill. Martha and Mary
Sent for Jesus. Jesus waited two days.
Lazarus died. Jesus walked two miles from
Jerusalem to Bethany. Christ wept.
The Navarre Bible notes are instructive.
"This is the shortest verse in the Bible."

Jesus raised Lazarus from the dead.
Jesus showed power over death. This is
A sign of our future resurrection.

Saint Augustine saw risen Lazarus
As everyone's reconciliation.
Lazarus came out of the tomb still bound.
We go to Confession still guilty.
Lazarus became loosed. We're forgiven.

Jesus the Son Reveals God the Father

John 14:1-6

Jesus predicted Peter's denial.
That seemed to have depressed the apostles.
Jesus wanted them to be joyful. So,
He told them, "that He is going away
To prepare a place for them in heaven"
Despite shortcomings, failures, and setbacks.

The quotes are from the Navarre Bible notes.

Jesus "is Life because from all eternity he shares in divine life with the
Father... through grace" we can have divine life.

Christ spoke in iambic pentameter:
Poetry, ten syllables in each line.

"I am the way and the truth and the life.
No one comes to the Father, but by me."

Dialogue between Pilate and Jesus

John 18:33b-37

Jesus answered Pilate's question with a
Question, even though Jesus was not Irish.
Jesus had a spiritual mission.
He did not seek independence from Rome.
This was hard for Pilate to understand.

Christ's kingdom prepares us for Judgment Day.
From the "Roman Missal," Preface of the
Mass of Christ the King, we know that the king-
dom of Jesus really is truth and life;
Holiness and grace; justice, love, and peace.

From the Workbook for Lectors," we know that,
"The humble service and total sacri-
fice of Christ the King is the truth that res-
cues humanity from itself and re-
stores the dignity of the human race."

Jesus Christ did not need Perry Mason.

Jesus Appeared to the Apostles Twice

John 20:19-31
Christ gave the apostles a commission.
He started the sacrament of Penance.
When Jesus appeared to the apostles
For the first time, Thomas was marked absent.

Tom doubted what the apostles told him.
He would even have questioned a football coach.
When Jesus appeared to the apostles
Again, Thomas became a believer.

Navarre Bible notes sum up John's purpose,
"To have people believe that Jesus is
The Christ, the Messiah announced by the
Old Testament prophets (and) the son of God."

This passage has two great quotes. Christ said, "Peace
Be with you." Tom said, "My Lord and my God."

The Catch of One Hundred Fifty-Three Fish

John 21:1-14

John loved Jesus Christ and recognized Him.
Peter got to Christ before the others.
When Jesus ate with them, He proved Himself.
Jesus was not a ghost; He had risen.

Saint Paul wrote, "Love is patient. Love is kind."
Saint Josemaria wrote, "Love, love is
Farsighted. Love is the first to appre-
ciate kindness." Sir Paul McCartney wrote
And sang, "Love doesn't come in a minute."

From the Navarre Bible notes, we know that,
"The boat is the Church, whose unity is
Symbolized by the net that does not tear;
The sea is the world; Peter in the boat
Stands for supreme authority in the Church."

PART FIVE: SPEECHES

IT'S WORTH SAYING

"After we had our senior prom at the Edgewater Beach Hotel, it had to be demolished. Maybe it was just coincidental."

—Patrick McCaskey

The speeches presented here have been given to many different audiences. I speak to Bears' fans, community groups, schools, charities, churches, clubs, men's groups, and other venues. You may recognize some of the material here from topics already covered in this book and my other books, but we wanted you to see the speeches in their entirety.

My Most Important Class

On Monday, January 14, 1974, I started the most important class of my life. It was Theater 315, Oral Interpretation II at Indiana University. We met on Monday, Wednesday, and Friday at 11:30 a.m.

Doctor Hawes was the teacher. The students were Cathie Atz, Barb Campaigne, Joyce Campbell, Linda DeRoo, Windell Mattheu, Carol Reid, Sue Rodelius, Pat McCaskey, and Jim Westerhouse. Doctor Hawes said that everyone in the class would choose a writer for a concert reading. I chose me.

Doctor Hawes respected my decision. That was a confidence builder. I still have the evaluations from Doctor Hawes and my classmates. Doctor Hawes taught us to stand up straight, project to the back of the class, and be off the script 90% of the time. To that I would add, forget about yourself.

Patrick McCaskey

Chicago Bears' History

My grandfather, George Stanley Halas, a founder of the Chicago Bears and the National Football League, was born on February 2, 1895, to Barbara and Frank Halas in an apartment on 18th Place and Wood Street in Chicago. He was the youngest of eight children, but of those eight, only four survived infancy: George, his brothers, Walter and Frank, and his sister, Lillian.

In the fall of 1914, Grandpa set out for the University of Illinois and hoped to impress the freshman football coach. He enrolled in civil engineering, and the fraternity got him a job as a waiter. However, Grandpa's freshman season on the gridiron didn't turn out quite as well as he had hoped it would. He ended up being a reserve halfback. He then turned his attention to baseball and he made the freshman team.

Grandpa returned to Chicago for the summer and he resumed working for Western Electric. On July 24, 1915, Western Electric was holding its annual picnic in Michigan City, Indiana. So like many of the other employees, Grandpa purchased a ticket to cross Lake Michigan on the excursion ship, called the Eastland, for the trip to Michigan City.

Fortunately for Grandpa, he overslept. Then his brother Frank asked him to step on the scale and check his weight just as he was about to leave the house to get on the Eastland. Grandpa checked in at 163 pounds, and the delay ended up saving Grandpa's life. When he got to the dock, he learned that the Eastland had capsized. The loss of life was appalling; 844 people died when the Eastland went down.

An alert reporter obtained a passenger list, and the next morning Grandpa's name appeared as one of the fatalities. That night the doorbell rang, and when Grandpa answered it, two of his fraternity brothers, Elmer Strumpf and Walter Straub, stood there, thinking they were going to extend their condolences to Grandpa's grieving mother. But they were delighted to find Grandpa alive! Suddenly, the magnitude of Grandpa's good fortune overwhelmed him and he readily agreed to his mother's suggestion that he say a Rosary of gratitude before he went to bed. Sometimes it's okay to be late.

The United States entered World War I in April 1917, and the country had little time for anything else. The newspapers were full of stories about our armed forces. Grandpa felt that it was his duty to enlist, but his mother kept pleading with him to get his degree before doing so.

Grandpa's mother was adamant about her son receiving his degree, but he wanted to serve his country. Since Grandpa much preferred the navy to the army, he decided to enlist, thereby obtaining a choice in which branch he would serve. And thankfully, the University of Illinois was very cooperative; since Grandpa had never failed a subject, he was told to go ahead and enlist, and his diploma would be mailed to his home in June. This pleased his mother, but Coach Ralph Jones wasn't very happy. Grandpa finally got Coach Jones to agree that winning the war was more important than winning basketball games.

After Grandpa had worked out all of the details confirming his graduation, he went up to the Great Lakes Naval Training Station and enlisted as a

Carpenter's Mate Second Class. It didn't take him long to find out that they had an officer's school there, so he applied for admission.

Grandpa never saw any combat duty at sea. Great Lakes Naval Training Station was very active in sports. So Grandpa's tour of duty consisted of him becoming Great Lakes' recreation officer, which involved playing and coaching football as well as playing basketball and baseball. It may not have helped the war effort, but playing and coaching for the Great Lakes teams was what he was ordered to do.

The team's biggest thrill came when it was invited to play the Mare Island Marines in the Rose Bowl on January 1, 1919. The Marines had an excellent team that came into the game undefeated at 10-0 with no ties. Great Lakes, meanwhile, had won six games and tied two.

That day, Grandpa thought he played the best game of his life. He was always wary of ever calling himself a star, but on this particular day, Grandpa was a star. His tackling was terrific on defense, and on offense he scored a touchdown on a 45-yard pass from Paddy Driscoll. Grandpa also intercepted a pass and ran it back 77 yards.

Great Lakes went on to win 17-0, and Grandpa was named Most Valuable Player. And we won the war.

New York Yankees scout Bob Connery had paid Grandpa a visit while he was playing outfield for Illinois during his junior year. Connery also came out to see some of the Great Lakes games in which Grandpa had played, and he recommended him to the Yankees organization for a tryout. The Yankees invited Grandpa to spring training, and he accepted with alacrity. He made the team but he didn't play until the 11th game of the season.

SPORTSMANSHIP

After Grandpa had played in 12 games for the Yankees, Manager Miller Huggins called Grandpa in to see him. He thought Grandpa needed more experience, so the Yankees planned to send him to St. Paul of the American Association. Naturally, Grandpa was heartbroken, but he always remembered the way Miller Huggins handled the situation. Whenever Grandpa had to cut a player throughout the years, he tried to emulate Huggins's grace and empathy. Grandpa decided to make the best of it, go to St. Paul, and do the best he could.

That same night, Grandpa managed to catch a train to St. Paul, and the next day he reported to Mike Kelly, a man who became his friend as well as a mentor and coach. Kelly was terrific at handling young ballplayers and helping them improve their weaknesses. Thanks to Kelly's coaching, Grandpa had a pretty good year at St. Paul. At the end of the season, Kelly told Grandpa that he would like him to return to St. Paul the following season. However, St. Paul's pay scale called for a reduction in his salary from $400 a month to $300 a month. The Yankees told him they had a youngster they planned to use in right field named Babe Ruth, but they thought Grandpa would be ready to move up to the parent club after another year of seasoning at St. Paul. Grandpa believed that an additional year with Mike Kelly would prepare him for a return to the big leagues, and he'd certainly stick with the Yankees the second time around.

Grandpa felt he was ready for the majors. He had a great arm, he was fearless, and Lord knows he had the desire. Faced with a 25 percent pay cut, Grandpa finally decided that it wasn't in his best interests to spend another year playing in St. Paul, so he didn't return. And the Yankees decided to go with Babe Ruth.

With professional baseball no longer in his plans, Grandpa went back to Chicago. He ended up working for the Chicago, Burlington, and Quincy Railroad as an engineer in the bridge department, but the desire to compete in the athletic arena still burned in him. Eventually, he learned a semipro football team, the Hammond Pros, was holding tryouts. Grandpa ended up making the team and he received $100 per game—a nice chunk of money at that time.

Grandpa was thrilled to pocket the $100 Hammond paid him for his professional debut. At that time, he sought some financial security, and the money he received was more than twice the amount he made working an entire week at the railroad. All told, Grandpa played between six and seven games for Hammond that fall, and the paycheck he received each week really got him excited about professional football.

On March 18, 1920, George Chamberlain met with my grandfather in Chicago. Chamberlain was the general superintendent of the A. E. Staley Manufacturing Company in Decatur. Chamberlain offered Grandpa the opportunity to learn the starch business and be the company's athletic director and football coach. He could also play on the Staley football and baseball teams.

On Friday, September 17, 1920, the original meeting for what is now the National Football League took place. The site was Ralph Hay's Hupmobile Showroom in Canton, Ohio. That's why the Pro Football Hall of Fame is located there. Hay was the owner of the Canton Bulldogs football team. Since there weren't enough chairs in the showroom, Hay and Halas and the other founding fathers sat on the running boards and the fenders of the cars. In the fall of 1920, the team was called the Decatur Staleys.

SPORTSMANSHIP

In the fall of 1921, there was a recession. The company couldn't afford to subsidize the football team anymore. (My grandfather was up for a promotion in the glucose department.)

On Thursday, October 6, 1921, Mister Augustus Staley gave the team $5,000 worth of advertising to move to Chicago with the stipulation that the team nickname Staleys be retained for that season. (Grandchildren of Mister Staley sometimes wonder what their lives would have been like if their grandfather had sold the company and kept the team.)

In 1921, the team was the Chicago Staleys. The team won the Championship based on the standings. On January 28, 1922, the Chicago Staleys became the Chicago Bears at a League meeting.

For the 1925 season, each NFL team was limited to 16 players. On Sunday, November 22, 1925, the Bears signed Red Grange and played the Green Bay Packers at Wrigley Field. The Bears won 21–0.

From November 26, 1925, through January 31, 1926, the Bears went on a coast-to-coast tour and played 19 games. This gave pro football national recognition.

On Saturday, November 5, 1932, Bears' rookie center Ookie Miller made his first trip to New York. He went to the Cotton Club to see Cab Calloway the night before the Bears played the Giants. When he returned to his room, there was a note on his door, "Ookie, when you get in, come see me, George."

When he saw Halas, he said, "Hey, Ookie did you have a good time last night?" Miller explained that it was his first trip to New York, etc. and Halas said, "Don't worry about it Kid, it will only cost you $100."

Miller told his teammates, if he wasn't going to get paid, he wouldn't play. One of them told him he had the same experience and after he'd played a good game, Halas rescinded the fine. So Miller said okay he'd play. The next day, the Bears won 28–8. After the game, Halas came down to where Miller was dressing and said, "Ookie, I think I'll fine you $100 before every game—you play better." Miller did not get a refund.

The 1932 Championship was to be based on the standings. The Bears and the Portsmouth Spartans finished the 1932 regular season tied for first place. On Sunday, December 18, 1932, the Bears played the Portsmouth Spartans at the Chicago Stadium for the Championship. The Bears won 9–0. The team had a deficit of $18,000.

After the season, George Halas asked Ookie Miller to come in to discuss a contract for 1933. Miller had played 60 minutes in most games so he was pretty confident he could get a raise.

Halas greeted Miller with, "Gee Kid, you had a great season and '33 should be better, but we lost money in '32. I was going to cut everyone's salary, but you had such a great year, I'll keep your salary the same as last year and we'll consider this a raise." Miller left feeling as if he had received a raise.

On Saturday, October 7, 1933, Bronko Nagurski had a sore hip and Ookie Miller had a charley horse. When the team arrived in Brooklyn, Halas arranged for Jack Dempsey's trainer to work on Nagurski and Miller before the game. Halas bought a bottle of Absorbine Junior to use on their injuries. That turned out to be very beneficial.

The next day, the Bears played the Brooklyn Dodgers in Brooklyn. The Bears won 10–0.

Riding back to Chicago on the train, Halas was paying Miller off in cash as was customary in those days. After he was finished, Miller said, "George, you are a dollar short."

Halas said, "That's for the bottle of Absorbine Junior."

And Miller said, "Yeh, but it was also used on Bronk."

And Halas said, "Yeh, but you kept the bottle."

On Sunday, December 17, 1933, the Bears played the New York Giants at Wrigley Field for the Championship. The Bears won 23–21.

On December 8, 1940, the Bears played the Washington Redskins in Washington for the Championship. In the fourth quarter, the referee came to my grandfather and said, "Please don't kick any more extra points. We're running out of footballs."

The Bears won 73–0.

On Sunday, December 21, 1941, the Bears played the New York Giants at Wrigley Field for the Championship. The Bears won 37–9.

On Sunday, December 26, 1943, the Bears played the Washington Redskins at Wrigley Field for the Championship. The Bears won 41–21.

The University of Chicago used to be in the Big Ten. When Alonzo Stagg was the football coach, they were a national power. There is a street through the center of the campus called Midway Plaisance. They were the original Monsters of the Midway.

Then the university president de-emphasized football. In 1946, they left the Big Ten. The Bears became the second Monsters of the Midway.

At the start of the 1946 training camp, Coach Halas said to the players, "You men have had a lot of discipline during the war. For this season, all training rules are off. You All Americans have an equal chance to make the team."

On Sunday, December 15, 1946, the Bears played the New York Giants in New York for the Championship. The Bears won 24–14.

Bill Osmanski got his teeth knocked out. He later became a dentist.

George McAfee wrote, "One thing I remember about Mister Halas. I took myself out of a game. Mister Halas asked why. I told him I think I broke my nose. Mister Halas said are you sure? I said well maybe. He told me to go back in until I'm sure."

In 1956, the Bears began their quest for a new stadium in Chicago. My grandfather also went to Green Bay to encourage the people to vote for a bond issue for a new stadium in Green Bay. On April 3, 1956, the referendum passed and the Packers got a new stadium.

On Sunday, October 20, 1963, the Bears played the San Francisco 49ers in San Francisco. The Bears lost 20–14.

During the flight home, Bill Wade moved to the forward part of the airplane and poured his sorrow out to Coach Halas, who patiently listened and said, "Who do we play next week?"

Bill wrote that Halas had the "great ability to constantly push forward and look ahead through hardship and defeat, heartache and disappointment."

On Sunday, November 17, 1963, the Bears played the Green Bay Packers at Wrigley Field. J.C. Caroline made a great tackle on a kickoff. The Bears won 26–7. In the film session the next week, the team gave J.C. Caroline a great round of applause.

On Sunday, November 24, 1963, the Bears played the Pittsburgh Steelers in Pittsburgh. In the fourth quarter, Mike Ditka caught a pass from Bill Wade and broke six tackles to set up the tying field goal. Roger

LeClerc kicked an 18-yard field goal. The Bears tied 17–17. Mike had seven receptions for 146 yards.

On Sunday, December 29, 1963, the Bears played the New York Giants at Wrigley Field for the Championship. Bill Wade scored two touchdowns on quarterback sneaks. The Bears won 14–10.

My father recalled this Stan Jones story. "After the Bears had won the 1963 Championship, Mayor Daley invited the team to City Hall to show appreciation. He said that a gift to everyone would be forthcoming.

"Stan and his wife, Darlis, went home and waited for it. With playoff money, they bought a glass table. Every day he would ask Darlis, 'Did the gift come from the Mayor?'

The answer was no for several weeks. "One day Darlis said, 'Stan, Mayor Daley's gift arrived.' In his haste to open the package, it slipped out of his hands and broke the glass table. The gift was a City of Chicago paperweight."

On January 22, 1972, my grandfather spoke in Washington, DC. Here is part of the speech that my father and I wrote for him.

Football has been my life. I drifted into it a long time ago with no preparation except four years under Zuppke at Illinois and an abiding itch. Fifty years ago I fell in love with the kickoff sound of a foot striking leather and I have been struck with it ever since....

How could I dream those short 50 years ago that 65 million people would see the Dallas Cowboys play the Miami Dolphins in Super Bowl VI? How could I dream that in 1972 the Gallup Poll would reveal football as America's No. 1 spectator sport?

I could not and I did not.... The miracle to me is not that football has grown to be the No. 1 spectator sport, but rather the important place that football has in the lives of millions of Americans. Today, with so much of the earth destroyed, damaged, or at least endangered, with heartache and turmoil surrounding us, a man's courage can easily fail him. Surrounded as we are by a sea of bad news, how does one find the strength to continue?

I have long been fascinated by the adventures of Jacques Cousteau, who tells us that the sea is dying. He has been down there, so he must know. Many say our cities are dying, and if the cities die, so will civilization as we know it. But we must never despair, for despair is no good for any of us...and so I would suggest to you that professional football has become a beacon of light for the millions of American who thrill to its excitement.

Recently, Commissioner (Pete) Rozelle authorized Louis Harris and Associates to undertake a survey of a cross section of sports fans in the country. When asked "What does pro football do for you?" the fans surveyed answered in a manner which I found fascinating.

For example: "entertainment and enjoyment"..."relaxation and recreation"..."thrilling and exciting"..."draws the family together when we watch it"..."gives us something to talk to friends about"..."an outlet for letting off steam"..."something to look forward to on the weekend"..."makes me feel young!" That's my favorite, "makes me feel young!"

Once I had a great friend who passed for too short a time on this earth, in this country, in this city. Once he said: "Football symbolizes the attributes of America: stamina, courage, teamwork, self-denial, sportsmanship, selflessness, and respect for authority."

My friend's name was Vince Lombardi.

270

SPORTSMANSHIP

Several hours after the Chicago Bears drafted Walter Payton in the 1st round of the 1975 NFL Draft, I drove to O'Hare Airport to meet him. However, he ended up not making the flight. Instead of nursing a grudge, I married a nurse.

Walter was certainly elusive on and off the field—and well known for playing practical jokes. He would light firecrackers in the middle of the night at training camp. He untied referees' shoelaces during games.

Here's Walter's impersonation of me at the office. "Let me answer the phone. Give me something to do."

When Tim Weigel interviewed Walter on television after a game, Walter said, "Our offensive line blocked so well that even Tim 'White Shoes' Weigel could have rushed for a lot of yards."

After a game in 1983 in Tampa in which Walter and Matt Suhey each rushed for over 100 yards, Brad Palmer pointed out to Walter that he was within a few receptions of Mike Ditka on the Bears' all-time receiving list.

Walter said, "No wonder we ran the ball so much."

On another occasion, he said, "All those McCaskeys look alike."

When Walter answered the phone in my father's office, he'd say in a high voice, "This is Bernice. Mister McCaskey can't come to the phone right now because I'm giving him a full body massage."

Walter was the best football player I've ever seen. He blocked, he ran, he caught, he punted, he kicked, he passed...and he tackled if he threw an interception on those occasions when he was called to throw a halfback-option pass. He played halfback, but he was a fullback, quarterback, receiver, kick returner, cheerleader, receptionist, and director, too.

There was a lot of Harpo Marx in Walter Payton. When reporters interviewed Walter, he often picked their pockets. He was the best on the team at throwing rolled up socks in the locker room after practice. And he did great impersonations of Buckwheat and Stevie Wonder.

One of the things that kept me busy was speaking at Walter Payton award ceremonies. It was a privilege to have him in a Chicago Bears' uniform. He personified the word superstar, and he was one of the most humble and soft-spoken gentlemen you'd ever meet.

The day after he rushed for 275 yards in a game, for example, he volunteered for the scout team. We can continue to extend his legacy through commitment to excellence and having a lot of fun.

When Mike Ditka was a Bears' player, there was great competition between the Bears' defense and the Bears' offense. When Mike was the Bears' coach, he promoted great cooperation between the Bears' defense and the Bears' offense. Doug Plank called the program, "Bring an offensive player to lunch."

In preparation for Super Bowl XX, Coach Ditka wanted me to take care of the people who really matter: the coaches and the players. My responsibility was to take care of them in terms of meals, meetings, and practices.

When I came into the locker room before one practice, Walter Payton told one of the security guards to check me out. He did and everyone involved had a good laugh.

When I met Jim McMahon's father, the day before the Super Bowl, I said to him, "You should have given Jim more spankings."

He replied, "I know."

SPORTSMANSHIP

Throughout the season, and particularly in the week before the game, everyone in the Bears' organization: management, coaches, and players, contributed to the Championship.

Patrick McCaskey

Faith Based Education

My great, great grandfather, J.P. McCaskey, was a teacher and a principal for over 50 years at Boys High School in Lancaster, Pennsylvania.

To each graduate of the high school he gave a portrait of himself with this inscription: "The best of men that ever wore earth about him was a patient sufferer, a soft meek, tranquil Spirit, the first true gentleman that ever breathed." That was written about Jesus. My great, great grandfather never even met me.

A great grandson of the great man was my father, Ed McCaskey. He recalled, "He had a habit of asking, 'What did you learn in school today?' If you said, 'nothing,' he replied, 'let's learn something.' Then you were obliged to memorize prose, poetry, or a Bible quote.

According to my father, "When J.P. was 96, I was 12. He used to talk to me a lot at lunchtime. One day when I came home from school, he said, 'Young man, I've been looking over my life. I've made three mistakes. I swore once. I smoked a cigar once. When I was 80, my wife died. I should have remarried for mine is good seed.'"

On another occasion, he said to my father, "The most important column in the newspaper is the obituary column because it marks the start of man's eternal journey." He died September 19, 1934, at the young age of 97 just short of his 98th birthday. On May 3, 1938, the new John Piersol McCaskey High School was completed and dedicated in Lancaster. My uncle, Jim McCaskey, unveiled J. P.'s portrait.

My grade school teachers were Sister Carlene, Sister Amata, Miss Marke, Sister Martha, Sister Mercy,

274

Sister Bertille, Sister Irma, Sister Verona, and Sister Arthesma.

The teachers encouraged the students to be positive role models. They usually seated the students in alphabetical order. There were times when misbehaving students were seated next to students who behaved. Don Nevins often sat next to me. He is now an excellent priest.

On my eighth birthday, April 30, 1957, I went to school in the morning. Sister Amata announced to the class that my father was taking me out of school in the afternoon. He was taking me to see the movie "Around the World in 80 Days" at the Michael Todd Theater in Chicago.

On May 3, 1957, the Saint Mary's second graders made their First Confessions. I said, "Bless me Father for I have sinned. Three days ago I played hookey. I ask for penance and absolution."

On May 5, 1957, the Saint Mary's second graders made their First Communions. On April 20, 1959, the Saint Mary's fourth graders received the Sacrament of Confirmation. My grandfather, Dick McCaskey, was my sponsor. My Confirmation name was Paul.

After Mass on First Fridays, we were allowed to stand at tables in the school hall and eat breakfast with hot chocolate that cost 10 cents a cup. The proceeds went to the missions.

We were also allowed to buy candy at lunchtime in that hall. The proceeds went to the missions.

We saw many good movies in that hall for 10 cents that went to the missions. We saw "The Bells of Saint Mary's," "The Glenn Miller Story," "The Pride of the Yankees," "The Spirit of St. Louis," and "The Student Prince."

When I was an altar boy at Saint Mary's Church, I talked to another altar boy during Mass one day. Father Richard Maginot confronted me afterwards. I denied it, but my conscience has been bothering me long enough. If I remember correctly, I said, "Father Maginot is a wonderful priest."

Don Nevins and I often volunteered to serve 6:30 a.m. weekday Mass. One morning I complained to Sister Amata about having to get up so early. She calmly explained that she woke up much earlier than I did.

Later in the day, she gave me a copy of a book entitled *Mangled Hands*. It was about Father Isaac Jogues. He was a missionary to the Iroquois Indians. They hacked off his thumbs with tomahawks. Yet he continued to try to convert them to Christianity. I didn't complain anymore.

We grew up about two miles from Maryville Academy, an orphanage in Des Plaines. When my parents' children were children, we had the mandate each Christmas of giving one of our gifts to Maryville. One Christmas I received a new baseball glove. I wanted to give it to Maryville. My parents asked if I was sure I wanted to do that. I was.

The next spring Art Contreras was wearing that glove when he struck me out. My heroes are the people who accept God's grace and mercy and forgive those who trespass against them. I'm not bitter.

When I complained about the conditions in my home one time, my mother asked me, "How would you like to live at Maryville for a while?"

The idea was somewhat intriguing because Maryville had great athletic teams. I played for Saint Mary's School. We never beat Maryville's A teams.

I wanted my parents to adopt Art Contreras because I thought he would make Saint Mary's much stronger athletically. I guess my parents felt that they had enough children. It's difficult for me, but I publicly acknowledge that Art was a better basketball player than I. Of course, he had his own gym.

When I was in seventh grade, I started at forward on the eighth grade basketball team. We had one victory. Saint Joseph the Worker got way ahead and put in their second string. Before they could recover, we won 14–12. We lost to Saint James 46–1. I led the team in scoring that game.

As a 5-foot-10 eighth grader, I had to choose between basketball and speed skating. Basketball had cheerleaders.

Before the start of the basketball games, they would go to the visitors' fans and exclaim, "H-E-L-L-O, HELLO."

"V-I-C-T-O-R-Y Saint Mary's Spartans, that's our cry. La-di-da, Our Spartans are the best. La-di-da, La-di-da, La-di-da, La-di-da"

"One, two, three, four, five, six, seven, all good players go to heaven. When they get there they repeat, Saint Mary's, Saint Mary's, can't be beat."

When I was in eighth grade, the basketball team was 15–7. We lost three games to Saint Stephen's. We won the Maryville Academy/Don Bosco Tournament at the end of the season. Then we had an eighth-grade assembly in the school hall. When I presented the trophy to our pastor, Father Bird, he asked me, "What do you want me to do with it?" I'm glad that he didn't give it to the missions.

We also had our 8th grade party in the school hall. I was president of Class 8A. Before I gave the welcoming speech, Mrs. Siffermann asked me if I was nervous. When I said yes, she told me to take off my glasses. Then I wouldn't be able to see the audience. I followed her advice and it seemed to work out fine.

When the Saint Mary's School, Class of 1963, graduated, Father Bird had an interesting speech. Among other things, he said, "This is the last time this group will be together. No matter how hard you try, you won't be able to get everyone together again. Some will die. Some won't be interested. You won't be able to find some people. This is the last time this group will be together."

My parents wove a pattern of hard work and discipline for the lives of their children. They stitched this pattern with love.

My mother always found it amusing when someone asked her how much hired help she had. That was probably the reason my father nicknamed her "Laughing Girl." She did all the cooking and laundry and housework. The only real time she got a break was when she went into the hospital to have another baby.

During those refreshing interludes, Mrs. Passarelli took care of us. Instead of dinners of hamburgers or hot dogs, she prepared homemade pizza or spaghetti and meatballs. While waving a wooden spoon covered with meat sauce, she would yell, "You kids stop fighting."

She never had to tell on us because my parents knew us very well. There were many fights in our home and my parents used belts, fly swatters, spatulas, and pizza paddles as instruments of discipline. When my father's discipline was thought to be too severe, we buried one of his watches in the vegetable garden.

Our version of family planning was to have the children born during the Chicago Bears' off-seasons. We had seven victories and four ties.

SPORTSMANSHIP

Education was very important in our home and chores were an essential part of our training. Grass had to be mowed and snow had to be shoveled. Dog pens had to be cleaned and vegetable gardens had to be cultivated.

My father was not a straw boss. He worked harder than any of his sons. When he cultivated a vegetable garden with a pitchfork and found one of his watches, he could see the humor in the situation.

All of us were raised with discipline and love and each of us was a special case.

My father considered it a privilege to help his father in the garden. One of the things I really appreciate about my father is that he never gave up on his children. There were times when we didn't want to work in the garden. My father encouraged us to do it anyway.

When I was a boy, I didn't always appreciate the change of seasons and the cycle of nature. My father said, "In the summer, we get ready for winter. In the winter, we get ready for summer."

Now that I am a man, I am reminded that my father never gave up on his children and that I should never give up on mine.

My parents have had the most influence on my spiritual development. They sacrificed to send their eleven children to parochial grade schools and high schools. Some of us even went to Catholic colleges and universities. During childhood Lents, we prayed the family Rosary out loud together on our knees, in the family living room. When we misbehaved, we were strongly reminded, "This is the family Rosary!"

I wanted to get married when I was in eighth grade because my parents had a great marriage. That was in 1963. My parents' marriage was in its 20th orbit.

I have sympathy for anyone who is in high school. I remember what it was like. High School was rough.

I was on the freshman football team. I was calling out the signals as quarterback one game and my voice cracked. I said, "Ready," (in a deep voice) "Set." (in a high voice)

The guy playing right end for our team fell on the ground laughing. I had to call time out to give him a chance to recover. The delay killed our momentum on that drive. We only won the game 50–0.

I was on the freshman basketball team. I didn't go to the Bears' 1963 NFL championship game because I had practice. When I used that as an illustration to my sons as to how dedicated they should be to their teams, they said, "Dad, you made a mistake."

I was on the freshman baseball team. I was late for practice one day because of detention. I didn't take the time to put on a protective cup before I caught batting practice. A foul ball made me wish I had.

I was on the sophomore football team. I started at end, halfback, fullback, and kicker. Then I didn't have to call signals.

I was on the sophomore basketball team. I didn't start against Glenbrook North, but I fouled out before the half.

I didn't make the sophomore baseball team. I'm not bitter.

At the start of my junior football season, I failed the physical because of a hernia. Remember that foul ball? My voice cracked that day.

Instead of going out for basketball, I worked out with the swimming team. I nearly drowned every practice.

After I had finished my homework, I ran laps around Cornell Park in Des Plaines. There were couples parked in cars, but I couldn't tell what they were doing because the windows were steamed. Maybe they were saying the Rosary.

When the laps became tiresome, I changed to a five-mile loop through the streets. I ran south on Wolf Road, east on Thacker, north on Pearson, west on Prairie, and north on Wolf Road. One of the things that kept me going during those runs was the possibility that maybe someday I'd be able to tell the story. I guess today's the day.

I was on an intramural 3-man basketball team with Tom Bunzol and Dick Rafferty. We won every game. We had to play during the second half of our lunch hour because the school basketball teams needed the gym to practice after school. We only had one gym.

There was barely time to eat lunch, hop into a pair of sneakers, play the game, jump back into my street clothes, and make it to my first afternoon class. This particular afternoon, after a hard-fought victory, I was very sweaty and tired. My shirt was hanging out, not only because I was sloppy, but also to cover the pockets of my Levi's that were illegal to wear. I barely made it to study hall before the second bell rang.

Since I was so physically exhausted, I merely laid my books on my desk and laid my head on top of them in the fond hope of falling immediately asleep. However, the study hall monitor, Coach White, was a strict disciplinarian and he had other plans for me. He roused me from my deep sleep and commanded me to free my mind to God's will by disciplining it through study.

Then I discovered how dry my mouth was. Barely audible, I said, "I thirst."

Coach White realized that I was sinful and separated from God. Since he cared about me, he wanted me to know God's love and God's wonderful plan for my life. So he wrestled me out of my desk. My response was, "My God, my God, why hast thou forsaken me?"

In an attempt to prove to me that "the wages of sin is death," Coach White took me by my shirt collar and brought me into the hallway. Father Schuneman happened to be walking by. Coach White said to him, "Maybe you can do something with McCaskey."

Father Schuneman didn't say anything for a long time. He waited for me to say something. In the interim, The Holy Spirit worked a miracle in my life. I felt compassion and understanding for Coach White. His behavior was not a problem; it was an opportunity to show God's love. I came down to his level to help him, just as Christ became man to save us, so many football seasons ago.

I said to Father John Schuneman, "Father, forgive him for he knows not what he does."

The entire incident earned me a Saturday detention. "It is finished."

When I went out for track, the distant runner's coach, Father Devlin, said that I ran like a football player. I took that as a compliment. I rode my bike 25 miles from Des Plaines to Wheaton to see Louise Raymond. She wasn't home.

At the end of the season, I was seeded tenth in the conference mile. I took fifth and won a medal. We won the conference meet.

When I was a senior, I was quarterback on defense and offense. My voice did not crack. We won every game by an average of 29 points. I was a Catholic New World All American.

I was a track co-captain. I was seeded third in the conference mile. I took second and won a medal. We won the conference meet by 29 points. I was most improved runner.

Father John MacLoraine was the founding pastor of Saint Emily's Parish. My father came up with the idea of a fundraising record. On one side was Johnny Desmond singing "Ave Maria." On the flip side was a message from Father MacLoraine.

Father MacLoraine had been an Army General and he was rather gruff. The gist of his message was "Hello. This is Father MacLoraine. We need money."

In the summer of 1966, I worked for Saint Emily's. I mowed the lawn and I painted classrooms. At the end of the summer, when Father MacLoraine paid me, he asked me, "What are you going to do with all of this money?"

I gave him an honest answer. I said, "I don't know."

Then he asked me, "Why don't you give it to Maryville."

I like to think that I quoted my mother and said, "We'll see."

My conscience bothered me for over 40 years. Then I wrote a check to the Ed McCaskey Scholarship Fund at Maryville Academy for $278.

During Easter week of 1977, the television movie "Jesus of Nazareth" was aired. For Easter Sunday dinner, I drove my grandfather to my parents' home. After dinner, I suggested that we watch the final installment of "Jesus of Nazareth." After the program, Grandpa said to me, "Thank you for having us watch that."

Different Tests

As a 5-10 eighth grader,
I had to choose between basketball and speed skating.
Basketball had cheerleaders.

After high school and only three more inches,
I had to give up football
Because of eye problems.
So I ran cross-country.
After two seasons,
I had to give up cross-country
Because of allergy problems.
So I wrote humor.
After ten years,
I became immune to many allergies,
But not kryptonite.
So I started running again.
My test was easier than Job's.
His was essay.
Mine was multiple choice.

When I got married and when my sons were baptized, my Saint Mary's classmate, Father Don Nevins, was the priest. He is a very unusual priest; he has never asked me for a penny. The most valuable part of our Saint Mary's School, Class of 1963, 25-year reunion, was his homily.

He was tempted to talk exclusively about things that happened 25 years ago, but he did not yield. He urged the congregation to look forward with something in common. He pointed out that we grew up in the same classrooms and in the same community. The kind of education that we received was very worthwhile.

Father Nevins cited George Gallup's poll of the contribution of Catholic education. "First, Catholic education had great quality. It was always first class. It offered a great deal to the community. Second, Catholic education lifts people up to a future that can lift the next generation up. People obtain a sense of self-esteem and confidence.

"Third, because of the size of Catholic education, it created a sense of community, the meaning of life itself. Fourth, Catholic education focused on values that are focused on Jesus. Values have to be passed on from one generation to another.

"Jesus shared His Life with His Apostles. That life brought the people together as one. As we come together, we ask all of you to pass on the values. People who hear the word of the Lord should share it with one another."

As soon as my sons got out of their cribs, I had them switching hands on the dribble. For several years, I didn't want to coach my sons on their sports teams because I coach them a lot at home. It's still a game of courtesy and grammar. I wanted them to get a different perspective. Besides, every time they did something right in a game, I'd want to call time out and shellac the ball.

When my sons were in seventh and eighth grade, I was one of their football coaches. I was an expert for a long time. Then I became a coach. Before most games, I said to my sons, "Good luck. Do your best because God doesn't grade on a curve. If you do your best, you're a winner regardless of the score."

When my son, Ed, was in eighth grade, we were in second place. When my son, Tom, was in eighth grade, we were in first place. When my son, James, was in eighth grade, we were in first place.

Tommy Rees was our best quarterback. Then he played quarterback for the University of Notre Dame. I gave him a postgame quote that he never used. I wanted him to say, "I was very well coached in junior high."

I taught him what Bill Wade taught me: footwork and follow through. I also taught him to be a servant leader like Jesus Who washed the feet of His Apostles.

My goal as a sports parent was to show interest without meddling. Any playing time was a great opportunity. I took notes at my sons' games. My approach was you were given this much playing time and this is what you did with it. I provided accountability and encouragement. I showed my notes to my sons, but I didn't bother their coaches. Taking notes at the games helped keep me quiet. Then I didn't have as much time to coach or officiate from the stands.

I think the worst thing I ever yelled at an official was, "Jesus died for your sins."

All previous games were preparation for the next one. When my sons played, I thought their coaches were great.

I have insisted that my sons go to church every week. I have also insisted that my sons go to faith based schools at every level: grade school, high school, college, and university. We want to win championships and we want to get to heaven.

Reading and Writing

Mark 8:22-26. "When they arrived at Bethsaida, they brought to him a blind man and begged him to touch him. He took the blind man by the hand and led him outside the village. Putting spittle on his eyes he laid his hands on him and asked, 'Do you see anything?'"
"Looking up he replied, 'I see people looking like trees and walking.'

"Then he laid hands on his eyes a second time and he saw clearly; his sight was restored and he could see everything distinctly. Then he sent him home and said, 'Do not even go into the village.'"

From *Contact Lens History*, we know that "George Jessen became interested in optics because his father was blind."

George "started work as a lens technician surfacing spectacle lenses."

He went to the Chicago College of Optometry which is now the Illinois College of Optometry. One of his lecturers was Newton Wesley.

George did "six years of research in his basement to get lenses to fit and correct Wesley's keratoconus. When successful, they formed the Plastic Contact Lens Company from the same basement. This developed into Wesley-Jessen which, at one time, supplied 90% of all the contact lenses used in the world. They also had a contact lens practice which Jessen ran as the clinician whilst Wesley ran the business. They set up the National Eye Research Foundation and were jointly responsible for the contact lens education of a great many practitioners and for developing the contact lens market around the world."

When I was in second grade at Saint Mary's School in Des Plaines, the school had eye exams in the school hall. I was very nearsighted. That probably began when I used to read at night under the covers with a flashlight. After I got my glasses, I was amazed at how clear everything looked. I started wearing glasses in the spring of 1957 in time to see the movie "Around the World in 80 Days" at the Michael Todd Theater in Chicago. Thank you Doctor Krefft.

I started wearing contact lenses in July 1963. I was working for the Chicago Bears as an office boy. Doctor George Jessen was the Bears' optometrist. So he took great care of me.

After I had lost many contact lenses, Doctor Jessen wrote a letter to my grandfather, George Halas. "I hope that Pat plays football as well as he loses contact lenses."

After my grandfather had a chat with me, I was more careful. It was a very short meeting.

I was a normal Catholic boy. I wanted to play quarterback for the University of Notre Dame. When I was a student at Notre Dame High School, Father Peter Sandonato said to me, "McCaskey, you have a unique writing talent. You should develop it."

I replied, "Father, I have to get to practice."

I was on the sophomore basketball team. I didn't start against Glenbrook North, but I fouled out before the half.

I was perhaps a little too intense and my classmates didn't seem to like me. I wanted to transfer. My parents would have allowed me to transfer, but first they wanted me to talk with my grandfather. He was not a great listener generally, but he was that day.

After he had heard me out, he said, "This is a small test. If you run from this, you'll run when something really difficult happens later in your life. Those fellows are jealous of you because you have a lot of talent. So get in there and show them."

I followed his advice and stayed at Notre Dame. Things didn't get better right away. When I was a junior, I failed the football physical because of a hernia. I played quarterback for the last two plays of the last game. I handed off twice.

When I was a senior, I was the defensive signal caller, right outside linebacker from scrimmage and on the punt return team, blocking back on the punting team, L-2 on the kickoff team, and quarterback. I knew what every position was supposed to do on every play.

Our team finished 9–0, outscored our opponents 341–80, and ranked as one of the top prep teams in the country. I was fortunate enough to be named to the Catholic New World All-American team as a quarterback. It turned out that Grandpa was right.

1966 Notre Dame H.S. Championship Roster

10 Pat McCaskey	Quarterback
12 Bill Harrington	Quarterback
13 Roy Vana	Quarterback
14 Tom Lange	Quarterback
20 Steve Hurley	Halfback
21 Mike Newton	Halfback
22 Owen Bauler	Halfback
23 Kevin Host	Halfback
24 Tom Newton	Halfback
30 Gary Aylesworth	Halfback
31 Charlie Bilodeau	Halfback
32 Dan Governile	Halfback
33 Kevin Saint Dennis	Halfback
34 Pat Hughes	End
35 Gary Lund	Halfback
36 Gary Keating	Halfback

41 Mark Havlis	Fullback
42 Tom Bunzol	Fullback
43 Rich Simko	Fullback
44 Greg Luzinski	Fullback
50 Tom Kusmerz	Center
51 Mike Fragale	Halfback
52 Kevin Murninghan	Center
53 Sam Zuccaro	Center
54 Mike Shaw	Center
55 John Nadolski	Guard
60 Jim Weides	Guard
61 Bill Marquardt	Guard
62 Bob Blaney	Guard
63 Mike Hughes	Guard
64 Glenn O'Grady	Guard
66 Dick Ryglowski	Guard
67 Bob Allen	Guard
68 Bruce Scacco	Guard
69 Gerry Bannon	Guard
71 Rick Rammon	Tackle
72 Brian Kelly	Tackle
73 Bob Rammon	Tackle
74 Jerry Jasinski	Tackle
76 Tom Zizak	Tackle
77 Pete Newell	Tackle
78 Greg Szymanski	Guard
79 John Debbout	Tackle
80 Joe Petricca	End
81 Mike Rolnicki	Tackle
82 Jim Lannon	End
83 Frank Urban	End
84 John Ellefson	End
85 Bob Feltz	Halfback
86 Bob Dorsch	End
87 Ken Powers	End
88 Jim King	End
89 John Clausen	End

SPORTSMANSHIP

University of Notre Dame assistant football coach, Joe Yonto, advised me to go to Cheshire Academy in Connecticut to get another year of playing experience. If I played well at Cheshire, then Notre Dame would seriously consider me for a scholarship.

Coach Yonto wrote a letter about me to Steve Kuk, the Cheshire varsity football coach. Based on that letter, Coach Kuk designed a pro-style offense with me passing often. To prepare for the 1967 Cheshire football season, I ran the mile in 4:37.9, the day after the prom.

While playing catcher that summer, I had a lot of passed balls. When my father asked me why, I said, "I can't follow the ball." On August 28, 1967, my eye doctor, George Jessen, asked me how much my football career meant to me. I said, "It means a lot to me."

He asked, "Does it mean so much to you that you'd risk losing your sight?"

I replied, "No."

After I got home, I quietly and slowly put my clippings and trophies in the garbage.

In a letter dated August 31, 1967, Doctor Jessen wrote to my father.

Dear Ed:
This is a report of our efforts with Patrick these past few days.
He has developed a serious eye problem called keratoconus, a non-inflammatory condition that is a stretching of the cornea. This tissue has a dual function, first it is the front wall of the eye and second it is the major focusing portion of the eye.
As it stretches, it becomes irregular, and double, triple, or more images are seen of every object. Vision becomes similar to a normal person trying to see

beneath the surface of the sea when the water is a little choppy.

A contact lens to keratoconus is like a glass-bottomed boat to the surface of the sea, it remarkably reduces the waviness.

I've enclosed photos of the surface of Pat's eyes. The white circles, that are the photoflash target, are all irregular while actually they should be perfectly round and clear.

Electron microscopic studies of corneal tissue indicated that the outermost layer of the cornea, the epithelium, is effected first and gradually the changes spread throughout the total cornea. The problem, therefore, becomes to avoid further irritation to the epithelium.

Dust, strain, and stress are the three most important things to avoid because when the eyelids squeeze the weakened tissue, they could cause it to stretch to the point of rupture. Therefore, football, baseball, basketball, weightlifting or play or work in dusty surroundings are definitely contraindicated.

We made Pat two pairs of lenses designed to contain the keratoconus. These differ from ones he had previously. Former lenses were designed to stay in place during sports.

He's a fine young man and he could have a great life in spite of the eye condition. My partner, Newton Wesley, is one example of how well a man can do with keratoconus. He's known to the ends of the earth for his work and research in the eye field.

An example closer to your field is Franklin Mieuli of the Warriors and 49ers. He has built quite a name in San Francisco in sports and radio despite keratoconus.

SPORTSMANSHIP

The main thing in these conditions is the proper frame of mind of Pat and his family. Shed no tears, this may be a blessing in disguise. This is usually an affliction of the talented serious person who can and will make a worthwhile contribution to society for a long time to come.
Sincerely yours,
George N. Jessen, O.D.

Because of severe eye problems, I could no longer play contact sports. That's why I try to be nice to everyone. My father said, "The steel of manhood is tempered in the fire of adversity. Everybody has something wrong with them. Everyone's handicap is different because all of us are unique. When we are strong in an area in which others are weak, we are our brother's keeper."

My grandfather told me how he started out in baseball, but had to give that up because of a hip injury. It was only because of the baseball injury, he said, that he turned to football full time. He declared, "It doesn't matter what you do as long as you excel."

Since I had to give up playing football right before I left for Cheshire, I was tempted to feel like Marlon Brando in the movie, "On the Waterfront." Brando said, "I coulda been a contender."

Then something happened so that I did not yield. Before classes started at Cheshire, I was standing in line at the bookstore one day. One student said to another student, "We were going to have a great football team, but the quarterback had to give up football."

I started to get all puffed up with pride. Then the other student asked, "What's his name?"

I fully expected to hear my name. Then the first student replied, "Jeb Swift; he hurt his knee."

Then I saw a notice on the bulletin board about going out for cross country. After getting clearance from Doctor Jessen, I went out for the team.

One meet was against Choate and Stony Brook at Choate. I surprised the leader, Alan Swanson of Stony Brook, as I came from the back of the pack in the rain and passed him. Then he tried to pass me twice. We ended up tied for first at the finish line. At the social, after the race, I found out that he had played quarterback, but he had to give up playing football because of a knee injury from snow skiing.

I placed 14th in the New England championship race and won a medal. I won the conference championship race that finished on the track around the football field at halftime of the homecoming game. I had 13 races and I won nine, while setting seven course records. My nickname was Roadrunner.

I had my College Board scores sent to Indiana University, Miami University in Oxford, Ohio, and Ohio State University. I was accepted at each of these schools. I was all set to go to Ohio State because that is where James Thurber went. The summer before college I began working for Doctor Jessen. His son, Mike, and Mike's wife, Kaaren, had gone to Indiana University. Over the summer, they convinced me to go there, too. I went there sight unseen.

IU had an excellent optometry school and an excellent literature department. They were also the reigning Big Ten cross-country champions.

When I first went to college, I wanted to be an optometrist because of the way Doctor Jessen helped people. He often quoted Jack Benny who said, "I just need these glasses to see."

When he worked in the lab on contact lenses, he often sang "Life is Just a Bowl of Cherries" and "Accentuate the Positive."

In the mornings, when he worked on his correspondence, he often exclaimed, "Paper work is the bane of my existence."

The 1968 IU cross-country team had an A team and a B team. At the beginning of the season, I was the worst runner on the B team. The freshmen had meets at IU, Purdue, the University of Chicago, and IU. By the end of the season, I was the best runner on the B team. The highlight for me was running four miles at the University of Chicago under 22 minutes.

After the season, I had to give up running for 10 years because of eye and allergy problems. During that period, my grandfather, Doctor Halas, kept after me to seek medical solutions. He urged me to remain optimistic and to persist in trying to improve myself.

In the fall of 1969, I was home from college because of eye problems. I worked part-time for Doctor Jessen and I went to Loyola University Chicago part-time.

Without contact lenses, I couldn't see clearly more than six inches. Binoculars magnified a television so much that it appeared as if the screen was six inches from me. So when I was unable to wear my contacts, I could watch television. I started doing that since I discovered the optical illusion by accident in 1969.

In the spring of 1970, I returned to IU and McNutt Quad, which was a co-ed dorm. During the day, I would play the typewriter. At night, I would go over to the ladies' side and read them my bedtime stories to help them sleep better.

In the fall of 1970, I called home from college and said, "I want to be a writer."

My father replied, "It's hard to make a living as a writer. Why don't you do that as an avocation?"

I became an English major, but I really majored in James Thurber and E. B. White. I read their books and the articles about them in the wonderful library on Tenth Street and Jordan Avenue at IU. They had shared an office at *The New Yorker* magazine. They wrote a book together; it was entitled *Is Sex Necessary?*

White helped Thurber with his style. White also saved Thurber's cartoons from the wastebasket. Thurber performed a revue of his work on Broadway. White had an aversion to public speaking. He never accepted his many awards in person.

Thurber had eye problems and he eventually went blind. White had a terrible time with allergies. Two performances that White did give were the readings of two of his classic children's novels, *Charlotte's Web*, and *The Trumpet of the Swan*, on record.

My favorite Thurber fable is "The Little Girl and the Wolf." At the end, "the little girl took an automatic out of her basket and shot the wolf dead. Moral: It's not so easy to fool little girls nowadays as it used to be."

My favorite White essay is "Freedom." In it is this sentence. "Or to an older youth, encountering for the first time a great teacher who by some chance word or mood awakens something and the youth beginning to breathe as an individual and conscious of strength in his vitals."

I also studied Mark Twain as a performer because of the Hal Holbrook recordings. When I am forced into hearing a person talk incessantly, I remember a Mark Twain line. "It's a terrible death to be talked to death."

In the summer of 1971, I had more eye and allergy problems. So I moved back into my parents' home and commuted to Loyola University Chicago for 2 years. In the fall of 1971, instead of playing quarterback for the University of Notre Dame, I had an essay and a poem published in the Loyola literary magazine, *Cadence.*

The editor my first year had a running argument with the editor my second year about whether my essay or my poem was the best thing ever published in the magazine. I was non-committal.

When I had gathered my strength, I went back to Indiana University for my final two semesters. I lived in Alpha Epsilon Phi Sorority with seventy ladies as their houseboy.

During my first sorority semester, in the fall of 1973, my writing professor, Scott Sanders, suggested that I start my own humor publication. So I mimeographed my writings for the ladies. Each Thursday night, after midnight, I put an essay or a poem in their mailboxes.

During the second sorority semester, in the winter and spring of 1974, after I had found out that I was allergic to duplicating fluid, I performed collections of my writings on Friday evenings in the dining hall while the ladies were eating dessert.

My oral interpretation professor, Doctor Hawes, had each student choose a writer for their concert reading at the end of the semester. I chose me. I still have evaluation notes from my classmates and my teacher.

I gave up living in a sorority to work for the Chicago Bears.

Because of eye and allergy problems, it took me 6 years to complete my undergraduate class work. My last class at IU was Thursday, June 20, 1974. I started working for the Bears full time the following Monday.

I went to the Bears' training camp as the publicity assistant. My father introduced me to the Bears' press corps and asked me, "Would you like to show these guys some of those poems that you've been writing?"

I replied, "Not at this time."

The players later went on strike.

It was a great privilege to work with George Halas on a day-to-day basis. There were no problems, only opportunities.

One morning at the office, I was telling my Uncle Mugs and my father that I had had speaking engagements the last three nights in a row. My grandfather happened to be walking by and overheard the conversation. He asked, "Where are you speaking tonight?"

I replied, "I don't have a speaking engagement tonight."

He said, "That's too bad."

In February 1977, he sent me a wonderful note. "Long ago I determined that work exceeds talent. Work every day by writing every day. Make me even more proud than I am of you. Love, George."

One of my father's favorite Bible passages was Sirach 3:12-14, "My son, take care of your father when he is old; grieve him not as long as he lives. Even if his mind fails, be considerate with him; revile him not in the fullness of your strength. For kindness to a father will not be forgotten, it will serve as a sin offering – it will take lasting root."

Fullness of Strength

When Peter and John arrived
At the Tomb,
John let Peter enter first
Because
He was the elder.
John had run
And
Peter might have told John that
He should do some stretching
Before entering.
When you are spiritually attuned,
God gives you the strength
To be obedient to His will.
When you are no longer living
In your parents' home
And
Your father asks you
To help him
With the gardening,
Remember:
Only a fool forgets his roots.

Different Tests

As a 5-10 eighth grader,
I had to choose
between basketball and speed-skating.
Basketball had cheerleaders.
After high school and only three more inches,
I had to give up football
because of eye problems.
So I ran cross-country.
After two seasons,
I had to give up cross-country

because of allergy problems.
So I wrote humor.
After ten years,
I became immune to many allergies,
but not kryptonite.
So I started running again.
My test was easier than Job's.
His was essay.
Mine was multiple choice.

One day my grandfather called me into his office.
He said, "Get a master's degree."
I asked, "Will you pay for it?
He said, "Yes."
It was a very short meeting. During the off-seasons, I went at night to DePaul University. I earned a master's degree in the interdisciplinary studies of business, writing, and performing.

In 1980, the Bears had a half mile run to start training camp. After I had finished eighth, my grandfather was very mad at me because I didn't win.

In 1981, the Bears had a half mile run to start training camp. One player, Kris Haines, finished ahead of me. He was later cut.

In 1982, I received a promotion. The Bears had a mile and a half run to start training camp. After I had finished first, Walter Payton said to me, "I tried to stay with you. Then I said, 'That boy is crazy.'"

That made all the training worthwhile. The players later went on strike.

On Thursday, July 25, 2001, I ran the National Masters 5000 meters at Louisiana State University. I finished first in my age group. So I was a national champion.

SPORTSMANSHIP

My father kept after me to get corneal transplants. On Monday, April 7, 2003, Doctor Rubenstein gave me a right corneal transplant. On Monday, February 9, 2004, he gave me a left corneal transplant. I don't know who the donors were, but my father was the inspiration. After those two corneal transplants, along with two cataract surgeries, my eyes are fine now. I don't need glasses or contact lenses for anything, but I still can't play quarterback for the University of Notre Dame. I'm not bitter.

When my eye doctor, Jon Rubenstein, was a boy, he went to Bears' games with his father. Jon's sister complained that she never got to go to a game. The weather happened to be cold and rainy on December 12, 1965, so Rubenstein said that his sister could go to the game against the San Francisco 49ers in his place.

Well, Jon undoubtedly wished he could have attended the game his sister witnessed. The Bears throttled the 49ers 61–20 as Gale Sayers scored six touchdowns.

Here are some lines from the Hebrew poet Yehuda Amichai. "The passing years have calmed me and brought healing to my heart and rest to my eyes."

Thank you to Doctor Rubenstein for restoring my vision.

Patrick McCaskey

Sports and Faith

When I was a student at Saint Mary's School in Des Plaines, the City of Destiny, I was in the Bluebirds Reading Group. I used to enjoy getting up in the front of the class and reading to my classmates.

When I was a sophomore at Notre Dame High School in Niles, the All-American City, my writing teacher, Father Sandonato, said to me, "McCaskey, you have a unique writing talent. You should develop it."

I replied, "Father, I have to get to practice."

For my high school graduation, my parents gave me a typewriter. A few years later, I called home from Indiana University and I said to my father, "I want to be a writer."

My father said, "That's wonderful."

Now I get to read what I have written.

The Ten Commandments of Football

I. Football is a wonderful game. There's blocking and tackling and much, much more. Be enthusiastic.

II. Weddings, births, and vacations should take place during the off-seasons.

III. Remember the Hupmobile and the original meeting.

IV. All previous games are preparation for the next one.

V. Obey the personal conduct policy.

VI. Work for the good of the league.

VII. Win championships with sportsmanship.

VIII. You shall not criticize the officials.

IX. You shall not covet other teams' coaches or players.

X. Game times are tentative and subject to flexible scheduling.

SPORTSMANSHIP

The gifts of football are stamina, courage, teamwork, self-denial, sportsmanship, selflessness, and respect for authority.

If the Apostles had played football, they would have been a great team. Jesus would have been the coach like George Halas.

Peter would have been the quarterback like Bill Wade. Andrew was Peter's brother. They would have been used to playing catch in the yard. Let's put Andrew at tight end like Mike Ditka.

James the son of Zebedee and his brother, John, were known as the sons of thunder. They would have been the running backs like Walter Payton and Matt Suhey.

We don't know much about Philip, Bartholomew, James the son of Alphaeus, Thaddeus, and Simon the Canaanean. So, they would have been the linemen like Jim Covert, Ted Karras, Jay Hilgenberg, Tom Thayer, and Bob Wetoska.

Thomas and Matthew would have been linebackers like Bill George and Mike Singletary. If Mike Singletary had been an Apostle, the other Apostles wouldn't have slept in the Garden of Gethsemane.

Matthias, who replaced Judas, would have been the punter like Maury Buford.

Paul would have been a writer and a speaker like me. He wrote a lot of letters even though the Corinthians were the only ones who ever wrote back. Everywhere he spoke there was either a revival or a riot.

What did William Shakespeare's father say to William Shakespeare?

Make plays.

My grandfather, George Halas, started the Chicago Bears in 1920. He played on the team for 10 years. He coached the team for 40 years. He was the owner of the team for 62 years, until he died in 1983 at the age of 88. He left the team to his family. We are trying to extend his legacy. That legacy has two parts: win championships and help other people.

I started going to Bears' games when I was five. My brothers and I sat on an army blanket next to the Bears' bench while my grandfather coached. My grandfather once said to an official, "No man is completely worthless. You can always serve as a horrible example."

After the games, we waited for Grandpa outside the Bears' locker room. Regardless of the outcome of the game, he said to each of us, "Hi Pal, how about a kiss for Grandpa?"

Sometimes I was allowed to accompany my grandfather to the Pink Poodle press room at Wrigley Field where he met with reporters after the games. Once, after he had let out a string of profanities following a particularly painful loss, he remembered that I was sitting next to him. Then he said, "Now fellas, all of that was off the record."

I started going to Bears' training camps when I was seven. George Blanda taught us how to kick. Bill George taught us how to play linebacker. Bill Wade taught us how to play quarterback.

When my grandfather coached the Bears, the players had to start training camp with the Halas Mile. That's how I got interested in running. As busy as he was, he knew the value of daily exercise. His motivational slogan was, "Never go to bed a loser."

When Grandpa received the Sword of Loyola in 1979, he said, "...Sixty years ago I offered my heart and my helmet to the Lord. My heart is still beating and my helmet still fits. I pray the Divine Coach finds me worthy to be on His first team..."

The last 5 years of Grandpa's life, his grandchildren took him out to dinner on his birthday. On Wednesday, February 2, 1983, his eighty-eighth birthday, we should have known that something was amiss because he told us that he did not swear anymore. He also said, "May the Good Lord grant all of you as long and as wonderful a life as I have had."

Before the Bears play a game, Mass and Chapel Service are available in the team hotel. We try to get the Pope because we think our games are important. We offer $100 and two tickets. Chuck Simpson said, "He probably doesn't know who to bring."

True or false: Martin Luther King Junior played quarterback for Morehouse College. True

True or false: His team was constantly penalized for delay of game because he kept making speeches in the huddle. False

For the first 6 years of my parents' marriage, I was not here. I only know the legend. Three wise men from the East, Bert Bell, Bill Lennox, and Art Rooney, followed a bright star until they found my father, Ed McCaskey, at the University of Pennsylvania Theater. They approved of him, much to the despair of Chief Papa Bear.

My mother's Indian name was Laughing Girl. My father put my mother on a donkey and they fled to Baltimore and they got married. In lieu of money, they gave the donkey to the priest. More than ten months after the wedding, my brother Mike was born in Pennsylvania. He was wrapped in an army blanket and laid in an open footlocker.

Across the Atlantic Ocean, Hitler had captured much of Europe. My father had heard that Hitler's ultimate plan was the capture of Ireland. So my father defeated Hitler with a sling and five smooth stones.

Upon my father's return to Pennsylvania, he met my brother Tim who cried and cried at the introduction. My sister Ellen was also born in Pennsylvania. When my mother was pregnant with me, the family moved to Illinois.

When I was seven months in my mother's womb, she received the blessing for expectant mothers. When my parents brought me home from the hospital, the lilacs in the side yard were in beautiful full bloom. Mary, Ned, Anne, George, Rich, Brian, and Joe were also born in Illinois.

In 1966, I went to the Bears' training camp at Saint Joseph's College in Rensselaer, Indiana, with my high school football teammate Ken Powers, my brother Ned, and my brother George. At the start of the visit, Grandpa called us over to his golf cart after practice. He gave us some pocket money. When tight end Mike Ditka observed the transaction, he came over to participate. Mike asked, "Hey Coach, how about some of that for me?"

Grandpa replied, "Never mind."

His favorite parable was the one about the workers in the vineyard.

When I was a high school senior, I was an All-American quarterback and a 4:37 miler. While playing catcher the summer after graduation, I had a lot of passed balls. When my father asked me why, I said, "I can't follow the ball."

On August 28, 1967, my eye doctor, George Jessen, asked me, "How much does your football career mean to you?"

I said, "It means a lot to me."

He asked, "Does it mean so much to you that you'd risk losing your sight?"

I replied, "No."

My father said, "The steel of manhood is tempered in the fire of adversity. Everybody has something wrong with them. Everyone's handicap is different because each of us is unique. When we are strong in an area in which others are weak, we are our brother's keeper."

In the fall of 1971, instead of playing quarterback for the University of Notre Dame, I had an essay and a poem published in *Cadence*, the literary magazine of Loyola University Chicago.

When I was a senior at Indiana University, my oral interpretation professor, Doctor Hawes, said that everyone in the class would give a concert reading of the writer of their choice. I chose me.

I was living in a sorority as a houseboy for seventy ladies. I gave that up to work for the Bears.

In the summer of 1974, I was fresh out of college and I went to the Bears' training camp as the publicity assistant. My father introduced me to the Bears' press corps and asked me, "Would you like to show these guys some of those poems that you've been writing?"

I replied, "Not at this time."

The players later went on strike.

In 1981, the Bears had a half mile run to start training camp. One player, Kris Haines, finished ahead of me. He was later cut.

In 1982, the Bears had a mile and a half run to start training camp. After I had finished first, Walter Payton said to me, "I tried to stay with you." Then I said, 'That boy is crazy.'"

That made all the training worthwhile. The players later went on strike.

For my 33rd birthday, I received permission to date. After nine months of prayer, I met Gretchen through mutual friends. Four months later, we looked at a house that was for sale. After the tour, Gretchen asked me, "Why are you looking for a house?"

I crossed my mouth with the back of my right hand and muttered, "In case you want to get married." She accepted my invitation.

We have been blessed with three sons: Ed, Tom, and Jim. They were named after my father and his brothers in the same birth order.

In 2003, I had a right corneal transplant. In 2004, I had a left corneal transplant. My eyes are fine now, but I still can't play for the Bears. Mitch Trubisky is wearing my number.

I left the swing set up on purpose because I was hoping for grandchildren. I was mocked and scorned. Now that I am a grandfather, I am a man of vision: Christopher Columbus, the Wright Brothers, Pat McCaskey.

When I started working for the Bears, my hair was brown, curly, and thick. Now my hair is white, straight, and thin. God is protecting my marriage. I was too good looking.

I've had the good fortune to be associated with the Bears all my life. In the process, I've learned how to appreciate it and cope with it.

The football business is an emotional rollercoaster. God is constant.

Since I am Catholic, I attend Saint Mary's and Saint Pat's Churches in Lake Forest, the City of Trees. Because my wife, Gretchen is Protestant, I escort her to Christ Church Lake Forest. As a result of going to those churches, I have a more abundant life. It's good to get a second opinion.

Catholic homilies are short. Protestant sermons are long. Catholics sing two or three verses of a hymn. Protestants sing every verse two or three times. Protestants have excellent children's nurseries.

Gretchen and I are also active in Bible Studies. You may have read about my wife in Proverbs 31; verses 10-31 describe the ideal wife. When I need a break from my wife's efforts to improve me, I say, "That's enough reformation for awhile."

Her only fault is that she tells me how to drive. After she apologizes to me, I say, "That's all right. That's okay. We'll stay married anyway."

I sort of have two wives: Gretchen and the Navigation Lady. My wife is Protestant, but she's the only one who would marry me.

There are 1,328 chapters in the Bible. If we read 26 Bible chapters a week, we can read the Bible in 51 weeks and have a week off for Christmas break. We can use that week to write thank you notes for our Christmas gifts. When we need to know the truth, we need to read the Bible. We can read the newspapers for information. We can read the Bible for inspiration.

As one out of many Bears' inheritors, I have prayerfully considered the future of the team. Here is what I have discerned.

George Halas was my grandfather and that's a great legacy. I work for the Bears and that's a great opportunity. I have it made because Christ died for my sins which we don't have time to discuss right now.

I believe that God has a plan for everyone and for every family. We have the freedom to be obedient. I think that God's plan for me is to work for the Bears. I choose to be obedient.

309

God gave me faith, a wonderful family, and a great legacy. As a mature Boy Scout, I feel prepared.

I hope that we never sell the team even though that would give us a lot of money. Satan offered Jesus all the kingdoms of the world. The Waltons never sold Waltons' Mountain.

From Robert Pinsky's essay, "Responsibilities of the Poet," we know this. "So one great task we have to answer for is the keeping of an art that we did not invent, but were given, so that others who come after us can have it if they want it, as free to choose it and change it as we have been."

The same responsibility applies to our Bears' legacy. With God's faith, I try to be obedient to His plan for my life. With God's hope, I try to be a voice of encouragement. With God's love, I try to exemplify Jesus.

Sports Faith International recognizes people who are successful in sports while living exemplary lives. We honor high school, college, and professional athletes, coaches, and teams on Pentecost Vigil.

In His Steps
We are not called
To walk on water
Or change water into wine
Or multiply loaves and fishes
Or raise the dead
Or be scourged
At the pillar
Or walk to Calvary
With a cross
On which
To be crucified.
We are not called

SPORTSMANSHIP

To do
What is impossible
For us.
Christ performed all
Of those heavenly deeds
At a three-year pace.
It is
For us to follow in His steps.
Live for righteousness
Without being self-righteous.

Moving On
In relation
To the parable
Of the prodigal son,
I have been the younger son.
I have been rebellious.
I have been the older son.
I have been resentful.
Now my goal is to be the father.
Forgive others as I have been forgiven.

When I was a child, there was a series of books called "Vision Books." They were about saints and other wonderful people. My mother gave us these books for ourselves and for our friends when we were invited to their birthday parties. My two favorite books in this series were *Champions in Sports and Spirit* and *More Champions in Sports and Spirit.* Ed Fitzgerald wrote both books.

Regardless of what happens on the field, let's behave like champions in sports and spirit. Let's not analyze. Let's not denigrate. Let's not second guess. Let's not diagnose injuries before we've read the x-rays. Let sportsmanship prevail.

The Beatitudes of Football

Blessed are the champions in sports and spirit, for they watch the games with sportsmanship.

Blessed are they who attend funerals, for they provide condolences.

Blessed are they who do not fight, for they will not be penalized.

Blessed are they who hunger and thirst for fitness, for they have a healthy lifestyle.

Blessed are the helpful, for they will improve the game.

Blessed are they who play clean, for they are doing God's will.

Blessed are the foot-washers, for they will be called servants of God.

Blessed are they who go to Church, for they hear the wonderful news of salvation.

Blessed are you when they mock and scorn you because of your faith. These are opportunities to live the gospel.

The Packers have 13 championships; the Bears have nine. This is disconcerting. The Packers are doing very well for an expansion team.

We want to win championships with sportsmanship. We do good works quietly, for God's glory. We fear God and we respect our opponents. We are trying to keep the Bears going until The Second Coming. We work diligently and we trust God for the results. Like the Magi who followed the great star, we go forward in faith.

We are grateful for at least the following: God created a wonderful world in six days; Jesus died for our sins, including fumbles; when we need The Holy

Spirit, He is there. He is even there when we think that we don't need Him.

We are hopeful that the world will not end until the Bears have the most championships. Instead of the Super Bowl Most Valuable Player saying that he is going to Disney World, he could say that he is going to church or mosque or temple. After the presentation of the trophy, The Second Coming would be a great postgame show.

We want to play our games with cooperation that is like an Amish barn-raising. We go to Church and Bible Study and have daily devotions. Our mandate is to love God and each other. In our attempts to love, we are often funny.

Halas Hall is a place of work and not a den of thieves. It is a halfway house to heaven. Instead of saying, "Please be quiet," we say, "Please become a mime."

We give away the credit and we take the blame. We criticize privately and we praise publicly. Instead of singing as soloists, we sing as a chorus. We provide accountability and positive reinforcement for each other.

From William Bennett's book, *The Moral Compass*, we know that "Goethe once said that you must labor to possess what you have inherited. 'If we are not grateful for our gifts and opportunities, we are not likely to value them, and if we do not value them, we are not likely to work hard to preserve them and improve them.'"

If you know some people who are not Bear fans, don't be discouraged. Some of the greatest Christians started out as atheists. Jesus forgave the good thief. All they have to do is repent.

A Bears' Prayer

Bitterness is spiritual cancer.   Forgiveness is
spiritual rapture.
Weather is a reminder that God is The Boss.
The Spirit strengthens us, even after a loss.
Jesus Christ is The Man; Salvation is the plan.
When we dance God's dance, He gives us
another chance.
God's work is efficient; His food is sufficient.
Here's a part of my prayers; bear down, Chicago
Bears.

Jesus Came to Establish Division

Our division is the NFC North.
We often play Lions, Packers, Vikings.
When you turn the other cheek, stand your
ground.
Let's establish a solid running game.

Some attend every game; some do not.
Let there be amnesty for the no shows.

Jesus did not come to establish peace.
That's why football is a collision sport.
Some root for the Cubs; some root for the Sox.
The important thing is we're all Bear fans.

Jesus was here to divide households.
Thank God for homilies to explain why.
We must follow the voice of Jesus Christ
from conception to a natural death.

PART SIX: RESOLUTIONS

Resolution for Pete Newell and Joe Petricca

STATE OF ILLINOIS
COUNTY OF LAKE
RESOLUTION

WHEREAS, Pete Newell and Joe Petricca matriculated at Saint Paul of the Cross School and Notre Dame High School, and

WHEREAS, Pete Newell and Joe Petricca played on the 1966 Notre Dame High School varsity football team that was 9–0 and outscored opponents 341–80, and

WHEREAS, Pete Newell had a 38-yard interception return for a touchdown versus Saint Francis in the homecoming game on Friday, October 14, 1966, and

WHEREAS, Joe Petricca was the only junior to start every game on defense, and

WHEREAS, Pete Newell had 69 tackles, 3 fumble recoveries, and 1 interception on the 1966 team, and

WHEREAS, Joe Petricca had 55 tackles, 1 fumble recovery, and 3 interceptions on the 1966 team, and

WHEREAS, Pete Newell played football for the University of Michigan, and

WHEREAS, Joe Petricca played football for the University of Utah, and

WHEREAS, Pete Newell coached football at Fenwick High School, and

WHEREAS, Joe Petricca coached football at Palatine High School, and

WHEREAS, Pete Newell and Joe Petricca served with distinction on the Notre Dame College Prep Governance Board, and

WHEREAS, Pete Newell and Joe Petricca were not allowed to talk in the huddle, but they made up for it in the board meetings.

NOW THEREFORE BE IT RESOLVED that Sports Faith International adopts this Resolution to honor and hold in high esteem Pete Newell and Joe Petricca. Adopted the 28th day of August 2018.

Patrick McCaskey

Loyola Academy

Loyola Academy in Wilmette, Illinois, opened in 1909 offering Jesuit education to boys. It moved from Chicago to Wilmette and has become co-ed. Sought after for its excellent academic programs, the Loyola Ramblers have a history of success in sports. The school boosts several NFL players. The Ramblers football team were recent 8A Champions.

Resolution for Loyola Academy

STATE OF ILLINOIS
COUNTY OF LAKE
RESOLUTION
WHEREAS, the Loyola Academy Football Team became the 8A State Champions on Saturday, November 24, 2018, and
WHEREAS, in order to attain this position of being the finest 8A high school football team in the state of Illinois, the 2018 Loyola Academy Football Team had to practice long and arduous hours and dedicate themselves totally to achieve this goal, and
WHEREAS, the 2018 Loyola Academy Football Team represented the Chicago Catholic League in an exemplary fashion that brought gratitude and a sense of community spirit to our entire area, and
WHEREAS, the 2018 Loyola Academy Football Team won every playoff game, and
WHEREAS, the 2018 Loyola Academy Football Team worked very well with Misericordia, and
WHEREAS, the 2018 Loyola Academy Football Team let me speak at their banquet.
NOW THEREFORE BE IT RESOLVED that Sports Faith International adopts this resolution to honor and

hold the 2018 Loyola Academy Football Team in high esteem.
Adopted the tenth day of December 2018.
Patrick McCaskey

Resolution for Kevin Matthews

STATE OF ILLINOIS
COUNTY OF LAKE
RESOLUTION

WHEREAS, Kevin Matthews was born on March 12, 1956, and

WHEREAS, Kevin Matthews and his wife, Debra, have two children, Trevor and Teage, and two grandchildren, Trynn and Rhett, and

WHEREAS, Kevin Matthews is a well-known ABC and CBS radio personality in Chicago, and

WHEREAS, Kevin Matthews was the drive-time radio host for seventeen years on AM 1000 The Loop and ABC and CBS radio, and

WHEREAS, Kevin Matthews was the voice of his sports commentator, Jim Shorts, and other characters, and

WHEREAS, Kevin Matthews wrote the book "Broken Mary" a story of his early years in radio and stand-up comedy, his successful career, his struggle with MS, his awakening to the dignity of women, and, importantly, his chance encounter with a broken statue of Mary left next to a dumpster and all that happened as a result, and

WHEREAS, Kevin Matthews told the story with signature good humor, this confession of the brokenness of mankind is touchingly honest, personally inspiring, and full of hope, and

WHEREAS, Kevin Matthews receives the Semper Altius Award from Everest Academy.

NOW THEREFORE BE IT RESOLVED that Sports Faith International adopts this Resolution to honor and hold in high esteem Kevin Matthews.

Adopted the 9th day of February 2019.
Patrick McCaskey

Patrick McCaskey

Resolution for Ben Ruf

STATE OF ILLINOIS
COUNTY OF LAKE
RESOLUTION
WHEREAS, Ben Ruf was born November 29, 1956, in Seattle, Washington, and
WHEREAS, Ben Ruf was the godson of former light heavy weight champion of the world, Melio Bettina and Ben's aunt, Lillian,
WHEREAS, Ben Ruf chose John Mary Vianney for his Confirmation name because of the underdog story, and
WHEREAS, Ben Ruf was a student at Sacred Heart School in Saratoga, California, and
WHEREAS, Ben Ruf played tennis and basketball and ran track for De Smet Jesuit High School in Saint Louis, and
WHEREAS, Ben Ruf met his wife, Linda, when he was a senior in high school and she was a junior, and
WHEREAS, Ben and Linda had a good time at the prom, and
WHEREAS, Ben and Linda went to the University of Notre Dame which was named after God's Mother, and
WHEREAS, Ben earned an MBA and a law degree from Washington University in Saint Louis, and
WHEREAS, Ben taught high school biology, coached basketball, and was the athletic director at Northridge Prep, and
WHEREAS, Ben & Linda married each other on January 3, 1981, and
WHEREAS, Ben & Linda have been blessed with six children and five grandchildren, and
WHEREAS, Ben was a lawyer for two years in Saint Louis, and

SPORTSMANSHIP

WHEREAS, Ben has retired from Credit Suisse after working there for thirty years as a bond salesman and sales manager, and

WHEREAS, Ben & Linda live in Sauganash in Chicago and go to Queen of All Saints Church, and

WHEREAS, Ben has been in Chicago Legatus for six years, including two years as president, and

WHEREAS, Ben is a consultant for life for Chicago Legatus, and

WHEREAS, Ben is a fan of the group Mercy Me, and

WHEREAS, Ben has renounced Satan and all his works and all his empty promises.

NOW THEREFORE BE IT RESOLVED that Sports Faith International adopts this Resolution to honor and hold in high esteem Ben Ruf.

Adopted the 28th day of March 2019.

Patrick McCaskey

Resolution for Mark Balasa

STATE OF ILLINOIS

COUNTY OF LAKE

RESOLUTION

WHEREAS, Mark Balasa was born July 2, 1958, in Petoskey, Michigan, and

WHEREAS, Mark Balasa was the godson of his uncle, Bob Beales, and his aunt, Lillian Marshall, and

WHEREAS, Mark Balasa chose John for his Confirmation name because his cousin, John Gibes, was his sponsor, and

WHEREAS, Mark Balasa was a student at Saint Francis School in Petoskey, and

WHEREAS, Mark Balasa wrestled and ran track for Petoskey High School, and

WHEREAS, Mark Balasa went to Central Michigan University for undergraduate work and the College of Denver for a master's degree, and

WHEREAS, Mark Balasa is a certified public accountant and a certified financial planner, and

WHEREAS, Mark Balasa has his own firm, Balasa, Dinverno, Foltz, LLC, that does wealth management, and

WHEREAS, Mark Balasa met his wife, Laurel, at a Catholic Alumni Club in 1983, and

WHEREAS, Mark & Laurel married each other on July 6, 1985, and

WHEREAS, the Chicago Bears won the 1985 Championship, and

WHEREAS, Mark & Laurel have been blessed with two sons, and

WHEREAS, Mark & Laurel live in Palatine and go to Saint Theresa Church, and

SPORTSMANSHIP

WHEREAS, Mark has been in Chicago Legatus for six years, including two years as president, and

WHEREAS, Mark is a consultant for life for Chicago Legatus, and

WHEREAS, Mark has renounced Satan and all his works and all his empty promises.

NOW THEREFORE BE IT RESOLVED that Sports Faith International adopts this Resolution to honor and hold in high esteem Mark Balasa.

Adopted the 28th day of March 2019.

Patrick McCaskey

Resolution for Father Conyers

STATE OF ILLINOIS
COUNTY OF LAKE
RESOLUTION

WHEREAS, Rich Conyers was born on October 7, 1942, at Holy Cross Hospital in Chicago, and

WHEREAS, Rich Conyers was baptized at Saint Margaret of Scotland Church in Chicago, and

WHEREAS, Rich Conyers chose Francis for his Confirmation name in honor of Saint Francis of Assisi, and

WHEREAS, Rich Conyers chose a family friend, Ted Asetek, to be his sponsor, and

WHEREAS, Rich Conyers went to Saint Gilbert School in Grayslake and Saint Joseph School in Round Lake, and

WHEREAS, Rich Conyers went to Holy Cross Seminary in Notre Dame, Indiana, and

WHEREAS, Rich Conyers went to the novitiate in Jordan, Minnesota, and

WHEREAS, Rich Conyers was a philosophy major at the University of Notre Dame, and

WHEREAS, Rich Conyers led the acapella choir and taught Gregorian Chant at Holy Cross Seminary, and

WHEREAS, Rich Conyers earned a master's degree in theology at Holy Cross College in Washington, DC, and

WHEREAS, Rich Conyers was ordained a deacon at Moreau Seminary in South Bend and was assigned to Little Flower Parish in South Bend as a deacon, and

WHEREAS, Rich Conyers was ordained as a priest at Sacred Heart Basilica in South Bend on April 12, 1969, and

WHEREAS, Father Conyers was a full-time student in the doctoral studies of the History of Art and

Architecture at the State University of New York-Binghamton, including one semester on the island of Malta, and

WHEREAS, Father Conyers was a rector for ten years at Keenan Hall at the University of Notre Dame, and

WHEREAS, Father Conyers taught the History of Art and Architecture and Biblical Foundation at Holy Cross College and Saint Mary's College, and

WHEREAS, Father Conyers did landscaping and was the Chairman of the Fine Arts Department and the Theology Department at Notre Dame College Prep, and

WHEREAS, Father Conyers begged to stay at Notre Dame College Prep, and

WHEREAS, Father Conyers was a liturgical consultant at Notre Dame Parish in Clarendon Hills, and

WHEREAS, Father Conyers was at Notre Dame College Prep for over twenty years and was the catalyst for the Holy Cross Congregation to remain associated with the school, and

WHEREAS, Father Conyers has celebrated many, many Don Baptisms, weddings, and funerals, and

WHEREAS, Father Conyers has renounced Satan and all his works and all his empty promises.

NOW THEREFORE BE IT RESOLVED that Sports Faith International adopts this resolution to honor and hold in high esteem Father Conyers.

Adopted the 13th day of April 2019, fifty years and a day after his ordination.

Patrick McCaskey

Resolution for Nancy Saviola

STATE OF ILLINOIS

COUNTY OF LAKE

RESOLUTION

WHEREAS, Nancy Rizzo was born April 14, 1919, in Melrose Park, Illinois, and

WHEREAS, Nancy Rizzo attended elementary school in Melrose Park, and

WHEREAS, Nancy Rizzo loved school and singing and she had a beautiful voice, and

WHEREAS, Nancy Rizzo had six sisters and one brother, and

WHEREAS, Nancy Rizzo worked at a women's clothing store, Allison's, in Hillside until she got married, and

WHEREAS, Nancy Rizzo married her childhood sweetheart, David Donald "Doc" Saviola at Our Lady of Mount Carmel in Melrose Park in 1939, and

WHEREAS, Nancy Saviola has received the sacraments of Baptism, Confession, Holy Communion, Confirmation, and Matrimony, and

WHEREAS, Nancy Saviola is not in a hurry to receive the sacrament of Extreme Unction, and

WHEREAS, when Doc returned from World War II, which we won, she was ironing at night and she was so excited that she walked into a screen door, and

WHEREAS, Doc & Nancy Saviola had five children, eighteen grandchildren and many, many great grandchildren, and

WHEREAS, Doc & Nancy were married from 1939 until Doc died in 2004, sixty-five years, and

WHEREAS, Nancy Saviola was a really, really good cook and had an extremely clean stove, and

WHEREAS, Nancy Saviola liked fashion and clothing and was always dressed beautifully, and

SPORTSMANSHIP

WHEREAS, on April 14, 1978, the Bears traded Wally Chambers to the Tampa Bay Buccaneers for a 1979 1st round draft choice, Dan Hampton, and

WHEREAS, Nancy Saviola has been to the Bears' training camp while wearing her pearls in her nineties, and

WHEREAS, Nancy Saviola has been going to Bears' games up until 2001, and

WHEREAS, Nancy Saviola went to Mass regularly and was devoted to the Pope who also went to Mass regularly, and

WHEREAS, Nancy Saviola has renounced Satan and all his works and all his empty promises.

NOW THEREFORE BE IT RESOLVED that Sports Faith International adopts this Resolution to honor and hold in high esteem Nancy Saviola.

Adopted the 14th day of April 2019.

Patrick McCaskey

Jessica Noonan's Agent

Resolution for the Metropolitan Water Reclamation District

STATE OF ILLINOIS
COUNTY OF LAKE
RESOLUTION

WHEREAS, the Metropolitan Water Reclamation District is an award-winning, special purpose government agency responsible for wastewater treatment and stormwater management, and

WHEREAS, the Metropolitan Water Reclamation District's mission is to protect the health and safety of the public, the quality of the water supply source (Lake Michigan), improve and protect the quality of water in watercourses, protect businesses and homes from flood damages, and manage water as a vital resource, and

WHEREAS, Commissioner Mariyana Spyropoulos has honored the Chicago Bears with a Resolution celebrating the team's 100th season.

NOW THEREFORE BE IT RESOLVED that Sports Faith International adopts this resolution to honor and hold in high esteem the Metropolitan Water Reclamation District of Greater Chicago.

Adopted the 6th day of June 2019.
Patrick McCaskey

Resolution for Cheshire Academy

STATE OF ILLINOIS
COUNTY OF LAKE
RESOLUTION

WHEREAS, Cheshire Academy was founded in 1794 as the Episcopal Academy of Connecticut, and

WHEREAS, in 1917, the school was renamed the Roxbury School, and trained young men exclusively for the purpose of attending nearby Yale University, and

WHEREAS, later known as Cheshire Academy, the school was the first private academic institution to accept international students dating back to the 1850s, and

WHEREAS, Cheshire Academy is currently the only independent school to offer the International Baccalaureate Diploma Programme in the state of Connecticut, and

WHEREAS, Cheshire Academy is a selective, co-educational college preparatory school located in Cheshire, Connecticut, and

WHEREAS, Cheshire Academy currently enrolls 362 students from approximately 30 countries and 13 states in grades 9 through 12 plus a postgraduate year, and

WHEREAS, Cheshire Academy has a campus of 104 acres and is located in the center of the town of Cheshire, and

WHEREAS, the campus includes five residential dormitories and facilities including the John J. White '38 Science & Technology Center and the Humanities Building, and

WHEREAS, all areas of the campus are equipped with wireless access and fiber optic network with 30 mb access to the internet, and

WHEREAS, in the fall of 2011, Cheshire Academy saw the dedication of the new Simosa track and field, and

WHEREAS, Cheshire Academy is accredited by the Connecticut Association of Independent Schools, the New England Association of Schools and Colleges, and the Association of Boarding Schools, and

WHEREAS, Cheshire Academy holds memberships in the National Association of Independent Schools, the Secondary School Admission Test Board, and the IB Diploma Programme, and

WHEREAS, Alumni, Parents, Students, Faculty, and Friends of Cheshire Academy have a weekend-long celebration to commemorate its historic 225th Year Anniversary, June 7-9, 2019.

NOW THEREFORE BE IT RESOLVED that Sports Faith International adopts this resolution to honor and hold in high esteem Cheshire Academy.

Adopted the 8th day of June 2019

Patrick McCaskey

Class of 1968

Resolution for John Perkins

STATE OF ILLINOIS

COUNTY OF LAKE

RESOLUTION

WHEREAS, John Perkins is an inspiration to athletes and everyone who need courage, and

WHEREAS, John Perkins got married and started a family, and

WHEREAS, John Perkins was ordained a Baptist minister in 1959, and

WHEREAS, John Perkins orchestrated social and religious programs to counter racial hatred and debased conditions of minorities, and

WHEREAS, John Perkins helped the people rebuild Mendenhall, Mississippi, the way that Nehemiah rebuilt the walls of Jerusalem, and

WHEREAS, John Perkins rebuilt Mendenhall with Bible studies and branched out, and

WHEREAS, John Perkins had ministries that developed affordable housing and worked to have people develop a more worldly vision of their faith, and

WHEREAS, John Perkins helped inspire the development of a thrift store, low-cost food for the poor, tutoring programs, and other initiatives, and

WHEREAS, John Perkins encouraged indigenous leadership, and

WHEREAS, John Perkins built up the entire social network and earned the nickname, "Father of Christian Community Development," and

WHEREAS, John Perkins established numerous programs for the poor: after-school tutoring, Bible studies, an award-winning technology center, summer day camp, youth internship programs, and a college scholarship program, and

WHEREAS, John Perkins advanced the principles of Christian community development and racial reconciliation throughout the world, and

WHEREAS, John Perkins has published a book entitled "He Calls Me Friend."

NOW THEREFORE BE IT RESOLVED that Sports Faith International adopts this Resolution to honor and hold in high esteem John Perkins.

Adopted the 1st day of October 2019.

Patrick McCaskey

Resolution for Bill Kanzer

STATE OF ILLINOIS
COUNTY OF LAKE
RESOLUTION
WHEREAS, Bill Kanzer was born October 15, 1949, in Norwood Park to Dorothy & Emil Kanzer, and
WHEREAS, Bill Kanzer received the Sacrament of Baptism to godparents Edmund Marek and Lucille Newby, and
WHEREAS, Bill Kanzer made his First Confession in 1957 at Saint Juliana Church in Edison Park,
WHEREAS, Bill Kanzer made his First Communion in 1957 at Saint Juliana Church in Edison Park, and
WHEREAS, Bill Kanzer received the Sacrament of Confirmation in 1963 at Saint Juliana Church in Edison Park, and
WHEREAS, Bill Kanzer attended Saint Juliana School, Notre Dame High School, and DePaul University, and
WHEREAS, Bill Kanzer was in the Band, the Jugglers, the Melodons, the Pep Club, and YCS at Notre Dame High School in Niles, and
WHEREAS, Bill Kanzer graduated from DePaul University in Chicago with a Bachelor of Science in Management, double majoring in Business and Music, and
WHEREAS, Bill Kanzer worked as a professional drummer and studio musician in California, and
WHEREAS, Bill Kanzer played the Hollywood Bowl while touring with Seals and Croft in California, and
WHEREAS, Bill Kanzer worked as a Marketing Manager for "Billboard Magazine" and "The Economist" in Chicago, and

WHEREAS, Bill Kanzer was President and Chief Operating Officer of Intermarket Publishing in Chicago, and

WHEREAS, Bill Kanzer served as President and CEO of executive search firm Kanzer Associates Incorporated in Chicago, and

WHEREAS, Bill Kanzer was the on-site coordinator of premium distribution at Chicago Bears games for the benefit of the Notre Dame High School Track, and

WHEREAS, Bill Kanzer currently serves as a Project Manager for the Archdiocese of Chicago, and

WHEREAS, Bill Kanzer met Celia Carvalho at the wedding of Richard & Lynn Rushkiewicz in 1975, and had their first date on October 31, 1975, and

WHEREAS, Bill Kanzer proposed marriage to Celia Carvalho on December 31, 1975, and

WHEREAS, Bill Kanzer was married to Celia Carvalho on October 9, 1976, at Saint Peter's Catholic Church in Skokie, and

WHEREAS, Bill & Celia were blessed with three children: Ashley, Myles, and Brice; one son-in-law: Jeffrey; and two grandsons: Quinn and Ford, and

WHEREAS, Bill Kanzer has been a member of Saints Faith, Hope & Charity Parish since 1982, and

WHEREAS, Bill Kanzer serves as the lector coordinator and a member of the Parish Council for Saints Faith, Hope & Charity Parish in Winnetka, and

WHEREAS, Bill Kanzer is getting closer to heaven.

NOW THEREFORE BE IT RESOLVED that Sports Faith International adopts this Resolution to honor and hold in high esteem Bill Kanzer.

Adopted the 12th day of October 2019.

Patrick McCaskey

Photo and Illustrations Credits

All photographs are reproduced with permission (unless public domain).

Page	Photo Description	Source
Cover	George Halas and Vince Lombardi	Getty Images
Page 18	1963 Chicago Bears Championship Roster	Author
Page 35	1985 Chicago Bears Championship Roster	Author
Page 36	Hupmobile.	Library of Congress
Page 67	Walter Payton Statue	Kamil Krzaczynski, UP/Alamy Live News
Page 68	George Halas Statue	Kamil Krzaczynski, UP/Alamy Live News
Page 74	Benjamin Franklin,	Library of Congress, Maurin Lithograph of painting by Joseph-Siffrède Duplessis
Page 78	Paul Bauer	Chicago Police Department
Page 80	Broken Mary Procession	Courtesy of the Canons Regular of St. John Cantius
Page 87	Red Grange	Library of Congress
Page 115	Matt Cullen, Pittsburgh Penguins center	Andy Martin, Jr. Alamy Stock Photo
Page 116	Mark Twain	Library of Congress
Page 142	Fred Allen	New York Library
Page 145	Illustration from the Wonderful Wizard of Oz	W.W. Denslow Illustration Library of Congress
Page 176	James Thurber Home	Nyttend, released to the Public Domain
Page 289	1966 Notre Dame H.S. Championship Roster	Author

Index

A. E. Staley Manufacturing Company,
12, 70, 264
A.G. Spanos Companies, 71
Abandoned to God, 149
ABC radio, 319
Aberdeen, Scotland, 149
Abrahams, Harold, 124-125
Absorbine Junior, 266-267
Academic All-American, 122
Academy Award, 149, 178
acapella choir, 324
Accentuate the Positive," 293
Achaia, 183
Acho, Sam, 14
Acts 18:24-28, 183
Adams, Anthony, 14
Adams, Don, 154
Adoration of the Three Magi, 190
African American coaches, 3
Agee, James, 140-141
agrege en Philosophie, 171
Air Medal with four oak clusters, 105
Albany, New York, 165
Aleck, Jimmy, 186
Aleichem, Sholom, 141
Alex Spanos (poem), 72-73
Alex: The Life of a Child, 61-62
Alexandria, 183
"All in the Family," 154
All the King's Men, 178
All-American basketball player at
Purdue, 184
All-American quarterback, 306
all-American soldier and citizen, 103
All-American, 122, 147, 306
Allen, Bob, 290
Allen, Fred, 143, 185
Allen, Woody, 186
Allison's, 326
All-NFC in 1985, 33
All-Pro, 2, 4, 6-16, 19, 21-22, 24, 26-
27, 30, 32-33, 37-38, 40-47, 49-55,
105, 123
All-Rookie team, 12
Alpha Epsilon Phi Sorority, 297
altar boy, 7, 151, 276
AM 1000 The Loop, 319

Amate House, 117
American Professional Football
Association, 26
"American Sholom Aleichem," 141
Amherst College, 180
Amherst, Massachusetts, 155-156,
Amichai, Yehuda, 124, 144, 301
Anaheim, 112
Andrews, Tom, 35
Anderson, Brad, 35
Anderson, Hunk, 17, 32, 40, 52, 61,
130-131
Anderson, Ken, 92
Anderson, Neal, 32
Angell, Roger, 144
Angelo, Jerry, 24, 111
100th Anniversary of Bears, 65, 328
Anoka, Minnesota, 160
anti-Semitism, 124
7th Anti-Submarine Group, 104
Apollos, 183-184
Arab-Israeli war, 144
Archdiocese of Chicago, 56, 57, 93,
94, 334
Archdiocese of Kampala, 121
Archy the cockroach, 164
Arendt, Mike, 121
Arizona Cardinals, 44, 90
Arizona State University-Tempe, 158
Armed Forces Benefit Game, 40
Army Air Corps, 154, 174, 181
Army Air Force flight program, 103
"Around the World in 80 Days," 275,
288
Art Institute of Chicago, 159
Arthritis, 155
Artoe, Lee, 9
Asetek, Ted, 324
Asher, Bob, 29
Associated Press, 112, 168-169
Association of Boarding Schools. 330
Atchison, Kansas, 122
Atkins, Doug , 18, 19, 31, 55
Atlanta Falcons, 42
Atlanta Hawks, 182
Atlanta, Georgia, 151, 185
Atlantic Monthly, The," 172

attack on Pearl Harbor, 51
Attempt to Stone Jesus Was
    Postponed, The, 252
Atz, Cathie, 259
Auburn, Indiana, 152
Augustana College, 92
Augustus Eugene Staley, 42, 70, 265
Aurora, 32
Austin, Texas, 166
Avellini , Bob, 91
Aveni, John, 3
Ayanbadejo, Brendon, 34
Aylesworth, Gary,
B-17, 105
B-24 Liberator, 104
B-24, 104, 105
Babich, Bob, 31
Balasa, Dinverno, Foltz, LLC, 322
Balasa, Laurel, 322
Balliol College University of Oxford,
    159
Balmoral Castle in Scotland, 163
Baltimore Colts tryout, 57
Baltimore Ravens, 76, 122
Baltimore, Maryland, 5, 57, 166, 174,
    304
Bang the Drum Slowly, 158
Bannon, Gerry, 290
baptism of John, 183
Baptist minister, 133, 331
Barb Campaigne, 259
Barile, Dan, 1
Barnett, Steve, 18
Barrington (IL), 95
Baschnagel, Brian, 35
Batavia High School, 156
Batavia, New York, 156
Bates, D'Wayne, 16
Bath, New York, 165
Battle of Little Bighorn, 132
Bauer, Commander Paul, 77
Bauler, Owen, 289
Baum, Frank, 146
Baxter, Ted (Ted Knight), 187
Beales, Bob, 322
Bears' Prayer (poem), 314
Bears—see Chicago Bears
Beatitudes of Football, v, 312
Beattie Feathers, 32, 51
Beaufort, South Carolina, 151
Becker, Kurt, 35
Bee, Clair, 146-147
"Begin the Beguine," 186

Bel Air, 5
Belfast, Ireland (Northern Ireland),
    161
Belgium, 171
Bell, Bert, 305
Bell, Upton, 30
Bellarmine Jesuit Retreat House, 95
"Bells of Saint Mary's," 275
Ben Ruf, 320-321
Benchley, Robert, 147
Benedictine College football team,
    122
Bengals and Paul Brown, 92
Bennett, William, 313
Benny, Jack, 186, 187, 293
Benton, Jim, 54
Beowulf, 156
Berkow, Ira, 147-148
Berra, Yogi, vi
Berry, Connie Mack, 16
Berry, Wallace, 165
Best Father Ever, 158
best picture, 164, 178
Bettina, Lillian, 320
Bettina, Melio, 320
Bettis, Tom, 18
Beverly Review, 97
Bible Commentary, Navarre, 191-196,
    199-210, 213, 215-217, 219-221,
    223-226, 228-231, 233-237,239-
    243, 249, 252-253, 254-257
Bible stories, 113
Bible study, 7, 95, 182, 309, 313, 331
Bible, 7, 84, 85, 95, 113, 125, 149,
    150, 157, 163, 182, 183, 185, 190,
    253,274, 298, 309, 313, 331
Biblical Foundation, 325
Biblical passage used in Seamus
    Heaney essay, 158
Biblical principles, 125
Big Bad John, 136
Big Ten, 267, 293
"Bill Dana Show," 154
Bill Walsh quarterback qualities, 92
Bill Walsh social responsibilities of
    coach, 92
Bill Walsh: Son of an Autoworker, 91-
    92
"Billboard Magazine," 333
Bilodeau, Charlie 289
Bishop Fulton J. Sheen, 171-172, 209
Bishop of Rochester, 172
Bishop Thomas Foley, 79

Bishop Tom Paprocki, 123
Bishop, Bill, 20
Bivins, Charlie, 11, 18, 44
Black Death, 151
Blacklock, Hugh, 42
Blanda, George, 31, 41, 65, 304
Blaney, Bob, 290
Blessed Virgin Mary, 58
Blind, 117, 165, 177, 198, 251, 287, 294
Bloomington, Illinois, 171
Bloomington, Indiana, 148
Blue Hill Falls, Maine, 174
Bluebirds Reading Group, 302
Body of Christ, 59, 102
Bogart, Humphrey, 185
490th Bomb Group, 104
851st Bomb Squadron, 104
bomber pilot, 174
Book of James, 182
Booker, Marty, 16
book-runner at the Boston Public Library, 143
Bortz, Mark, 7, 35
Boston, 143, 154
Bourbon Street, 59
Bourbonnais, Illinois, 65, 66, 171
Bowen High School, 13
Boys High School, 274
Bradds, Dave, 63
Bradleys, 85
Bradshaw, Terry, 89
Brady, Tom, viii
Brando, Marlon, 292
Brian Piccolo Award—see Piccolo Award
Brian Piccolo Golf Tournament Banquet, 154
"Brian's Song," 154
Bridge of San Luis Rey, 181
Brisbane, 128
British Army, 144
Broken Mary, 81, 381
Broken Mary: A Journey of Hope, 81, 381
Brooklyn Dodgers in Brooklyn, 266
Brooklyn, 266
Brooks, Mel, 118, 286, 218
Brosnan, Jim, 148
Brother Rice High School, 166
Brown University, 170
Brown, Alex, 23
Brown, Ed, 27, 45

Brown, Jim, 43
Brown, Lester, 82
Brown, Mike, 7, 15
Brown, Paul, 82-83, 92
Brown's "best 11 men," 83
Brumbaugh, Carl, 11, 45
Brupbacher, Ross, 15, 20
Buffalo All-Americans, 51
Buffalo Bills, 33, 122-123
Buffone, Doug, 16, 26
Buford, Maury, 35, 58, 302
Bukich, Rudy, 9, 18
Bull, Ronnie, 15, 18
Bunzol, Tom, 281, 290
"Bury the Dead," vi
Butkus, Dick, 4, 27, 30, 50, 51,
Butler, Kevin, 29, 35, 38
"By the Skin of Our Teeth," 181
Bynner, John, 186
Cabral, Brian, 35
Cadence, literary magazine of Loyola, 297, 307,
Cadile, Jim, 18, 29
Caine Mutiny, 185
Cairo, Egypt, 150
Calendar of Noteworthy Events in Bears History, 1-55
California Institute of the Arts, 158
California, 133, 149, 154, 158, 173, 174, 178, 320, 333
Call of Matthew and Many Others, 196
Calland, Lee, 20
Calloway, Cab, 265
Cambridge University, 170
Cambridge, Massachusetts, 143
Campbell, Father Dwight, 121
Campbell, Joyce, 259
Canton Bulldogs, 88
Canton, Ohio, 38, 264
captain in the Naval Reserve, 39
Captain Kavanaugh, 103
Captain T. DeWitt Carr, 128
Cardinal George, 117
Carlin, George, 186-187
Carmichael, Hoagy, 148-149
Carolina Hurricanes, 112
Carolina Panthers, 42, 112
Caroline, J. C., 3, 18, 23, 49, 268
"Carousel," 157
Carpenter's Mate Second Class, 261
Carrier, Mark, 17
Carroll, Bob, 103

Carter, Virgil, 92
Casares, Rick, 18, 24, 27, 38
Castledawson, Northern Ireland, 158
cataract surgeries, 299
"Catbird Seat," 177
Catch of One Hundred Fifty-Three
Fish, 257
Catcher in the Rye, 168
Catholic Alumni Club, 322
Catholic faith, 57, 121
"Catholic Hour" radio program, 171
Catholic New World All-American,
282, 289
Catholic New World, 56, 282, 289
Catholic University of America, 172
Catholic Youth Organization (CYO)
champion, 97
7th Cavalry, 132
CBS radio, 319
Celebrating the Great Ones, 124
Center Line, Michigan, 122
Central Division crown, 50
Central Michigan University, 322
Chairman of the Fine Arts
Department, 325
Chamberlain, George, 12, 264
Chamberlin, Guy, 14, 51
Chambers, Oswald, 149-151,
Champions in Sports and Spirit
(book), 311
Champions in sports and spirit, 5, 76,
82, 92, 311
chapel services, 7, 95, 182
chaplain for the Chicago Bears, 56-58
"Chariots of Fire," 124-125
Charleston, South Carolina, 151
Charlotte's Web, 157, 179-180, 294
Chase, Salmon, 175
Chaucer, Geoffrey, 151
Cheshire Academy, 94-95, 291, 293,
329-330
Cheshire varsity football coach, 291
Chesney, Chet, 40
Chicago Bears, 1, 4, 23, 39, 48, 56,
57, 65, 66, 67, 76, 88, 90, 91, 95,
105, 110, 112, 123, 126, 131, 210,
260, 265, 270, 272, 278, 288, 297,
302, 313, 322, 333, 334
Chicago Bears 1,000th game, 42
Chicago Bears (Staleys) 1921
Championship, 5, 6, 14, 33, 37, 46,
51, 265

Chicago Bears 1932 Championship,
1, 5, 11, 24, 30, 37, 41, 43, 45-47,
52, 54, 266
Chicago Bears 1933 Championship,
1, 4-5, 10-11, 15, 19, 24, 30, 37,
41, 43, 46-47, 50, 52-54, 267
Chicago Bears 1940 Championship,
1, 4-5, 10-12, 14-15, 17, 20-22, 24-
25, 28, 31, 34, 37, 39, 40, 43, 46,
47, 49, 50-51, 54, 105, 130, 267

Chicago Bears 1941 championship,
1- 2, 4- 5, 6, 9, 10-12, 14-15, 20-22,
26, 28-29, 31, 34, 37, 39, 46-47,
49, 50-51, 54, 105, 267
Chicago Bears 1943 championship,
1- 2, 4- 5, 6, 9, 10-11, 15-17, 21-22,
25-26, 28,37, 40, 46-47, 49-52, 46-
47, 49, 50-52, 54, 267
Chicago Bears 1946 championship,
1-2, 4-6, 10-12, 14, 16-17, 26, 29,
37, 40, 46, 49-54, 105, 268
Chicago Bears 1963 championship,
1, 3, 5-6, 9-13, 15-16, 18-24, 26-28,
33-34, 38, 41-42, 44-46, 50, 52, 54-
55, 61, 269, 280
Chicago Bears 1985 Championship,
1, 2, 6, 7, 10, 12-14, 17, 19, 24, 26,
28-30, 32-36, 40, 43-46, 52, 54, 89,
322
Chicago Bears 300th victory, 45
Chicago Bears 500th victory, 49
Chicago Bears assistant coach, 2, 4,
6, 10, 11, 12, 13, 17, 24, 26, 39, 42,
50, 105
Chicago Bears Bourbonnais training
camp, 65
Chicago Bears captain, 12, 15, 16
Chicago Bears Care Gala, 21
Chicago Bears Chairman George
McCaskey
Chicago Bears chapel services
speaker, 182
Chicago Bears coast-to-coast tour,
50, 265
Chicago Bears first televised game,
43
Chicago Bears flight versus train
story. 39-40
Chicago Bears general manager, 2,
7, 24, 37, 53, 110
Chicago Bears half mile run, 97, 298,
300, 307

Chicago Bears Head coach, 2, 3, 4, 7, 8, 26, 30, 38, 44
Chicago Bears headquarters at Halas Hall
Chicago Bears History speech, 260-271
Chicago Bears longevity list, 2, 203
Chicago Bears mile and a half run, 300, 307
Chicago Bears offices at 111 West Washington, 9
Chicago Bears orange Cs, 38
Chicago Bears retired numbers, 5, 10, 11, 13, 22, 24, 25, 30, 43, 44, 45, 46, 47, 49, 52, 123
Chicago Bears rookie rushing record per game, 16, 17
Chicago Bears special teamer, 3, 16, 23, 34,
Chicago Bears training camp, 28, 31, 65, 97, 267, 271, 297, 300, 304, 306, 327
Chicago Bears traveling secretary, 2
Chicago Bears white Cs on helmets, 38
Chicago Bruins basketball, 184
Chicago Bulls, 182
Chicago Cardinals, 44, 50, 51, 52, 61, 90, 104
Chicago Cardinals-Pittsburgh Steelers, 51
Chicago Catholic League, 317
Chicago Catholic, 56
Chicago College of Optometry, 287
Chicago Fellowship of Christian Athletes, 182
Chicago Lakefront 67
Chicago Police Commander Paul Bauer, 77
Chicago River, 127
Chicago Stadium, 53, 266
Chicago Staleys –see Staleys
Chicago Tribune, 126, 160
Chicago White Sox, 21
Chicago, 9, 12, 13, 14, 21, 43, 48, 57, 60, 67, 77, 79, 81, 88, 95, 108, 117, 121, 126, 136, 140, 146, 147, 164, 166, 169, 179, 260, 264, 265, 268, 275, 288, 317, 319, 321, 324, 334
Chicago, Burlington, and Quincy Railroad, 264
Chicago's Water Tower, 81
Chico State College, 156

Child's Prayer, 106
Chip Hilton Sports Series, 146
Chittenango, New York, 146
Choate, 220, 292
Christ Church Lake Forest, 308
Christ is the Long Awaited Messiah, 198
Christ Is the One Who Reveals the Father, 248
Christ Reacts to the Death of Lazarus, 253
Christian apologetics, 161
Christian Broadcasting Network (CBN), 154
Christian community center, 133
Christian pilgrimages, 65
Christianity Today, 185
Christianity, 133, 162, 185, 276
Christmas at the Quinn's, 63-64
Christmas Sonnet: For One in Doubt, 168
Chuckles the Clown, 187
"Church Clips" column, 56
Church of Saint Mary in Lake Forest, 77
church sexton, 57
Cicero, Illinois, 127
Cincinnati, Ohio, 148, 157
Citadel, 151
City of Chicago paperweight, 269
City of Children orphanage, 122
Civil War, 132
Clarinda, Iowa, 164
Clark, Harry, 54
Clausen, John, 290
Clemons, Craig, 23
Clemons, Samuel, 177
Cleveland, Ohio, 43, 176, 122, 147
coach of the year, 44, 54
Coach White, 281-282
Coast Guard, 181
Cohen, Tarik, 20
Coia, Angelo, 16, 18
College All Star Game, 34
College All-Star queen, 63
College Church in Wheaton, 84
College of Denver, 322
Colonel, 132
Columbia Bible College, 185
Columbia Law School, 157
Columbia University, 130, 157, 168
Columbus Tigers, 50
Columbus, Christopher, 308

Columbus, Ohio, 177
Comiskey Park, 51
Commissioner (Pete) Rozelle, 270
Commissioner Mariyana
    Spyropoulos, 383
Commissioner Roger Goodell, 22
Concord Massachusetts, 175
conference championship race, 282,
    292,
conference meet, 283
conference mile, 282
Connecticut, 94, 173, 177, 181, 291,
    329, 330
Connecticut Association of
    Independent Schools, 330
Connery, Bob, 262
Connor, George, 31
Conroy, Pat, 151-152
Contact Lens History, 287
Contreras, Art, 276, 277
Conway, Curtis, 2
Conzelman, Jimmy, 24, 27, 37-38
Corbett, George, 43
1 Corinthians 12:12-30, 59
corneal transplant, 198, 251, 301,
    308,
Cornell Park in Des Plaines, 280
Cornell University, 175, 179
Cornish, New Hampshire, 169
Corporal Works of Mercy, vi
Cosell, Howard, 187
Costas, Bob, vi
Cotton Club, 265
counterintelligence work, 168
County Mayo, 97
Cousteau, Jacques, 270
Covert, Jim, 12, 35, 302
Cradle of Coaches," 82
Crathie Kirk, 163
Credit Suisse, 321
Croce, Ingrid, 152
Croce, Jim, 152
Crockett, Davy, 136
cross country, 95, 292
Cubs Park (re-named Wrigley in
    1926), 50
Cullen Children's Foundation (Cully's
    Kids), 114
Cullen, Bridget, 114
Cullen, Joe, 112
Cullen, Mark, 112
Cullen, Matt, 112-114
Cullen, Terry, 112-114

Cumberland train station, 63
Cuppy, Will, 152
Curran, Mark, 121
Custer, Elizabeth, 132
Custer, Lieutenant Colonel George
    Armstrong, 131-132
Cutler, Jay, 17, 48
Cystic Fibrosis Foundation, 62
cystic fibrosis, 62
Czechoslovakia, 4
Dakota Territory, 132
Dale Haase, 100-101
Dalhousie University, 93
Dallas Cowboys, 39, 49, 269
Dana, Bill, 153-155
Dana, Indiana, 167
Dangerfield, Rodney, 187
Daniel Webster Grammar School,
    153
Darling, Gertrude, 147
Dartmouth, 164
Daufuskie Island, 151
Davis, Al, 31
Davis, Harper, 40-41
Davis, Roger, 18, 25
Davis, Wendell, 1
Day Junior, Clarence, 155
De Smet Jesuit High School, 320
Death in the Family, 140
Debbout, John, 290
Decatur Staleys-see Staleys
Decatur, IL, 12, 42, 65, 264
Decline and Fall of Practically
    Everybody, 152
Deford, Alexandra "Alex," 61-62
Deford, Carol, 62
Deford, Frank, 61-62
DeGuire, Mike, 121
Delafield, Wisconsin, 31
DeLameilleure, Joe, 122-123
DeLong, Steve, 27, 32
Democratic National Convention, 126
Denney, Austin, 3
Dent, Richard, 6, 31, 35, 52
DePaul University, 300, 333
Des Plaines, IL, 62, 84, 135, 212,
    212, 248, 276, 280, 282, 288, 302
Dialogue between Pilate and Jesus,
    255
Dickinson, Emily, 155-156
Different Tests (poem), 283-284, 299-
    300
Diocese of Cleveland, 122

Diocese of Providence, 57
Distinguished Flying Cross, 105
Distinguished Public Service Award, 40
Ditka, Mike, 3, 18, 30, 44, 53, 58, 59, 192, 268, 271, 272, 302, 306
Divine Renovation Ministry, 93
Divine Renovation: From a Maintenance to a Missional Parish, 93
Doctor Hawes, 259, 297, 307
Doctor Jessen letter, 291-293
Doctor Krefft, 288
Doehring, John, 47
Doing the Dishes (poem), 85-86
Doing the Laundry (poem), 264
Doing the Will of God; Building on Rock, 195
Dolphin Stadium, 3
Dominican Republic, 126
Dons of Notre Dame H.S., 62, 94
Dorsch, Bob, 290
Dottley, John, 33
Doug, Plank, 10, 272
Douglas Testing Division, 154
Douglass, Bobby, 25
Doylestown, Pennsylvania, 157, 165
Dreesen, Tom, 187
Driscoll, Paddy, 2, 26, 27, 38, 40, 262
Dublin, Ireland, 164
Duerson, Dave, 7, 35
Dugan, Jimmy, vi
Dungy, Tony, 3
Dunn, Finley Peter, 187
Dunsmore, Pat, 35
Duty Calls Again, 128-129
East Hampton, Long Island, 161
Eastern Europe, 168
Eastland excursion ship, 127, 260-261,
"Economist," 333
Ed Block Courage Award, 14, 15, 16
Ed McCaskey Scholarship Fund at Maryville Academy, 283
Edelweiss," 157
Edinger, Paul, 16
Edison Park, 333
Edison, Thomas, 187-188
Edwards, Harry, 92
Egypt, 149, 150, 191
El Paso, Illinois, 171
Ellefson, John, 290
Elliott, Pete, 30

Ellis, Allan, 32, 39
Elmhurst, 62, 169
Emerson College, 154
Emmys, 154,
England, 151
English (school subject), 151, 154, 158, 164, 165, 178, 179, 294
Ephesus, 183
Episcopal Academy of Connecticut, 329
Episode of the Good Repentant Thief, 245
Eucharist, 77, 241, 244
European Parliament, 107
European Theater, 104, 167
Evans, Walker, 141
Everest Academy, 319
expansion-team Vikings first game, 90-91
Eye England, 104
Fair Oaks, California, 173
Faith Based Education, 274-286
Famiglietti, Gary, 28
familial amyloidosis, 98
Fanning, Stan, 24
Farley, Father John Francis, 57
Farrington, Bo, 3, 18
Father Bird, 210, 277, 278
Father Don Nevins, 275-276, 284
Father Dwight Campbell, 121
Father Isaac Jogues, 276
Father James Mallon and Healthy Faith-Life, 93-94
Father James McGovern, 79
Father John Francis Farley, 57
Father John MacLoraine, 283
Father John Schuneman, 282
Father John Smyth (poem), 136-139
Father John Smyth, 121, 135-139
Father Martin Luboyera, 121
Father Mike McGovern (poem), 79
Father Mike McGovern, 77-79
Father Nicholas Marro, 56-59
Father of Christian Community Development"
Father Peter Sandonato, 288, 302
Father Richard Maginot, 276
Father Smyth, a Remembrance, 135-139
FBI, 64
FCA summer conferences, 124-125
Fellowship of Christian Athletes, 113, 124-125, 182

Feltz, Bob, 290
Fencik, Gary, 24, 35
Fenwick High School, 315
"Fiddler on the Roof," 141
Fig Tree Shows Us the Kingdom of
 God, 243
Finding of Jesus in the Temple, 212
Finks, Jim, 7, 30, 205
first college draft, 60
First Communions, 275, 333
First Confessions, 275, 333
First Fridays, 248, 275
First Presbyterian Church of
 Northport, 163
First Quarter, 45-64
first sergeant, 131
first to pass for 400 yards in game,
 48
first trade in League (NFL), 50
Fischer, Chad, 67
Fisher, Jeff, 9, 35
Fitzgerald, Ed, 311
Flanagan, Walter, 50
Flanigan, Jim, 34
Flat Rock National Park, 169
Flight into Egypt; the Massacre, 191
Florida Panthers, 112
Florida State, 19
Florida, Missouri, 177
"For the Love of It All," 174
Forbes Field, 51
Ford's Theater, 163
Fort Abraham Lincoln, 132
Forte, Aldo, 34
Forte, Matt, 7, 16, 42, 105-106
Fortmann, Dan, 6, 15, 21, 31, 38
Fortunato, Joe, 13, 18, 28
founding (inaugural season) NFL
 teams, 90
Four Friends Help a Paralyzed Man
 Get Cured, 203
Fourth Quarter, 97-101
Fragale, Mike, 290
France, 104, 151, 180
Franny & Zooey, 169
Frazier, Les, 14, 35
Frederick, Andy, 35
"Freedom" essay by E. B. White, 179,
 296
From a Den of Thieves to a House of
 Prayer, 247
Fuller, Kyle, 12, 15
Fuller, Steve, 19, 35

Fullness of Strength (poem), 299
Gage, Maud, 146
Galesburg, Illinois, 169
Galimore, Willie, 13, 18
Gallagher, Dick, 39
Gallarneau, Hugh, 14
Gallup Poll, 269
Gallup's poll on Catholic education,
 284
Gardner, John, 156
Gardocki, Chris, 6
Gartenmayer, Charlie, 122
Gates, Lorette, 100
Gault, Willie, 35
Gayle, Shaun, 10, 35
general superintendent of Staley
 Company, 12, 264
"Genius" Walsh, 91
Gentry, Dennis, 6, 35
George Halas Courage Award, 38-39
George Halas Junior Sports Center,
 37
George Halas postage stamps, 32
George Halas Trophy, 2
George Halas, statue of, 66-67
George Halas's home 4356
 Washington Boulevard, 40
George Halas's Military Service, 127-
 129
George Mason University, 156
George, Bill, 18, 30, 45, 65, 303-304
Georgia, 132, 151, 166, 185
Geraldine, 189
German submarines, 128
Germany, 104, 144, 180
"Get Smart," 154
Gettsyburg Address, 162
ghosts of Christmas past, 63-64
GI Bill, 154
Gibes, John, 322
Gibron, Abe, 8
Gilliam, Joe, 31
Giving Thanks, 112-123
Glenbrook North, 280, 288
GLSA youth soccer, 101
Glueck, Larry, 18, 42
goat farm, 169
God, 58, 75, 85, 87, 94-96, 99, 102.
 106-107, 110, 114, 118, 120, 125,
 134, 137, 139, 149, 150, 157, 162,
 163, 172-178, 182, 183, 190,194-
 196, 201-202, 209, 211-212, 214-
 215, 217, 226-228, 230-231, 233-

235, 237, 238, 244-245, 249, 252, 254, 285, 299, 308-310, 312-314
"God's Grandeur," 159
Goethe quote, 313
Golden Gloves, 97, 121
Goldman, Eddie, 19
Good News: Fasting Is Not Everlasting, 197
"Good Old Soak," 165
Goodbye Pastor, 79
Goodell, Commissioner Roger, 22
Gordon, Dick, 103
Gordon, Wayne, 84
Gould, Robbie, 14
Governile, Dan, 289
Grace Kelly & Prince Ranier wedding, 60
Grafton, West Virginia, 146
Grammy, 8
Grange, Red, 5, 24, 37, 49, 50, 53, 265
Grant, Lou (Ed Asner), 187
Grbac, Elvis, 122
Great Lakes Bluejackets, 1
Great Lakes football team, 128
Great Lakes Naval Training Station, 128, 261-262
Great Lakes' recreation officer, 262
Great Santini, 151
Greatest Commandment, Greatest Gift of All, 202
"greatest generation," 103
Greece, 159
Green Bay bond issue for a new stadium, 268
Green Bay Packers, 13, 15, 32, 41, 47, 49, 53, 69, 90, 265, 268, 312
Green Bay, Wisconsin, 13, 173, 268, 344
Green, Bobby Joe, 18, 19, 22
Green, Cathy, 101
Green, Shecky, 187
Greenwich Village, New York, 152
Gregorian Chant, 324
Grendel, 156
Guide to Contentment, 172
Guthrie, Kentucky, 178
Haase, Dale, 63, 100-101,
Haase, Jeanne M. Eppers, 100
Haase, Matthew, 100-101
Haase, Meredith, 100-101
Hackett, Buddy, 127, 166
Haines, Kris, 29, 97, 300, 307

Hal Holbrook recordings, 177, 296
Halas Addendum, 129-131
Halas Hall, 9, 20, 241, 313
Halas Mile, 304
Halas, Barbara and Frank, 260
Halas, Frank, 2, 127
Halas, George, 1, 2, 5, 7, 12, 13, 15, 20, 21, 22, 23, 30, 31, 32, 33, 36, 37, 39, 46, 47, 49, 50, 54, 60, 61, 65, 66, 70, 123, 125-131, 184, 192, 220, 264-270, 288, 295, 298, 302, 309
Halas, Junior, George "Mugs," 25, 37, 53, 298
Halas, Lieutenant Commander, Commander George, 127-129
Halas, Lillian, 260
Halas, Min, 7, 26
Halas, Virginia, -see Virginia McCaskey
Halas, Walter, 127, 260
Hale, Dave, 25
Halftime, 76-86
Halifax-Yarmouth Diocese in Canada, 93
Hall, Indiana, 184
Hamden, Connecticut, 181
Hammerstein II, Oscar, 157
Hammond Pros, 21, 264
Hamner Family Cemetery, 157
Hamner, Earl, 157
Hamner, Jane Martin, 157
Hampton, Dan, 31, 36, 39, 327
Hanks, Tom, vi
Harold Abrahams and Eric Liddell, 124-125
Harper, Roland, 89-91
Harrington, Bill, 289
Harris, Mark, 158
Harris, Tommie, 17
Hartenstine, Mike, 35
Harvard University, 166, 172
Hathaway, Anne, 170
Havlis, Mark, 290
Hawaii, 60
Hawes, Doctor, 259, 297, 307
Head Tide, Maine, 168
Healey, Ed, 37, 39, 49, 50, 54
Heaney, Seamus, 158-159, 214, 250
Hebrew University, 144
"Heidi," 157
Heisman Trophy, 103
Helwig, John, 51

SPORTSMANSHIP

Here's to an Evening with Father James Mallon (poem), 93-94

Herndon, United Kingdown, 163

Herod Is Curious about Jesus, 223

Heroes, 64, 124-139, 276

Hester, Devin, 6, 16, 44, 48, 53

Hewitt, Bill, 30, 43

Higgins, Bob, 88

High School of Commerce in Boston, 143

Highland Farms, 157

Hilgenberg, Jay, 12, 35, 302

Hill, Harlon, 19

Hillside, Illinois, 326

History of Art and Architecture, 324-325

Hitler, 304-306

Hoagy Sings Carmichael," 149

Hodgenville, Kentucky, 162

Hodgkin's disease, 173

Hoffa, Portland, 143

Holbrook, Hal, 177, 296

Holy Cross College, 324-325

Holy Cross Hospital, 324

Holy Cross Seminary in Notre Dame, Indiana, 324

Holy Trinity Church (Stratford), 170

Holy Women Provide for Jesus, 222

Homecoming (novel), 157

homecoming queen at Maine West, 63

Hoosier Dome, 33, 38

Hope, Bob, 71-73,

Hopkins, Gerard Manley, 159

Host, Kevin, 289

How Green Was My Valley, 164

"How Little We Know," 149

How to Attract the Wombat, 153

How to Be a Hermit, 153

How to Become Extinct, 153

How to Get from January to December, 153

How to Tell Your Friends from Apes, 153

Howard, Jordan, 17

Hrusovsky, Anthony, 120

Hrusovsky, Joey, 120

Huggins, Miller, 263

Hughes, Mike, 290

Hughes, Pat, 289

Humility of Greatness, 103-104

Humphries, Stefan, 35

Hundred Years War, 151

Hungary, 153

Hupmobile, 36, 39, 246, 302

Hurley, Steve, 289

"I Get Along Without You Very Well," 149

"I'll Have to Say I Love You in a Song," 152

Idonije, Israel, 22, 99

If Apostles had played football, 192, 210, 302

Illinois College of Optometry, 287

Illinois poet laureate, 169

Immaculate Conception Knights, 62

impersonations of Buckwheat and Stevie Wonder, 271

In His Steps (poem), 310-311

"In the Cool, Cool, Cool, of the Evening," 149

In the Long Run, 170

In the Suicide Mountains, 156

In the Wake of the News," 160

inaugural season NFL teams, 22

Indiana University Library, 179, 296

Indiana University (IU), 76, 148-149, 167, 170, 179, 181, 259, 294-297, 302, 307

Indiana, Pennsylvania, 174

Indianapolis Colts, 3, 6, 38, 72, 76

Induction into Pro Football Hall of Fame, 31, 37-38, 45

"Inside the Bears," 14

Intermarket Publishing in Chicago, 334

international agribusiness, 70

International Baccalaureate Diploma Programme, 329

Interpretation of the Present Time, 232

intramural 3-man basketball, 281

Investigative Reporter Lila Rose, 106-107

Ireland, 306

Iroquois Indians, 276

Is Sex Necessary?, 179, 294

island of Malta, 325

It Looked Like For Ever, 158

It's Worth Saying, 258

Italy, 151, 180

IU cross-country team, 295

Jack Dempsey's trainer, 266

Jack: A Life of C. S. Lewis, 161

Japanese, 128

Jasinski, Jerry, 290

Jauron, Dick, 4

Jencks, Bob, 18, 28

Jennings, Keith, 20

Jerusalem, 144, 240, 240, 249, 253, 331

Jessen, George, 287-288, 291-295, 306

Jessen, Kaaren, 294

Jessen, Mike, 294

Jessica Noonan's Agent, 327

Jesuit education, 317

Jesuit, 95, 159, 317, 320

Jesus Appeared to the Apostles Twice, 256

Jesus Came to Establish Division, 314

Jesus Censures the Scribes; the Widow's Mite, 209

Jesus Christ Appeared in the Upper Room, 246

Jesus Christ Had a Hall of Fame Thursday, 244

Jesus Christ Taught the Fullness of the Law, 193

Jesus Christ Went Fishing for Disciples II, 215

Jesus Christ Went Fishing for Disciples, 192

Jesus Christ Wept Over Jerusalem, 240

Jesus Cured a Man Who Had Been Born Blind, 251

Jesus Cured a Man Who Was Deaf and Dumb, 206

Jesus Cures a Woman on the Sabbath, 233

Jesus Drove the Robbers from the Temple, 241

Jesus Gave the Apostles a Mission, 210

Jesus Has a Discussion on Fasting, 217

Jesus Makes Us Acceptable to God, 214

Jesus of Nazareth," 183

Jesus Prayerfully Chose the Twelve Apostles, 218

Jesus Reproached His Contemporaries, 199

Jesus the Son Reveals God the Father, 254

Jesus Told the Unjust Judge Parable, 239

Jesus Warns Us to Avoid Scandal, 207

Jesus Went from God to Jerusalem, 249

Jeter, Bob,20, 23

Jeter, Perry, 23

Jewish Mark Twain, 141

Jimenez, Jose, 153-154

Jimmy Stewart and His Poems, 174

Joan of Arc, 117

Jogues, Father Isaac, 276

John 10:31-42, 252

John 11:1-45, 253

John 14:1-6, 254

John 18:33b-37, 255

John 2:13-22, 247

John 20:19-31, 256

John 21:1-14, 257

John 6:37-40, 248

John 7:1-2, 10, 25-30

John 8:1-11, 250

John 9:1-41, 251

John J. White Science and Technology Center, 329

John M. Perkins Foundation for Reconciliation & Development, Inc., 133

John Piersol McCaskey High School, 165, 274

John the Baptist Preached in the Wilderness, 213

John the Baptist, 121, 205, 213, 223, 224, 252,

John, Gospel of, poems, 247-257

Johnny Desmond "Ave Maria," 283

Johnson, John, 18, 27

"Jolly Old Saint Nicholas," 165

Jonah and Saint Teresa of Avila, 231

Jones, Darlis, 261

Jones, Ralph, 30, 130, 261

Jones, Stan, 18, 30, 50, 269

Jordan, Minnesota, 324

Joseph, Dwayne, 23

Junior Miss Des Plaines, 63

Kansas City Chiefs, 122

Kanzer Associates, 334

Kanzer, Ashley, 334

Kanzer, Brice, 334

Kanzer, Celia Carvalho, 334

Kanzer, Dorothy, 333

Kanzer, Emil, 333

Kanzer, Myles, 334

Karr, Bill, 60

Karras, Ted, 18, 51, 302
Kavanaugh, Jr., Ken, 103
Kavanaugh, Ken, 4, 53, 102-105
Keating, Gary, 289
Keenan Hall at the University of Notre Dame, 325
Keillor, Garrison, 160, 166
Kelly, Brian, 290
Kelly, Jack, 64
Kelly, Mike, 263
Kentucky, 132, 162, 178
keratoconus, 287, 291-292
Kerr, Andy, 37
Keys, Tyrone, 35
Kilcullen, Bob, 18, 20, 30
Kindt, Don, 27
"King and I," 63, 157
King, Jim, 290
Kingdom of God Overruled Satan, 228
Kingston Trio, 64
Kinney, Harrison, 143
Klawitt, Dominic "Dick," 13
Knox College, 164, 169
Knox, Bill, 25
Knox, Ronnie, 23, 25
Knoxville, Tennessee, 140
Knute Rockne Memorial Trophy, 102-103
Kopcha, Joe, 30, 54
Krenk, Mitch, 37
Kreutz, Olin, 7, 23
Kuk, Steve, 291
Kusmerz, Tom, 290
Lake Forest College, 20, 28
Lake Forest, 9, 20, 77, 79, 117, 167, 308
Lake Geneva, Wisconsin, 167
Lambeau Field, 47
Lambeau, Curly, 13
"Lancaster Fencibles," 131
Lancaster, Pennsylvania, 69, 131, 165, 274
Lange, Tom, 289
Langley Air Base, 104
Lannon, Jim, 290
Lardner, Ellis Abbott, 160
Lardner, Ring, 160
Last Catholic in America, 167
Latta, Greg, 43
"Laughing Girl," 278, 305
Laughter Prescription, 155
Lawrence, David, 37

Layne, Bobby, 51
le Shima island, 167
"League of Their Own," vi
Learning from Father Maczkiewicz, 95-96
LeClerc, Roger, 9, 18, 42, 48, 269
Lee, Herman 10, 18, 34
Leeuwenburg, Jay, 25
Leeuwenburg, Rich, 25
Legatus, 195, 321, 323
Leggett, Earl, 18
Lennox, Bill, 305
Let Us Now Praise Famous Men, 141
"Letter to a Reader," 170
leukemia, 76
Lewis, C. S. 161-162
Libertyville Little League, 101
Liddel, Eric, 124-125
"Life is Just a Bowl of Cherries," 295
"Life Is Worth Living," 172
Life with Father, 155
Lila Rose (poem), 107
Lincoln Middle School in Park Ridge, 101
Lincoln, Abraham, 162-163, 169, 175, 184
Lindvall, Michael, 163
Lines from My Favorite Comedians, 186-189
Lipski, Bull, 126-127
literary translator, 180
Little Flower Parish, 324
"Little Girl and the Wolf," 177, 296
Little, Lou, 38
Live Action, 107
Livingston, Andy, 45
Llewellyn, Richard, 163-164
Lombard College, 169
Lombardi, Vince, 220, 270
London, 151, 163
Long Island University, 146
Long Season, 148
Long, Kyle, 20
Los Angeles Rams, 20, 20, 40, 46-48, 61
Los Angeles, California, 157, 174
Louis Harris and Associates survey, 270
Louisiana State University, 102, 178, 300
Louisiana Tech, 89
Louvain University, 171
Love & Marriage, 119-120

Loyeff, Olga, 141
Loyola Academy Ramblers, 317-318,
Loyola Academy, 317-318,
2018 Loyola Academy Football Team,
 317-318
Loyola literary magazine, "Cadence"
Loyola University Chicago, 37, 166,
 295, 297, 307
Luboyera, Father Martin, 121
Luckman, Sid, 37, 47, 48, 49, 53, 54,
 90, 130
Lujack, Johnny, 52
Luke 1:39-45, 211
Luke 10:1-19, 226
Luke 10:17-24, 227
Luke 11:14-23, 228
Luke 11:25-26, 229
Luke 11:27-28, 230
Luke 11:29-32, 231
Luke 12:54-59, 232
Luke 13:10-17, 233
Luke 13:22-30, 234
Luke 15:1-10, 235
Luke 15:1-3, 11-32, 236
Luke 16:1-13, 237
Luke 17:26-27, 238
Luke 18:1-8, 239
Luke 19:41-44, 240
Luke 19:45-48, 241
Luke 2:41-52, 212
Luke 21:20-28, 242
Luke 21:29-33, 243
Luke 22:14-23:56
Luke 23:35-43, 245
Luke 24:35-48, 246
Luke 3:10-18, 213
Luke 4:21-30, 214
Luke 5:1-11, 215
Luke 5:12-16, 216
Luke 5:33-39, 217
Luke 6:12-16, 218
Luke 6:17, 20-26, 219
Luke 6:27-38, 220
Luke 6:39-42, 221
Luke 8:1-3, 222
Luke 9:18-22, 224
Luke 9:28b-36, 225
Luke 9:7-9, 223
Luke Has Four Beatitudes and Four
 Woes, 219
Luke, Gospel of, poems, 211-246
Lund, Gary, 289
Luzinski, Greg, 290

Lyman, Link, 37, 50
Lynde, Paul, 64
MacArthur, Douglas, 129
MacArthur's Seventh Fleet, 128
Mack, Khalil, 8, 37
Maclean, Norman, 164
MacLoraine, Army General John, 283
MacLoraine, Father John, 283
Macon, Eddie, 10
Madison, Wisconsin, 181
Madlener, Dolores, 56, 58
Maginot, Father Richard, 276
Magnani, Dante, 11, 54
Maine West, 63, 101
Major Diocesan seminary in
 Baltimore, 57
major in the 20th Infantry, 132
Manders, Jack, 4, 53
Maness, James, 35
Mangled Hands, 276
Manhattan, New York, 168
Maniaci, Joe, 4, 39
"man-in-motion," 130
Mannelly, Pat, 16, 38
Manning, Payton, 32
Manske, Eggs, 4
Manual Academy Grant, 98-99
Marasco, Carl, 7
Marconi, Joe, 18
Mare Island Marines, 1, 128, 262
Marek, Edmund, 333
Mark 10:35-45, 208
Mark 12:38-44, 209
Mark 16:15-18, 210
Mark 2:1-12, 203
Mark 4:26-34, 204
Mark 6:14-29, 205
Mark 7:31-37, 206
Mark 8:22-26, 287
Mark 9:41-50, 207
Mark Balasa, 322-323
Mark Twain Courtyard, 59
Mark Twain Prize, 166
Mark, Gospel of, poems, 203-210
Marke, Miss, 274
marker of distinction, 39, 146, 169
Marlins, 181
Maroon Tales, 153
Marquardt, Bill, 290
Marquis, Don, 164-165
Marquis, Marjorie Potts Vonnegut,
 164
Marquis, Reina Melcher, 164

Marro, Father Nicholas, 56-59
Marro, Katherin, 57
Marshall, Lillian, 322
Marshall, Wilber, 19, 35
Martin Luther King Junior, 305
Martin, Billy, 18, 23
Martyrdom of Saint John the Baptist, 205
Marx, Harpo, 271
Mary Ellen Nolan Guardian Angel Award, 117
"Mary Tyler Moore Show," 187
Mary Went to Visit Elizabeth, 211
Maryville Academy, 135-137, 220, 276, 277, 283
Maryville Don Bosco basketball tournament, 100
Mass and chapel services, viii, 59, 95, 304
Mass with the Bears, 57
Mass, viii, 57-59. 63. 77. 95. 113, 151, 248. 255, 275, 276, 327
Massachusetts, 104, 143, 147, 153, 155, 156, 174, 175, 178
master's degree interdisciplinary studies, 300
Masterson, Bernie, 20, 31
Matt Forte (poem), 105-106
Mattheu, Windell, 259
Matthew 11:16-19, 199
Matthew 19:3-12, 200
Matthew 2:1-12, 190
Matthew 2:13-18, 191
Matthew 21:33-43, 45-46
Matthew 22:34-40, 202
Matthew 4:18-22, 192
Matthew 5:20-26, 193
Matthew 5:3-12, 5
Matthew 6:19-23, 194
Matthew 7:21-29, 195
Matthew 9:14-15, 197
Matthew 9:27-31, 198
Matthew 9:9-13, 196
Matthew, Gospel of, poems, 190-202
Matthews, Debra, 319
Matthews, Kevin, 81, 319
Matthews, Teage, 319
Matthews, Trevor, 319
Mayer, Larry, 1, 65
Mayes, Rufus, 28
Mayor (Richard J.) Daley, 269

Mayor Richard M. Daley City of Chicago's Lakefront Improvement Plan, 48
McAfee, George, 11, 39, 268
McCarthy, Gayle, 63
McCartney, Paul, 120, 257
McCaskey 40th anniversary wedding party, 155
McCaskey High School, 165, 274
McCaskey, Anne, 231, 306
McCaskey, Brian, 193, 306
McCaskey, Dick, 275
McCaskey, Ed (author's son), 85, 285, 308
McCaskey, Ed (author's father), 5, 17, 19, 30, 31, 45, 274, 305, 307
McCaskey, Ellen, 62, 306
McCaskey, George, 19, 65-66, 193, 306
McCaskey, Gretchen, 84-85, 185, 222, 308-309
McCaskey, J. P., 131, 165, 274
McCaskey, Jim (author's son), 285, 308
McCaskey, Jim (author's uncle) 274
McCaskey, Joe, 306
McCaskey, Margaret Piersol, 131
McCaskey, Mary, 306
McCaskey, Mike, 62-64, 126, 193, 305,
McCaskey, Ned, 62, 193, 306
McCaskey, Patrick, v, vi, 56, 65, 76, 87, 97, 102, 112, 124, 140, 186, 190, 258-259, 282, 288-289,302, 308, 316, 318, 319, 321, 323, 325, 327, 328, 330, 332, 334,
McCaskey, Rich, 193, 306
McCaskey, Second Lieutenant, Lieutenant Colonel, Major, Colonel, Brigadier General William Spencer, 131-132
McCaskey, Tim, 62, 193, 306
McCaskey, Tom, 285, 308
McCaskey, Virginia, 1, 5, 66
McCaskey, William Spencer, 131-132
McCaskey, William, 131
McCasland, David, 149
McClure, Ruth Ann, 169-170
McGarry in the Ring, 97-98
McGarry, Morgan, 98
McGarry's Boxing Club, 98
McGill University in Montreal, 178
McGovern, Father James, 79

McGovern, Father Mike, 77-79
McKie, Jason, 21
McKinnely, Phil, 28
McKinnon, Dennis, 33, 36, 38
McLean, Ray, 51
McMahon, Jim, 33, 35, 59, 272
McMichael, Steve, 35, 44
McNown, Cade, 16
McNutt Quad, 295
McRae, Bennie, 18
Medill School of Journalism, 148
Melrose Park, Illinois, 326
Mercy Me, 199, 321
Merton, Thomas, 58
Metamoros, Mexico, 122
Miami Dolphins, 34, 49, 269
Miami Marlins, 181
Miami University in Oxford, Ohio, 82, 148, 170, 294
Michael Todd Theater, 275, 288
Michener, James, 165-166
Michigan City, Indiana, 127, 260
Michigan State University, 174
Midway Airport, 66
Midway Plaisance, 267
Mieuli, Franklin, 292
Mighty Ducks, 112
Milburn, Glyn, 8
Miller, Dan, 121
Miller, Don, 37
Miller, Mary Margaret "Peg," 146
Miller, Ookie, 265-267
Miller, Zach, 15
Minneapolis, 50
Minnesota Vikings, 49, 50, 53, 90, 91, 314
Minnesota Wild, 113
Minnesota's Player of the Year (high school), 112
Minnis, Steve, 122
Minority Coaches Fellowship, 92
5 Minutes with Father, 56
Misericordia, 317
Mississippi River, 59
Missoula, Montana, 164
Mitch Miller singing group, 100
modified T Formation, 38, 130-131
Molesworth, Keith, 11
Moline Tractors, 42
Monday Night Football, 39
Monsignor Dempsey, 117
Monsters of the Midway, 99, 267

Monsters of the Midway" comic universe, 99
Montana, 132, 164
Montana, Joe, 92
Moorhead High School, 112
Moorehead, Emory, 37
Moral Compass, 313
More Champions in Sports and Spirits (book), 311
More than Coincidences, 123
Moreau Seminary, 324
Morehouse College, 305
Morris, Johnny, 18, 41
Morris, Larry, 18, 52
Morrissey, Jim, 35, 54
Morton Grove, Illinois, 148
most improved runner, 283
Most Valuable Player of NFL, 19, 30, 46, 49
Most Valuable Player of Rose Bowl, 1, 262
Most Valuable Player of Super Bowl XX, 52
Most Valuable Player of the 1963 championship game, 52
Mount Vernon, New York, 158, 179
Mountain Home Idaho, 104
Moving On (poem), 311
Mrs. Quinn Sold the House, 62-64
Mucha, Rudy, 29
multiple sclerosis, 81
Mundelein Seminary, 121, 123
Murningham, Mike, 290
Museum Campus Chicago Lakefront, 41
Musso, George, 15, 31, 37
Musso, Johnny, 29
MVP in the 1919 Rose Bowl, 128
My Favorite Writers, 140-185
My grandfather's legacy, 304-305, 309-310
My Most Important Class, 259
My Own "Temperance Movement," 94-95
Mystical Body of Christ, 102
Nadolski, John, 290
Nagurski, Bronko, 1, 37, 47, 53, 54, 126, 127, 266
Nagy, Matt, 2, 38, 69-70, 76
NAIA Hall of Fame Coach, 122
NAIA national championship game, 122
Nash, Frances Rider Leonard, 166

SPORTSMANSHIP

Nash, Ogden, 166
Nashville Predators, 113
Natchitoches, Louisiana, 152
National Business Hall of Fame, 13
National Eye Research Foundation, 287
National Football League Championship, 122
National Football League –see NFL
National Hockey League (NHL), 112
National Masters 5000 meters, 300
Native Americans, 132
Nativity of Our Lord Church in Bridgeport, 77
Navarre Bible commentary, 191-257
Navy Assignment, 128
Navy Lieutenant Gunnery Officer, 60
Navy, 39, 60, 128-129, 155, 185, 261
NBA, 7
NBC, 154
NDHS Band, 333
NDHS Dons, 62, 94
NDHS Jugglers, 333
NDHS Melodons, 333
NDHS Pep Club, 333
NDHS YCS, 333
Neal, Dan, 26
"Nearness of You," 149
Nevers, Ernie, 37
Nevins, Father Don, 275-276, 284
New England Association of Schools and Colleges, 330
New England championship race, 292
New England Patriots, 4
New Hebron, Mississippi, 133
New Orleans Saints, 4
New Orleans, 4, 59, 60
New York City, 57, 141, 143, 144, 147, 155, 157, 160, 166, 172, 180, 184
New York Giants, 28, 39, 46, 48, 53-54, 105, 265, 267-269
New York Rangers, 112
New York Times, 148
New York University, 168
New York Yankees, 21, 262
New Yorker magazine, 140, 144, 147, 152, 155, 160, 166, 168, 169, 173, 175, 177, 179, 294
Newell, Pete, 290
Newby, Lucille, 333
Newhart, Bob, 166, 187-188
Newhart, Virginia Quinn, 166

Newton, Bob, 20
Newton, Mike, 289
Newton, Tom, 289
NFC Champions, 2
NFC championship game, 2, 4
NFC Defensive Lineman of the Year, 40
NFC North crown, 53
NFC Rookie of the Year, 33
NFL 1920s All-Decade Team, 2, 5, 14, 17, 24, 26, 37, 40, 46, 54
NFL 1930s All-Decade Team, 11, 12, 15, 21, 32, 43, 47
NFL 1940s All-Decade team, 4, 10, 11, 37, 46, 49, 54, 105
NFL 1950s All-Decade team, 13, 45
NFL 1960s All-Decade team, 19, 22, 52, 55
NFL 1963 Championship, 1, 3, 5, 6, 9, 10, 11, 12, 13, 15, 16, 19, 20, 21, 22, 23, 24, 26, 27, 28, 33, 34, 37, 40, 42, 44, 45, 46, 50, 52, 54, 55, 61, 268, 269, 280
NFL 1970s All-Decade team, 30, 46, 52, 123
NFL 1980s All-Decade team, 12, 30, 40, 43, 46
NFL 2000s All-Decade team, 22, 24
NFL 75th Anniversary All-Time team, 15, 22, 30, 37, 44, 46-47, 52
NFL all-time rushing leader, 43
NFL attendance record, 47
NFL championship, 4, 14, 40, 280
NFL Coach of the Year, 44
NFL Comeback Player of the year, 22
NFL commissioner Roger Goodell, 22
NFL Defensive Player of the Year, 22, 37, 40, 43, 52
NFL Defensive Rookie of the Year, 17, 21
1975 NFL Draft, 112, 271
NFL Man of the Year Award, 7, 8, 30, 43
NFL Man of the Year, 7, 8, 30, 43
NFL Most Valuable Player, 19, 30, 46, 49
NFL Organization, vii, 1, 12, 14, 15, 17, 23, 256, 28, 32, 27, 28, 69, 76, 89, 90, 91, 98, 123, 126, 129, 260, 264
NFL record for most return touchdowns, 44

NFL Rookie of the Year, 15, 19, 44, 53

NFL Schedules History, 90-91

Nike Project, 154

Niles, Michigan, 160

Nobel Prize, 159

Nolting, Ray, 47

Normal Oklahoma Naval Base, 128

North Brooklin, Maine, 179

North Caldwell, New Jersey, 180-181

North Carolina, 70, 132, 169, 173

1667 North Humboldt Boulevard, 146

Northern Environmental Systems, 100

Northern Ireland, 158, 161

Northern Virginia, 104

Northfield Mount Hermon Chapel, 174

Northridge Prep, 320

Northwest Highway, 63

Northwestern University, 52, 148, 156, 157

Notebook, 173

Notre Dame College Prep Governance Board, 136, 245, 315

Notre Dame College Prep, 62, 94, 136-137, 288-290, 302, 315, 325, 333-334

Notre Dame High School (NDHS)— see Notre Dame College Prep

Notre Dame High School Roster for 1966, 289-290

Notre Dame Parish in Clarendon Hills, 325

Notre Dame—see University of Notre Dame

O'Bradovich, Ed, 18, 21, 27, 30, 31

O'Grady, Glenn, 290

O'Hare Airport, 112, 270

Oak Park, Illinois, 166

Oakland Raiders, 32, 37, 76

Oakland-Alameda County Coliseum, 32

Oberlin College, 156

Obtain Salvation through the Narrow Door, 234

Officer Training School, 128

Ohio State basketball team, 63

Ohio State University, 28, 177, 293

"Oklahoma," 157

Okon, Ken, 63

"Old Soak," 165

Olivet Nazarene University, 65-66

1924 Olympics, 124

Omaha, Nebraska, 173

On the Waterfront," 293

One Man's Meat, 180

Oologah, Oklahoma, 168

Oorang Indians, 47

Optometrist, 288, 294

original class of the Pro Football Hall of Fame, 37

original meeting of National Football League, 38, 254, 301

Orlando Magic, 182

Ortego, Keith, 34, 37

Oscar, 174

Osmanski, Bill, 44, 64, 268,

Ottawa Senators, 113

Our Lady of Knock Shrine, 97

Our Lady of Mount Carmel, 326

"Our Town," 181

Overtime, 3, 100, 102-111

Oxford University—see University of Oxford

Oxford, England, 164

Oxford, Ohio, 82, 148, 170, 294

Pace, Ryan, 2

Pacific Theater, 144, 167

Pagano, Chuck, 76

Pagano, Tina, 76

Palatine High School, 315

Palestine, 144

Pallbearer, 63

Palmer, Brad, 271

Parable about Integrity, 221

Parable of the Prodigal Son, 236

Parable of the Unjust Steward, 237

Parable of the Wicked Tenants, 201

Parables: The Lost Sheep and the Lost Coin, 235

Parmer, Jim, 17

PART FIVE: SPEECHES, 258-314

PART FOUR: BIBLICAL POEMS, 190-252

PART ONE: NOTEWORTHY EVENTS, 1-55

PART SIX: RESOLUTIONS, 315-344

PART THREE: PRAISEWORTHY, 123-189

PART TWO: THE GAME, 56-123

Pasadena, California, 133

Passarelli, Mrs., 278

patrol boy, 64

Paul Bauer and Father Mike McGovern, 77

352

SPORTSMANSHIP

Paul Brown: Son of a Railroad Man, 82-83
Paulsen, Pat, 188, 199
Payton, Brittney, 67
Payton, Jarrett, 30
Payton, Walter, 7, 8, 29, 30, 35, 42, 43, 46-49, 59, 66, 67, 88, 89, 90, 91, 112, 192, 208, 270, 271-272, 300, 303, 307
Payton's Great Mates, 88-90
Peace Corps, 158
Pearl Harbor, 51, 128-129
Pearson (street), 281
Penn State, 88-89
79th Pennsylvania Infantry, 131
Peppers, Julius, 10
Percival, Mac, 9
Perkins (poem), John, 133-135
Perkins, John, 133-135, 331-332
Perry, William, 35, 37
2 Peter 3:18, 119
Peter, Paul & Mary, 174
Peter's Faith and the Passion Announcement, 224
Peterson, Adrian, 27
Petitbon, Richie, 16, 20, 23
Petoskey High School, 322
Petoskey, Michigan, 322
Petricca, Joe. 290
Philadelphia 76ers, 182
Philadelphia Eagles, 43, 55, 69, 126
"Philadelphia Story," 174
Philadelphia, Pennsylvania, 69, 152
philanthropic family, 71
Philippians 1:3-6, 118
Philippians 3:14, 75
Philippines, 129, 132
Phillips Exeter Academy, 140
Phillips, Reggie, 35
Phillips, Ted, 22, 26
physics scholarship, 170
Piccolo Award, 7-10, 12, 17, 24-25, 33, 39
Piccolo, Brian, 25, 119
Piersol McCaskey, John, 131, 165, 274
Pilgrimage, 65
Pillars of the NFL, 82, 91
Pilot training, 104
Pink Poodle press room, 56, 304
Pinsky, Robert, 310
Pitcher, Anne, 148
Pittsburgh Penguins, 112-114

Pittsburgh Steelers, 51, 89, 268
18th Place and Wood Street, 260
Plague, 170
Plasman, Dick, 14, 25
Plastic Contact Lens Company, 287
Pledge of Allegiance, 121
Pleshette, Suzanne, 187
pogrom in 1905, 141
Point Barrow, Alaska, 168
Polo Grounds, 1, 53
Pool, Hamp, 10, 22
Pope John Paul II, 117, 172
Porter, Anne, 103-104
Porter, Cole, 186
Portland All-Stars in Portland, 5
Portsmouth Spartans, 53, 266
Poston, Tom, 166
Powers, John, 166-167
Powers, Ken, 290, 306
Prairie Avenue, 63
"Prairie Home Companion," 160
Pray with Humility and Confidence, 216
President of the National Football Conference, 12
Press On (poem), 75
"Pride of the Yankees," 275
Prince and the Revolution's "Kiss," 8-9
Princeton Theological Seminary, 163
Princeton University, 174, 181
Pro Bowl, 3, 7-8, 10, 12-14, 16-17, 19 20, 27, 30, 32, 33-34, 38-46, 50, 52, 55, 60, 122-123
Pro Football Hall of Fame, 2, 5, 6, 10-15, 19, 20-22, 24, 26, 29-31. 37-41, 43-47, 49-55, 123, 264
Professional Football Researchers Association (PFRA), 103
Pro-life, 108, 121, 191
Proverbs 31; verses 10-31, 309
Providence, Rhode Island, 57
Psalm 23, 85
publicity assistant, 297, 307
Pulitzer Prize, 140, 165, 178, 181, 185
Purdue University, 158, 184, 295
Pyle, Ernie, 18, 167
Queen of All Saints, 321
"Quiet Man," 97, 251
Quiet Olympics," 173
Quincy College, 100-101
Quincy High School, 154

Quincy, Massachusetts, 153
Quinn, Debbie, 63
Quinn, Diana, 63, 64,
Quinn, Honora, 62-63
Quinn, Jim, 62, 64
Quinn, Kenny, 63
Quinn, Kevin, 63
Quinn, Maureen, 62-63
Quinn, Sheila, 62-63
Quinn, Terry, 63
Racine, Wisconsin, 121
Radar, 104
Rafferty, Dick, 281
Rains, Dan, 35
Ralph Hay's Hupmobile Showroom, 39, 264
Rammon, Bob, 290
Rammon, Rick, 290
Rancho Mirage, California, 149
Randolph County North Carolina, 70
Raymond, Louise, 84, 282
Reading and Writing, 287-300
Red Smith: A Biography of Red Smith, 148
Redding, Connecticut, 177
Rees, Tommy, 285
Reid, Andy, 69
Reid, Carol, 259
Reinsdorf, Jerry, 58
relationship between sports and sportsmanship, 70
Rembrandt, 173
Rensselaer, Indiana, 31, 306
Resolution for Bill Kanzer, 333-334
Resolution for Cheshire Academy, 329-330
Resolution for John Perkins, 331-332
Resolution for Kevin Matthews, 319
Resolution for Mark Balasa, 322-323
Resolution for Nancy Saviola, 326-327
Resolution for Rich Conyers, 324-325
Resolution for the Ben Ruf, 320-321
Resolution for the Loyola Academy, 317-318
Resolution for the Metropolitan Water Reclamation District, 328
Resolution for the Pete Newell and Joe Petricca, 315-316
Responding to the Word of Jesus Christ, 230
"Responsibilities of the Poet," 310
Revelation about God's Kingdom, 238

Reverend Leroy, 189
Richardson, Mike, 35
Rickles, Don, 188
Rider College, 146
Riding My Bike on My Old Running Course (poem), 83-84
River Runs through It and Other Stories, 164
Rivera, Ron, 2, 19, 35
Rizzo, Nancy, 326
Roadrunner, 292
Robinson, Allen, 88
Robinson, Edwin Arlington, 168
Robinson, Marcus, 9
Robinson, Ray, 173
Rock Island Independents, 49, 50
Rockne, Knute, 130
Rodelius, Sue, 259
Roder, Mirro, 4
Rodgers and Hammerstein, 165
Rogers, Betty Blake, 168
Rogers, Will, 168
Roggeman, Tom, 28
Rolnicki, Mike, 290
Rome, 172, 178, 255,
rookie of the year, 15, 17, 19, 21, 33, 44, 53,
Rooney, Art, 305
Rosary, 81, 122, 128, 261, 279, 281
714 Rose Avenue in Des Plaines, 62
Rose Bowl,1, 128, 262
Rose, Lila, 106-107
Ross, Harold, 147
Roxbury School, 329
Rozelle, Commissioner Pete, 270
Rubenstein, Doctor Jon. 251, 301
Ruf, Linda, 320-321
Run to the Waterfall, 178
Rushkiewicz, Richard & Lynn, 334
Rutgers University, 146
Ruth, Babe, 263
Ryan, Buddy, 26
Ryan, Jim, 121
Rye, New York, 166
Ryglowski, Dick, 290
Ryken, Leland, 85
Sacrament of Confirmation, 275, 333
Sacred Heart Basilica, 324
Sacred Heart School in Saratoga, California, 320
Saint Andrews Seminary, 140
Saint Barnabas, 98
Saint Callistus, 57

Saint Catherine's High School, 121
Saint Charles Borromeo, 57
Saint Clement High School in Center Line, 122
Saint Dennis, Kevin, 289
Saint Emily's Parish, 63, 283
Saint Emily's School, 62
Saint Francis of Assisi, 324
Saint Francis School in Petoskey, 322
Saint Gilbert School in Grayslake, 324
Saint Ignatius High School, 77, 166
Saint James, 65, 124, 277
Saint John of God, 79
Saint John's Military Academy in Delafield, Wisconsin, 31
Saint John's Military Academy, 31
Saint Joseph High School in Cleveland, 122
Saint Joseph Parish in Libertyville, 122
Saint Joseph School in Round Lake, 324
Saint Joseph the Worker, 277
Saint Joseph's College in Rensselaer, Indiana, 31, 306
Saint Juliana Church, 333
Saint Louis Cardinals, 53, 90, 91
Saint Louis, 156, 320
Saint Margaret of Scotland Church, 324
Saint Mary's basketball team, 120, 124
Saint Mary's Church, 276
Saint Mary's College, 325
Saint Mary's School, 62-64, 100, 124, 135-136, 212, 248, 275-278, 284, 288
Saint Patrick Church in Lake Forest, 117
Saint Patrick Parish Peoria, 171
Saint Paul of the Cross School, 315
Saint Paul, 60, 75, 257
Saint Paul, Minnesota, 160, 171,
Saint Peter Canisius, 79
Saint Peter's Catholic Church in Skokie, 334
Saint Philip the Apostle Parishioners, 117
Saint Raphael the Archangel Parish in Old Mill Creek, 79
Saint Stephen's, 277
Saint Theresa Church, 322

Saint Viator College, 171
Saints Faith, Hope & Charity Parish, 334
Salaam, Rashaan, 16
Salinger, J. D., 168-169
Sammy Davis Visits the Bunkers," 154
San Antonio, 103
San Diego Chargers, 71-72
San Francisco 49ers, 39-40, 45, 48, 52, 92, 122, 268, 292, 301
San Francisco State College, 158
San Francisco, 39-40, 45, 48, 92, 268, 292
Sandburg, Carl, 163, 169
Sandburg, Lillian Steichen, 169
Sandburg's biography of Abraham Lincoln, 163, 169
Sanders, Deion, 44
Sanders, Ruth Ann McClure, 169-170
Sanders, Scott, 169-170, 297
Sanders, Thomas, 35
Sandonato, Father Peter, 288, 302
Santa Lucia-Santa Maria Incoronata, 57
Santa Monica, California, 154
Saturday Evening Post, 148, 160
Sauganash in Chicago, 321
Savannah, Georgia, 166
Saviola, David Donald "Doc," 326
Sayer, George, 161
Sayers, Gale, 22, 27, 30, 42, 50, 52, 54, 301
Scacco, Bruce, 290
Scalabrini seminary, 57
Scalabrinians (Missionaries of Saint Charles Borromeo), 57
Schaumburg, 64
Schmidt, Terry, 26
Schubert, Steve, 11
Schul, Bob, 170
Schuneman, Father John, 282
Schuyler, Virginia, 157
Scotch and Soda," 64
Scotland, 93, 149, 163
Seals and Croft, 333
Seattle Seahawks, 3
Seattle, Washington, 320
Second Quarter, 65-75
"Secret Life of Walter Mitty,"177
Seed and the Mustard Seed Parables, 204

seminary in Saint Paul, Minnesota, 171
Seminary of Christ the King, 93
Semper Altius Award, 319
Seventy Disciples Have a Mission, 226
Seventy Return; Jesus Gives Thanks, 277
Shakespeare at Halftime (poem), 109-110
Shakespeare, Anne Hathaway, 170
Shakespeare, William, 109-110, 163, 170-171, 302
Sharecroppers, 133, 141
Shaughnessy, Clark, 130
Shaw, Mike, 290
Sherman, Solly, 24, 43
Shinsky, Cindy, 122
Shinsky, John, 122
Shorts, Jim, 319
"Show Boat," 157
Siegal, John, 20
Sierra Leone, 158
Siffermann, Mrs., 217-218
Simeone, Matt, 1
Simko, Rich, 290
Simpson, Chuck, 305
Simpson, O. J., 123
Sinatra, Frank, 187-188
Singletary, Kim, 31
Singletary, Mike, 29, 31, 35, 43, 302,
Sinking Spring Farm, 162
Sioux encampment, 132
Sioux, 132
Sirach 3:12-14.
Sissman, L. E., 172-173
Sister Amata, 275-276
Sister Arthesma, 63, 275
Sister Bertille, 275
Sister Carlene, 274
Sister Irma, 275
Sister Martha, 274
Sister Mercy, 274
Sister Verona, 275
Skidmore College, 156
"Skylark," 149
Smith, Lovie, 3
Smith, Red, 148, 173
Smyth, Father John, 121, 135-139
Snyder, Bob, 6
Society for the Propagation of the Faith, 172
Soldier Field certified "green," 22

Soldier Field, 2-4, 21-22, 33-34, 37, 38, 40, 42, 44, 48, 49, 53, 55, 58, 65, 66,
Sometimes I Wonder, 149
Sons of Zebedee Make a Request, 208
Sorey, Revie, 38
Sound of Music," 157
South Carolina, 151
South Dakota State, 13
South Pacific," 157, 165
331 South York Street, 169
Southern Illinois University in Carbondale, 156
Southpaw, 158
Southwestern College, 178
Spanish-American War, 132, 155, 169
Spanos, Alex, 71-73
Spanos, Dean, 71
Spanos, Michael, 71
Sparks, Nicholas, 173
Spartanburg Phillies, 181
Spenser's Mountain, 157
Spirit of St. Louis,"275
Sports and Faith Series, 65
Sports and Faith Speech, 302-314
Sports and Faith: More Stories of the Devoted and the Devout, 94, 131
Sports Faith All-Star College Lifetime Achievement Award, 122
Sports Faith Awards Ceremony, 121-123
Sports Faith Collegiate Team of the Year Award, 122
Sports Faith Father Smyth Award, 121
Sports Faith High School Team of the Year Award, 121
Sports Faith International Committee, 117, 121
Sports Faith International, 310
Sports Faith Virtue of Saint Paul Award, 121
Sports Network All-American honors, 69
Sportsmanship, v, 56, 61, 70, 99, 125, 270, 301, 311-312
Springfield, Illinois, 123
Springfield, Massachusetts, 104
Sprinkle, Ed, 37
Spyropoulos, Commissioner Mariyana, 328

squadron commander in the Army Air Corps, 174
St. Augustine's Seminary, 93
St. Cloud State University, 112
St. Joseph's Catholic Church in Moorhead, 113
St. Paul of the American Association, 263
Stagg, Alonzo, 367
Staley Field in Decatur, 42
Staleys (Decatur-Chicago), 4, 5, 6, 14, 21, 33, 37, 42, 43, 46, 51, 65, 90, 265
Staleys' 1921 championship team, 5, 6, 14, 33, 37, 46, 51, 265
Stan Musial's funeral, vi
Standing Tall Foundation, 136, 137
Standlee, Norm, 29
Stanfel, Dick, 29
Stanley Cup Champions, 112
Stanton, Edwin, 175
Stardust Melody: The Life and Music of Hoagy Carmichael, 149
Stardust Road, 149
Stardust Road, 149
"Stardust," 149
state (boxing) champion, 97
state championship (football), 121, 317
"State Fair," 157
State University of New York at Binghampton
Stations of the Cross
Statues at Soldier Field 66-77
Steichen, Lillian, 169
Steinkemper, Bill, 54
Sternaman, Dutch, 5, 6, 42, 51
Sternaman, Joey, 5
Steve Allen Show," 154
Stewart, Gloria Hatrick McLean, 174
Stewart, Jimmy, 174
Stinchcomb, Pete, 33
stock market crash in 1929, 153
Stony Brook, 95, 220, 292
Stookey, Elizabeth, 174
Stookey, Paul, 174
Stratford, England, 159, 170
Stratford-upon-Avon, 170
Straub, Walter, 261
Strumpf, Elmer, 261
Student Prince," 175
Stuhldreher, Harry, 37

Stydahar, Jumbo" Joe, 6, 11, 12, 31, 60-61, 218
Sudhalter, Richard, 149
Suhey, Matt, 28, 35, 58, 88-90, 192, 208, 271, 302
Suhey, Steve, 89
Sullivan, Frank, 175
Sullivan, John Florence, 143
Sumner, Charlie, 44
Sun Life Stadium, 49
Super Bowl Shuffle, 7, 9, 19
Super Bowl VI, 269
Super Bowl XLI, 3, 6
Super Bowl XX, 52, 59-60, 85, 272
super doctorate" (agrege en Philosophie), 171
Susquehanna, Pennsylvania, 156
Swanson, Alan, 95, 220, 292
Swarthmore College, 165
Swiatek, Max, 2, 203
Swider, Mrs., 84
Swift, Jeb, 293
Swisher, Bob, 28
Sword of Loyola, 304-305
Szathmary, William, 153
Szymanski, Greg, 290
T Formation, 130
Taking Time to Praise, 190
Tales of the South Pacific, 165
Tampa Bay Buccaneers, 38, 41, 327
Tarkenton, Fran, 91
Taylor, Ken, 35
Taylor, Lionel, 32
Taylor, Rosey, 18, 27
TCF Bank Stadium, 53
Teachings about Love of Enemies, 220
Teammates in Christ (poem), 118
Temple Grafton,170
Ten Commandments of Football, 302
Tennessee, 132, 140
Thacker, 281
That's How the Ball Bounces, 126
Thayer, Tom, 32, 35, 58, 302
The game is all about character and sportsmanship, 56
"The Glenn Miller Story," 275
The Good News from North Haven, 163
The Government of the Tongue," 158
The Great Depression 129, 141, 155
Theater 315, Oral Interpretation II, 259

Therese Snow Sewer Lines Company, 100
Third Quarter, 87-96
Thomas, Calvin, 35
Thoreau, Henry, 175
Thorpe, Jim, 47
Thrift, Cliff, 19, 35
Thurber, James, 143, 160, 177, 179, 188, 232, 294, 296
Ticket for a Seamstitch, 158
Tillman, Charles, 7-8
Tokyo Olympics, 170
Tomczak, Mike, 35, 45
Tomlinson, Matt & Angela, 123
Toronto School of Theology, 93
Toscanini, 173
Touchdown Club, 102-103
Tower Hill School, 181
track co-captain, 282
Trafton, George, 37
Transfiguration of Jesus Christ, 225
Treadmill to Oblivion, 143
Trevathan, Danny, 13
Triangle Club, 174
Tribulation and the Second Coming, 242
Trinidad, 104
Trubisky, Mitch, 41, 308
Trumpet of the Swan, 179, 294
Trusting in God's Fatherly Providence, 194
Tuberculosis, 175
Tucker, Rex, 16
Turner, Bulldog, 10, 39, 46
Twain, Mark, 117, 141, 177, 188, 296
Two Sleepy People," 149
typesetting machine, 177
typhoid fever, 160
U. S. poet laureate, 169
U.S. Army Air Corps Intelligence, 181
U.S. Army Air Forces, 103
U.S. Army, 103, 146, 180, 181
U.S. Green Building Council, 22
U.S. Infantry, 132, 154, 167
U.S. Maritime Service, 146
U.S. Navy in the Pacific, 185
U.S. Team (hockey), 113
UCLA, 23, 184
Uganda, 121
Ukraine, 141
Umstadd, William, 37
Uncle Mugs (see also George Halas Junior), 298

Unclean Spirit and Seven Others, 229
Unique from Day One (poem), 108-109
United Club at Soldier Field, 21
United Nation's Commission on the Status of Women, 107
United States poet laureate, 180
United States Postal Service, 32
University of California, Berkeley, 178
University of Chicago Graduate School, 185
University of Chicago, 24, 152, 164, 181, 267, 295
University of Cincinnati, 157
University of Denver, 158
University of Detroit, 156
University of Illinois, 30, 100, 127,128, 260, 261, 262, 269
University of Iowa, 156
University of Michigan, 122, 163, 315
University of Minnesota, 158, 160, 178
University of Notre Dame, 94, 130, 137-138, 173, 285, 288, 291, 297, 301, 307, 320, 324-325
University of Oxford, 159, 161, 178
University of Pennsylvania Theater, 305
University of Pittsburgh, 158
University of Richmond, 157
University of Rome, 178
University of Southern California, 158
University of Utah, 315
University of Wisconsin, 163
Urban, Frank, 290
Urlacher, Brian
Ursinus College, 168
Valley Falls High School, 147
Vana, Roy, 289
Vanderbilt University, 178
Van Horne, Keith, 35
Vasher, Nathan, 48
Venice, 147
Vernon, Jackie, 188-189, 197
Very Purpose of Love and Marriage, 200
Vianney, John Mary, 224
Villanova University, 152
"Vision Books," 311
Visitation of Mary, 81
Vivante, Arturo, 178
Waddle, Tom, 8

Wade, Bill, 18, 54, 65, 192, 268, 269, 286, 303-304
Waechter, Henry, 35
Wagle, Gretchen—see McCaskey, Gretchen
"Waiting"(poem), 178
Wake Forest University, 181
Walden Pond, 175
Walden: or, Life in the Woods, 175
Walking to Commemorate Papa Bear, 65-66
Wall Street, 155
Walnut, Illinois, 164
Walquist, Laurie, 10, 41
Walsh, Bill, 91-92
Walston, Bobby, 25
Walter Payton award ceremonies, 272
Walter Payton, statue of, 66-77
"Waltons," 157, 310
Wannstedt, Dave, 3
War and Remembrance, 185
Ward, Artemus, 175
Warren, Robert Penn, 178
"wash out," 103
Washington Redskins, 29, 41, 51, 54, 130, 131, 267
Washington University, 156, 320
Washington, D.C., 51, 163, 171
Way of Saint James in Spain, 65
Waynesburg College, 146
wedding feast at Cana, 123
Weides, Jim, 290
Weigel, Tim, 271
Welfare and Recreation Officer, 128
Well, There's No Harm In Laughing, 175
Wellesley, 180
Wellfleet, Massachusetts, 178
Welsh Guards, 163-164
WERS, 154
Wesley, Newton, 287, 292.
Wesleyan, 180
Wesley-Jessen, 287
West Milton, Ohio, 170
West Virginia, 60, 146
Westerhouse, Jim, 259
Western Electric Summer picnic, 127
Western Electric, 127, 260
Western Electric's famed Hawthorne Works, 127
Western suburbs of Chicago, 81
Westover Field, 103

Wetnight, Ryan, 47
Wetoska, Bob, 18, 33, 302
"What a Friend We Have in Jesus," 59
"What I Gave at the Office," 173
Wheaton College, 84-85,
Wheaton Graduate School, 185
Wheaton, Illinois, 84, 282
Wheeling and Lake Erie Railroad, 82
"When We Clean the Latrine"?, 186
White Sox Park, 58
White, Allene, 180
White, E. B., 144, 179-180, 296
White, Katherine, 155, 180
Whitfield, Mal, 173
Whitsell, Dave, 18, 23, 24
Who do we play next week?", 268
Wicklund, Mister, 171
Wiggen, Henry, 158
Wilbur, Richard, 189-181
Wilcox, Larry, 122
Wilder, Thornton, 181
Williams College, 156
Williams, Dave, 89
Williams, Fred, 18
Williams, James, 13,
Williams, Pat, 181-184
Williams, Ruth, 182
Wilmette, Illinois, 317
Wilmington, Delaware, 181
Wilson, Flip, 189
Wilson, George, 50
Wilson, Otis, 35, 28
"Windhover," 159
Winds of War, 185
Wisdom, Larry, 69
Wolf Road, 281
Wonderful Wizard of Oz, 146
Wooden, John, 184
Wooden: A Lifetime of Observations and Reflections On and Off the Court, 184
Worcester, Massachusetts, 147
World Championships (hockey), 113
World War I, 128, 159, 261
World War II, 128, 144, 154, 186
Worthwhile Struggle, 98
Wouk, Betty Sarah Brown, 185
Wouk, Herman, 184-186
Wright Brothers, 308
Wright State University, 170
Wright, Steven, 189
Wrightman, Tim, 13, 35

Wrigley Field, 31, 43, 44, 45, 47, 48, 49, 50, 51, 52, 53, 54, 56, 104, 265, 267, 268, 304
Writing of Jesus Christ in the Dirt, 250
Xavier University, 148
Yale, 155, 178, 181, 329
Yancey, Phillip, 185
Yankees organization, 262
1,000-yard rusher in the NFL, 32
Year of Growth (poem), 119
100 Years of the NFL, 1, 66,
Yonto, Joe, 291
You Know Me Al, 161
Youngman, Henny, 189
Yuska, Dan, 1
Zeller, Joe, 19
Zizak, Tom, 290
Zuccaro, Sam, 290
Zuppke at Illinois, 269

Made in the USA
Monee, IL
21 February 2020